SAS® Text Analytics for Business Applications

Concept Rules for Information Extraction Models

Teresa Jade
Biljana Belamaric Wilsey
Michael Wallis

§.sas.

sas.com/books

The correct bibliographic citation for this manual is as follows: Jade, Teresa, Biljana Belamaric Wilsey, and Michael Wallis. 2019. *SAS® Text Analytics for Business Applications: Concept Rules for Information Extraction Models*. Cary, NC: SAS Institute Inc.

SAS® Text Analytics for Business Applications: Concept Rules for Information Extraction Models

Contents

About This Book

What Does This Book Cover?

The independent research firm Forrester recognized SAS as a leader in text analytics. The field of text analytics is rapidly growing, but effective use of models for information extraction (IE) is elusive. This book focuses on tips, best practices, and pitfalls of writing IE rules and creating IE models, with the goal of meeting the needs of a broad audience of users of text analytics products such as SAS Visual Text Analytics, SAS Contextual Extraction, and SAS Enterprise Content Categorization.

The primary goal of the book is to answer application questions, such as the following:

- What criteria were used for developing the predefined concept rules and what type of results are expected to be found in the data? (See chapters 2 and 3.)
- When it is appropriate to use each type of rule, and how do the different rule types interact? (See chapters 4–9 and 11.)
- What pitfalls should be avoided and what best practices should be kept in mind when one is developing IE projects by applying predefined and custom concepts? (See chapters 4–10.)

In answering those questions, this book provides details of concept rule creation using the proprietary SAS syntax called LITI, which stands for *language interpretation for textual information*. Because real-world examples are essential for increased relevance to users, the book presents best practices from seasoned practitioners through realistic use cases and real data as much as possible. The topic selection and discussions were informed by real questions from SAS customers. Important and helpful hints from SAS Text Analytics experts are presented through tool tip boxes.

Generally, more complex topics come after less complex ones, so if you find yourself lost, go back and master some earlier sections; then try the more advanced ones again. As you advance your own skills with IE, you will rely on different sections of the book to assist you. Progressing through the book will be an indicator of successful learning on your part, as will increased success with your IE models.

This book focuses on the underlying functionality of the SAS IE toolkit and not on the visual aspects that may change with software product or version. Although screen captures from current SAS Text Analytics tools are included, please refer to existing documentation to interpret interface components as necessary.

The information in this book builds on SAS Text Analytics documentation by taking a more detail-oriented approach. For example, components of the SAS IE toolkit, such as the basics of rule syntax, lists of predefined concepts, and part-of-speech tags, are described in the documentation for SAS Visual Text Analytics, SAS Contextual Analysis, and SAS Enterprise

Content Categorization. This book picks up where documentation leaves off, so you may find it useful to keep your documentation handy as you proceed, in case you need to refresh your memory of how a product feature works or where to find it in the graphical user interface (GUI). The documentation is accessible from the SAS Support website: https://support.sas.com.

Is This Book for You?

This book is for advanced beginner- or intermediate-level SAS Text Analytics products users who are technically savvy and want to leverage unstructured text analysis by using SAS IE tools. It is written primarily for those text analytics practitioners with some experience in text analytics, so it is assumed that you will have a basic familiarity with SAS Text Analytics products, interfaces, IE rule types, and format, as well as familiarity with finding documentation on how the rules work.

The book is conceptualized as a train-the-trainer technical reference. The topics in the book were chosen to demonstrate how SAS IE can bring value and insights derived from text data. Combined with practical experience and application, this knowledge empowers you to deepen your knowledge of IE methods and the SAS IE toolkit, as well as to become an expert and champion for harnessing text analytics to answer business questions. Additionally, by creating a community of SAS Text Analytics products champions, the book helps educate non-text-oriented practitioners about the rigor of text analytics processes and tools, demonstrating that text analytics is an important part of data science.

What Should You Know about the Examples?

This book includes examples for you to follow to gain hands-on experience with SAS. There are simple and complex examples of each of the LITI rule types and business scenarios combining various rule types into more realistic models. These examples and scenarios span various subject domains, including banking and capital markets, communications, energy and utilities, government, health care, insurance, life sciences, manufacturing, retail, and services.

"Pause and think" boxes have been incorporated throughout the book to provide opportunities for guided practice, review, and application of presented materials with real-life examples. These hands-on sections are a signal for you to pause your reading, try the rules and models yourself in your SAS Text Analytics product, and test your understanding of presented concepts. You can check your output with the output in the book and read the explanations that follow these sections to deepen your understanding.

Software Used to Develop the Book's Content

In the book, you will find examples from each of the SAS Text Analytics products that support creating custom LITI rules: SAS Visual Text Analytics, SAS Contextual Analysis, and SAS Enterprise Content Categorization. All examples can be duplicated in any of the three products, with exceptions noted. The concepts that are created with LITI rules can also be compiled and applied to data sources using Text Analytics DS2 code and Cloud Analytic Services (CAS) actions.

Example Code and Data

You are encouraged to follow along with the examples, run them in your SAS Text Analytics product, and examine the results. Because the text analytics products enable you to create and apply IE models both programmatically and through a GUI, you can also experiment with the examples in the book both ways. The book content includes input documents and rules that you can copy and paste into a taxonomy in your product's GUI to create and apply a model. Alternatively, the programmatic version of the rules and models is provided in the supplemental online materials accompanying the book. This code assumes that you are using SAS Viya and that you have access to the text analytics CAS action sets.

You can access the example code and data for this book by linking to its author pages at https://support.sas.com/authors.

We Want to Hear from You

Do you have questions about a SAS Press book that you are reading? Contact us at saspress@sas.com.

SAS Press books are written by SAS Users for SAS Users. Please visit sas.com/books to sign up to request information on how to become a SAS Press author.

We welcome your participation in the development of new books and your feedback on SAS Press books that you are using. Please visit sas.com/books to sign up to review a book

Learn about new books and exclusive discounts. Sign up for our new books mailing list today at https://support.sas.com/en/books/subscribe-books.html.

Learn more about these authors by visiting their author pages, where you can download free book excerpts, access example code and data, read the latest reviews, get updates, and more:
https://support.sas.com/jade
https://support.sas.com/belamaric-wilsey
https://support.sas.com/wallis

x

Acknowledgments

We thank SAS Press and our editor, Jenny Jennings Foerst, for believing in us and in this project. Our gratitude extends to the entire SAS Press team, which has contributed to making this book a reality, and to Cynthia Zender for her assistance with the graphs in chapter 12.

We also extend our appreciation to all our curious colleagues and customers who inspired us to find answers to their questions about information extraction and how our text analytics software works. Thanks to David Bultman for planting the seed for us to write this book. Thanks to Christina Hsiao, Tuba Islam, and Ann Kuo for connecting us to customers' concerns so that we could address them.

Special thanks to our colleagues and reviewers for their helpful comments, suggestions, and code: Tom Sabo, Kim Stott, Jim Cox, Fruzsina Veress, Da Young Lee, Lane Surratt, Nate Gilmore, Angela Jones, Laura Moore, Jason Loh, Seng Lee, Aaron Arthur, Seung Lee, and David Bultman. They kept us accountable for every word we wrote, but we made all our own mistakes.

We are grateful to our managers, Xu Yang, Praveen Lakkaraju, Saratendu Sethi, and Jared Peterson for their support and to developers, such as Janardhana Punuru and Jim Cox, for taking the time to answer our technical questions.

Much gratitude to Julie Legeros in the SAS Library, who made it possible to be more accurate and to find related references on information extraction.

We also thank our families for graciously holding the fort while we focused on the book. Writing a book is a marathon, not a sprint, and they were there to cheer us on around every bend.

Finally, thank you to our readers. We hope this book is a useful resource for your information extraction projects.

Chapter 1: Fundamentals of Information Extraction with SAS

1.1. Introduction to Information Extraction

At a recent analytics conference, a data analyst approached the SAS Text Analytics booth and asked whether her organization could derive value from unstructured text data. She came to the conference with a solid understanding that there is value in analyzing structured data but was not sure whether the same was true for unstructured text, such as free-form comments, surveys, notes, social media content, news stories, emails, financial reports, adjustor notes, doctor's notes and similar sources.

The answer to this question of deriving value from unstructured text is an unequivocal "yes, it is possible!" This book will show you how *information extraction* (IE) is one way to turn that unstructured text into valuable structured data. You will be able to use the resulting data to improve predictive models, improve categorization models, enrich an index to use in search, or examine patterns in a business reporting tool like SAS Visual Analytics.

This chapter introduces what IE is and when to use it in SAS Text Analytics products. Chapters 2, 3, and 4 give you the knowledge and understanding you need to leverage pre-built sets of rules that are provided in the software "out of the box." You learn how to build your own rules and models in chapters 12–14. Along the way, you will encounter many types of information patterns found in text data across a variety of domains, including health care, manufacturing, banking, insurance, retail, hospitality, marketing, and government. These examples illustrate the value that text data contains and how it can be accessed and leveraged in any SAS Text Analytics product to solve business problems.

1.1.1. History

The practice of extraction of structured information from text grew out of the theories and efforts of several scientists in the early 1970s:

- Roger C. Schank's conceptual dependency theoretical model of parsing natural language texts into formal semantic representations
- R. P. Abelson's conceptual dependency analysis of the structure of belief systems
- Donald A. Norman's representation of knowledge, memory, and retrieval

At this time, the concern was with two-way relationships between actors and actions in sentences (Moens 2006). For example, Company X acquired Company Y; the two companies are in an acquisition relationship. In the mid-1970s, through Marvin Minsky's theoretical work, the focus became frame-based knowledge representation: a *frame* is a data structure with a number of slots that represent knowledge about a set of properties of a stereotyped situation (Moens 2006). For example, for an acquisition, you can add slots like date, valuation, acquiring company, acquired company, and so forth. At the same time, logician Richard Montague and linguist Noam Chomsky were writing about transformational and universal grammars as structures for analyzing formal/artificial and natural languages syntactically and semantically.

By the 1980s, the Defense Advanced Research Projects Agency and the Naval Ocean Systems Center were fueling rapid advances through sponsoring biennial Message Understanding Conferences (MUCs), which included competitions on tasks for automated text analysis and IE (Grishman and Sundheim 1996). The texts ranged from military messages in the first few MUCs to newswire articles and non-English texts in the later ones (Piskorski and Yangarber 2013). The tasks continued the tradition of frames, as they still involved identifying classes of events and filling out slots in templates with event information, although the slots became more complex, nested, and hierarchical as the field advanced (Grishman and Sundheim 1996). In 1995, *named entity recognition* (NER) was introduced as a MUC IE task for the first time (Jiang 2012). NER models extract the names of people, places, and things. In chapter 2, you can learn more about NER and how the SAS Text Analytics products extract information by using techniques for NER.

In 1999, the successful MUC initiative grew into the Automated Content Extraction program, which continued encouraging the development of content extraction technologies for automatic processing of increasingly complex natural language data (Piskorski and Yangarber 2013). In the 21st century, other initiatives, such as the Conference on Computational Natural Language Learning, Text Analysis Conference, and Knowledge Base Population, also adopted the MUC approach to competitions that target complex tasks such as discovering information about entities and incorporating it into knowledge bases (Piskorski and Yangarber 2013; Jurafsky and Martin 2016).

Through the decades, the tasks in the field have grown in complexity in three major areas:

- *Source data.* The data being analyzed has become more complex: from only well-formed, grammatical English text-based documents of a single type (i.e., military reports, news) and document-level tasks, to extraction from various types of sources, well-formed or not (i.e., social media data), across large numbers of documents, in languages other than English, and in non-text-based media (such as images and audio files).
- *Scope of the core tasks.* The core IE tasks have changed from shallow, task-dependent IE to deeper analysis through entity resolution including co-reference (linking multiple references to the same referent), word sense disambiguation (distinguishing multiple meanings of the same word), and predicate-argument structure (linking subjects, objects, and verbs in the same clause).
- *Systems and methods.* The domain-dependent systems with limited applications have expanded to include domain-independent, portable systems based on a combination of rule-based and statistical machine/deep learning methods (supervised, semi-supervised, and unsupervised).

This gradual growth in the complexity of analysis necessitated additional resources for processing and normalization of texts because treating text-based data as a sequence of strings did not leverage enough of the embedded linguistic information. Such resources included tokenization, sentence segmentation, and morphological analysis (Moens 2006).

The SAS Text Analytics products leverage natural language processing (NLP) methods and pair them with a proprietary rule-writing syntax called *language interpretation for textual information* (LITI) to help you extract the information you need from your unstructured text data. This combination, with rule-building tools and support such as automatic rule generation, applies the best of what statistical machine learning has to offer with a rule-based approach for better transparency in extraction.

1.1.2. Evaluation

Another tradition that originally came out of the MUC program is the approach and metrics used for measuring the success of an IE model. In IE, the model targets a span of labeled text. For example, consider the following sentence:

Jane Brown registered for classes on Tuesday.

Possible spans of labeled text in this example include the following:

- "Jane Brown," which has two tokens and could be labeled Person
- "Tuesday," which is one token that could be labeled Date

In general, the most important things to know about a span of text identified by a model are as follows:

1. Is the span of text that was found an accurate representative of the targeted information?
2. Were all the targeted spans of text found in the corpus?

The first of these items is called *precision* and represents how often the results of the model or analysis are right, based on a human-annotated answer key. Precision is the ratio of the number of correctly labeled spans to the total that were labeled in the model. It is a measure of exactness or quality and is typically calculated by this formula:

$$\text{Precision} = \frac{\#\text{Correct spans in model}}{\#\text{Correct spans in model} + \#\text{Incorrect spans in model}}$$

If the model found only "Jane Brown" as Person, then the number of correct spans would be 1 and the number of incorrect spans would be 0, so precision would be 100%. Precision is easy to measure because you need to examine only the output of the model to calculate it.

The second of these items is called *recall* and represents how many of the spans of text representing a targeted entity that exists in the data are actually found by the model. Recall is the ratio of the number of correctly labeled responses to the total that should have been labeled by the model as represented in the answer key. It is a measure of completeness and is typically calculated by this formula:

$$\text{Recall} = \frac{\#\text{Correct spans in model}}{\#\text{Correct spans in key}}$$

In the example at the opening of this section, the number of correct spans in the model was 1 (i.e., only "Jane Brown" was found), but the number of correct spans in the key was 2. Therefore, recall is 50%. The model would have incorrectly missed "Tuesday" as a Date. Recall is more difficult to measure because you need to know all the correct spans in your answer key, so every span in the key must be examined, and all spans to be matched must be annotated.

There are some basic tradeoffs between recall and precision because the most accurate system in terms of precision would extract one thing and, so long as it was right, precision would be 100%, as illustrated by our current basic example. The most accurate system in terms of recall would do the opposite and extract everything, making the recall an automatic 100%. Therefore, when you are evaluating an IE system, reporting a balanced measure of the two can be useful. The harmonic mean of these two measures is called *F-measure* (F_1) and is frequently used for this purpose. It is typically calculated by the following formula, and it can also be modified to favor either recall or precision:

$$F_1 = 2 * \frac{\text{Precision} * \text{Recall}}{\text{Precision} + \text{Recall}}$$

In terms of these metrics, a good IE model will have a measure of the accuracy that shows a balance between precision and recall for each of the pieces of information it seeks to extract. It is also possible to use these metrics and a smaller annotated sample to estimate the accuracy of a model that is then applied to a larger data set. In other words, if you are planning to build a model to use on a large data set, you do not need to manually annotate the full data set to know the quality of your results.

For more information about setting up measurement for IE projects, see chapter 14.

1.1.3. Information Extraction versus Data Extraction versus Information Retrieval

The phrase "information extraction" is sometimes confused with either data extraction/collection or information retrieval (Piskorski & Yangarber 2013), but they are all different processes. *Data extraction and collection* describes the gathering of data in order to create a corpus or data set. Methods of data extraction include crawling websites, querying or collecting subsets of data from known data sources, and collecting data as it arrives in a single place. The corpus is usually created on the basis of the origin or purpose of the data, but sometimes it might be culled from a larger data collection by the use of keywords or a where-clause. The use of keywords makes the activity seem much like information retrieval, but the goal is to collect *all* items containing the keywords. Recall, not precision, is the focus when you are assessing the success of the collection effort. An example of collection without use of keywords is the collection of all call center notes in a single repository. This process may occur alongside other common processes to collect structured data, as well.

Information retrieval, in contrast, assumes that you already have a data collection or corpus to pull information from. The goal in this case is to align information with a specific information need or question. The result is a set of possible answers in the form of a ranked list, which is not normally intended to be a comprehensive collection of answers or related information. An information retrieval process is successful if at least one document toward the top of the list satisfies the information need. Precision, not recall, is the focus. Keywords and natural language queries are used to interrogate the original data collection.

After a process of data extraction or collection has been completed and a corpus or data set exists, *information extraction* pulls out specific hidden information, facts, or relationships from the data. You can use these facts and relationships as new information, structured data, directly in reports or indirectly in predictive models to answer specific business questions. Both precision and recall are usually in focus and balanced toward the particular use case. The use cases throughout this book illustrate various types of information you can extract as part of this process.

The differences between these terms can be summarized as follows:

- *Data extraction* or *collection* results in a data set or corpus of documents
- *Information retrieval* results in a ranked set of answers to an information question linked to documents
- *Information extraction* results in new structured data variables that can stand alone or be appended to existing data sets

1.1.4. Situations in Which to Use IE for Business Problems

You should use IE when you want to take information from an unstructured or semi-structured text data type to create new structured text data. IE works at the sub-document level, in contrast with techniques, such as categorization, that work at the document or record level. Therefore, the results of IE can further feed into other analyses, like predictive modeling or topic identification, as features for those processes. IE can also be used to create a new database of information. One example is the recording of key information about terrorist attacks that are reported in the news. Such a database can then be used and analyzed through queries and reports about the data.

One good use case for IE is for creating a faceted search system. *Faceted search* allows users to narrow down search results by classifying results by using multiple dimensions, called *facets*, simultaneously. For example, faceted search may be used when analysts try to determine why and where immigrants may perish. The analysts might want to correlate geographical information with information that describes the causes of the deaths in order to determine what actions to take.

Another good example of using IE in predictive models is analysts at a bank who want to determine why customers close their accounts. They have an active churn model that works fairly well at identifying potential churn, but less well at determining what causes the churn. An IE model could be built to identify different bank policies and offerings and then track mentions of each during any customer interaction. If a particular policy could be linked to certain churn behavior, then the policy could be modified to reduce the number of lost customers.

Reporting information found as a result of IE can provide deeper insight into trends and uncover details that were buried in the unstructured data. An example of this is an analysis of call center notes at an appliance manufacturing company. The results of IE show a pattern of customer-initiated calls about repairs and breakdowns of a type of refrigerator, and the results highlight particular problems with the doors. This information shows up as a pattern of increasing calls. Because the content of the calls is being analyzed, the company can return to its design team, which can find and remedy the root problem.

The uses of IE can be complex, as demonstrated by these examples, or relatively simple. A simple use case for IE is sentence extraction. Breaking longer documents down into sentences is one way to address the complexity of the longer documents. It is a good preprocessing step for some types of text analytics. For an example of an IE rule for transforming your documents into sentences, see section 8.3.2.

1.2. The SAS IE Toolkit

The SAS IE toolkit includes the following components:

- NLP foundation for IE
- LITI rule syntax
- Predefined concepts (out-of-the-box NER)
- Taxonomy of components for each model
- Three types of matching algorithms
- Graphical user interface (GUI) for building and testing models to sample data sets and a programmatic interface for building and applying models to large data sets

These parts of the IE toolkit operate together. They also integrate well with the larger SAS product suite including other SAS Text Analytics capabilities—categorization, for example—and SAS Viya products, such as SAS Visual Data Management and Machine Learning, SAS Visual Analytics, and SAS Model Manager.

1.2.1. NLP Foundation for IE

The first component in the SAS IE toolkit, NLP, involves computational and linguistic approaches to enabling computers to "understand" human language. Computers process character-by-character or byte-by-byte and have no conceptualization of "word," "sentence," "verb," or the like. NLP provides methods that help the computer model the structure and information encoded in human language.

Some of the foundational methods of NLP include tokenization, sentence breaking, part-of-speech (POS) tagging, lemmatization or stemming, misspelling detection, and grammatical parsing. These foundational NLP processes often feed information into higher-level processing types, such as machine translation, speech-to-text processing, IE, and categorization. The SAS Text Analytics products carry out many of these foundational NLP analyses behind the scenes and make the results available as part of the IE toolkit. Toolkit users do not directly see or participate in the NLP foundation but benefit in various ways, which are described in the next few sections.

Tokenization

One of the basic operations in NLP and a critical task for effective IE is *tokenization*. *Tokenization* refers to the process of analyzing alphanumeric characters, spaces, punctuation and special characters to determine where to draw boundaries between them. The pieces of text that are separated by those boundaries are called *tokens*.

Different text processing systems may approach tokenization differently. Some tasks may require that tokens be as short as possible, whereas others may produce better results if tokens are longer. Furthermore, natural languages have different conventions for certain characters such as white space and punctuation. For example, Chinese does not have white spaces between words, Korean sometimes has white spaces between words, and English usually has white spaces between words. These conventions play an important role in tokenization. Even if focusing only on English text, different tokenization approaches may produce different results.

Consider the following example sentence:

> Starting Dec. 21st, Mrs. Bates-Goodman won't lead the co-op any more.

Pause and think: Can you identify some words that could potentially be tokenized two or more different ways in the sentence above?

You may have identified some of the following possible differences in tokenization in the sentence:

- "Dec." could be 1 or 2 tokens: /Dec./ or /Dec/./
- "21st" could be 1 or 2 tokens: /21st/ or /21/st/
- "Dec. 21st" could possibly be 1 token if dates are important: /Dec. 21st/
- "Mrs." could be 1 or 2 tokens: /Mrs./ or /Mrs/./
- "Bates-Goodman" could be 1 or 3 tokens: /Bates-Goodman/ or /Bates/-/Goodman/
- "Mrs. Bates-Goodman" could possibly be 1 token if person names are important /Mrs. Bates-Goodman/
- "won't" could be 1, 2, or 3 tokens: /won't/, /won/'t/, or /won/'/t/ or even be turned into /will/not/
- "co-op" could be 1 or 3 tokens: /co-op/ or /co/-/op/

Furthermore, some systems may tokenize proper names like "Bates-Goodman" differently from words that may be found in a dictionary and contain a hyphen, such as "co-op." In other words, when you are tokenizing text, there are many decisions that must be made in order to present the most meaningful set of tokens possible to aid downstream analysis. For more information about how complex the tokenization of periods can be, see Belamaric Wilsey and Jade (2015).

The default SAS Text Analytics tokenization approach embodies one of these advanced systems that tries to get these decisions right. The tokens are optimized to represent semantic meaning. Therefore, if a character is a part of a series of characters that means something, then the goal is to make all of the series into a single token rather than keeping them as separate pieces of meaningless text. This approach is effective for enabling better POS tagging, which will be described in more detail in the next section.

Since at least 2016, the English language analysis tools in SAS have followed this approach of tokenization based on meaningful units. In order to limit the combinations, the SAS method of NLP follows two rules about putting together pieces with internal white space. First, there are no tokens with white space created during tokenization, so you can use special tags (described in the subsection "Part-of-speech Tagging" below), such as ":url" or ":time," and they will match tokens without white space only. Second, the only tokens containing internal white space come from a process known as *multiword identification*, a process whereby meaningful terms that have multiple pieces, but a single meaning and POS, are combined as a single compound token. For example, SAS NLP will analyze "high school" as a single token based on an entry in the multiword dictionary.

In English and many other languages, there is a process of word formation called *compounding*, which combines two separate words together to create a new expression with a different meaning than that comprised by the two words used together. It is common for this process to start with the two words used as a pair of words with a normal space between them, for example, "bubble wrap." Later, as users of the multiword become accustomed to the new meaning, the pieces may be hyphenated or even written as a single word, for example, "play-date," "suitcase," "nickname," or even "before." Analyzing these terms as a single token when they are still space-separated, but have a single meaning, improves POS tagging and topic identification.

Tokens are important for the SAS IE toolkit, because a token defines the unit over which an IE model will operate. The model can recognize and operate over a single token or a series of multiple tokens, but it will not easily recognize partial tokens, such as only "ing" in word endings. This tokenization limitation actually saves a lot of work, because the models can be based on semantically meaningful units rather than being cleaned up piece by piece before finally targeting the meaningful pieces.

If you are accustomed to modeling using only a regular expression approach to processing text data, you may find that this token-based approach to models seems to limit your options at first. However, if you shift your focus and strategy to target those larger tokens, you will likely find that you end up with a smarter and more easily maintained model in the long run. If that is not the case for your data, then you can still turn to the regular expression syntax in SAS code in procedures, such as the PRXCHANGE procedure, to identify partial-token matches.

Other Boundaries

Another type of division of the text that is provided as a part of the NLP foundation for IE is *sentence tokenization* or *sentence segmentation*. In this process, the data is broken up into sentence-level pieces, taking into account cues including punctuation, newline characters and other white space, and abbreviations in each language. All SAS Text Analytics products detect sentence boundaries and feed this information forward into the IE and categorization processes.

Some SAS Text Analytics products will also detect simple paragraph boundaries and pass that information into both IE and categorization. Additionally, detection of clause boundaries for IE is a planned feature on the development roadmap in order to enable even more refined IE models.

Part-of-Speech Tagging

Once the tokens, the units of analysis, have been determined in the NLP foundation for IE, it is useful to understand how they fit into the sentence from a grammatical viewpoint. For this task, a set of grammatical labels is applied that determine each token's POS. These labels, such as "noun," "verb," "adjective," "adverb," and so on are called *POS tags*, and they are fully documented in your product documentation. Assigning these labels to tokens is called *tagging*. There are also a few special tags that can be applied to tokens, which include the following: ":sep," ":digit," ":url," ":time," and ":date." These tags, explained in Table 1.1, are created for specific types of tokens that are not labeled with grammatical tags.

Table 1.1. Special Tags and Description

Special Tag	Description
:sep	Applied to any single punctuation character that stands alone as a token
:digit	Applied to any single or multiple numeric token; number
:url	Applied to URLs, email addresses, and computer path; digital location
:time	Applied to any string of characters without spaces that depicts a time
:date	Applied to any string of characters without spaces that depicts a date

Knowing a token's tag adds tools to your IE toolkit that enable you to refer to and capture tokens that appear in the same grammatical patterns in a sentence. For illustration, consider the following phrases: "a counteractive measure," "an understandable result," and "the predictable outcome."

Pause and think: How could you use tagging to extract these phrases in your IE model?

Because the phrases all follow the same POS pattern of a determiner followed by an adjective and noun, an IE rule that references those POS tags in a sequence will extract all three phrases, as well as any additional ones that follow the same pattern in the text. Leveraging POS tags makes IE rules more efficient and versatile.

Parenting

In addition to tagging, two other NLP processes that happen behind-the-scenes in SAS Text Analytics products help to group related tokens together into sets: identification of inflectional variation of terms (*lemmatization*) and misspelling detection. Inflectional variants are those words that come from a *lemma*, the base form of a word, and remain in the same basic POS family. For example, English verb paradigms can contain multiple forms:

- The base form, also called the infinitive, as in "be"
- The first person present tense "am"
- The second person present tense "are"
- The third person present tense "is"
- The first person past tense "was"

In the SAS IE toolkit, you can access these "sets" of words directly through a single form, called the *parent term*. See section 1.5.3 for more details about parenting.

Misspelling detection is the second process that adds word forms to the set of child terms under a parent. When users choose to turn on this feature, misspellings are automatically detected and added to the "sets" of words grouped under a parent term.

Hybrid System

The NLP processing that takes place to produce tokens, lemmas, POS tags, misspellings, and the like uses a combination of dictionaries, human-authored rules, and machine learning approaches. In other words, like most real-world NLP systems, it is a hybrid system. SAS linguists are continually working to improve and modernize the approaches used in the SAS NLP foundation. Therefore, an upgrade or move to a newer SAS Text Analytics product will likely result in differences in how this processing occurs or the results you may see on specific data. It is advised that you recheck any models that you migrate from system to system so that you can adjust your models, if needed, to align with the newer outputs.

It is important to note that, even though the quality of the results of SAS NLP is increasing over time, the specific results you may observe on a particular data set may vary in quality. Particularly, if you are using very noisy or ungrammatical data, the results may not always look like what you would expect them to. For example, POS tagging assumes *sentential* data, which is data containing sentences with punctuation. Therefore, examining POS tagging output on non-sentential data will often not provide expected results, because context is a critical part of the POS tagging analysis.

The SAS linguists strive to ensure that the NLP foundation works well on data from the common domain, as well as across all the domains of SAS customers, including health care, energy, banking, manufacturing, and transportation. Also, the analysis must work well on sentential text from a variety of document types, such as emails, technical reports, abstracts, tweets, blogs, call center notes, SEC filings, and contracts.

Because of the variety of language and linguistic expression, correctly processing all of these types of data from all the domains is an unusual challenge. The typical NLP research paper usually reports on a specific domain and frequently also addresses a single document type. SAS linguists have a higher standard and measure results against standard data collections used in research for each language, as well as against data that SAS customers have provided for testing purposes. If you have data that you want the SAS systems to process well, you are encouraged to provide SAS with a sample of the data for testing purposes. All of the supported languages would benefit from additional customer data for testing. You can contact the authors or SAS Technical Support to begin this process.

1.2.2. LITI Rule Syntax

The SAS IE toolkit leverages the hybrid systems in the NLP foundation, but centers on a rule-based approach for the IE component. This type of IE approach consists of collections of rules for extraction and policies to determine the interactions between those rule collections. The rules in the SAS IE toolkit leverage a proprietary programming language called *LITI*. Policies include procedures for arranging taxonomies and resolving match conflicts.

LITI is a proprietary programming language used to create models that can extract particular pieces of text that are relevant for various types of informational purposes. The LITI language organizes sets of rules into groups called *concepts*. Each group of rules can be referenced as a set in other rules through the name of the concept. This approach enables models to work like a well-designed building with foundational pieces that no one sees directly, such as electrical wiring and plumbing, as well as functional pieces that visitors to the building would readily identify, such as doors, elevators, and windows.

Each rule written in the LITI syntax is a command to look for particular characteristics and patterns in the textual data and return targeted strings of text whenever the specified conditions are met in the text data. You can use LITI to look for regular expressions, simple or complex strings, strings in particular contexts, items from a class (like a POS class such as "verb"), and items in particular relationships based on proximity and context. LITI syntax enables modeling of rules through different rule types, combinations of rule types, and operators, including Boolean and proximity operators.

The LITI syntax is flexible and scalable. One aspect of LITI that contributes to these attributes is the variety of rule types that are available. Many other IE engines take advantage of regular expression rules. In addition to this capability, LITI supports eight other rule types, which give you the ability to extract strings with or without specifying context and with or without extracting the context around those strings. In addition, the rules for fact matches allow you to specify and extract relationships between two or more matches in a given context. Finally, the LITI syntax enables you to take advantage of Boolean and proximity operators, such as AND, OR, SENT and others, to restrict extracted matches. The benefit of this set of rule types is that the user can target exactly the type of match needed efficiently, without using more processing than is required for that type of extraction.

The different types of rules and operators, as well as LITI rule syntax, are discussed in detail in chapters 5–11. For users who do not want to write their own rules, the next section discusses automatically generated rules, as well as pre-built rules.

1.2.3. Predefined Concepts

LITI rules can be written by a human or automatically generated. Automatically generated rules have been included in the SAS IE toolkit since 2018 and are available through the SAS Visual Text Analytics GUI starting in product releases in 2019. In addition, commonly used concepts for each supported language are predefined and provided out-of-the-box as part of the toolkit. All fully supported languages in SAS Text Analytics products support at least seven SAS-proprietary predefined concepts, including the following: Person Names, Location Names, Organization Names, Dates, Times, Currency Amounts, and Percentage Amounts. Additional predefined concepts, such as Measures or third-party open-source predefined concepts, may also be available in certain products. Some examples are provided in Table 1.2.

Table 1.2. Example Matches for Predefined Concepts

Predefined Concept	Example Match (in Bold)
Person Name	**Mayor Roland Ries** told XYZ television the gunman got inside a security zone to stage the terrorist attack in the French city of Strasbourg on Tuesday at 10am.
Organization Name	Mayor Roland Ries told **XYZ television** the gunman got inside a security zone to stage the terrorist attack in the French city of Strasbourg on Tuesday at 10am.
Location Name	Mayor Roland Ries told XYZ television the gunman got inside a security zone to stage the terrorist attack in the French city of **Strasbourg** on Tuesday at 10am.
Date	Mayor Roland Ries told XYZ television the gunman got inside a security zone to stage the terrorist attack in the French city of Strasbourg on **Tuesday** at 10am.

Predefined Concept	Example Match (in Bold)
Time	Mayor Roland Ries told XYZ television the gunman got inside a security zone to stage the terrorist attack in the French city of Strasbourg on Tuesday at **10am**.
Currency Amount	Stocks fell 3.5% and investors lost around **$1.1 trillion**.
Percentage Amount	Stocks fell **3.5%** and investors lost around $1.1 trillion.

These predefined concepts enable the immediate identification of information that many models need to find. They are built with general data sets and therefore have some limitations in terms of accuracy in specialized data sets. However, you can expand and constrain them through custom, user-written rules that refine their behavior in accordance with the specific characteristics of the data to which they will be applied. In other words, predefined concepts are a springboard for immediate text analysis and a solid foundation on which to build even more effective concepts for specific analytic needs.

SAS proprietary predefined concepts are introduced in chapter 2. The definition and results for each concept are described in detail in chapters 3 and 4.

1.2.4. Taxonomy of Concepts

Another piece of the SAS IE toolkit is the *taxonomy* of concepts. In the design stages of a model, each of the concepts, which are groups of LITI rules, is organized into a hierarchy, or taxonomy. This taxonomy serves as a blueprint for the model being built. It lays out the pieces and enables a visual depiction of their relation to one another. This feature is flexible and allows the model to be set up in a logical way for testing and maintenance of the particular rule sets used in the model.

For example, you will probably want to set up any reasonably complex model with two types of concepts. One type of concept will be used to produce your explicit results—to generate your extracted information data. This type of concept is a *functional* piece of the model, because it produces results that can be observed. Other pieces of the model could be constructed solely to support the output of these functional components, like the foundation of a building supports all the pieces that one can see and use directly. These supporting concepts can be called *foundational* or *helper* concepts. They have rules and produce results, but those results only feed into other concepts rather than producing resulting data from the model.

Taxonomy design and setting up projects is discussed in more detail in chapters 12–14. Best practices for identifying the concepts to use are in section 11.3, and how to set up more complex models is covered in chapters 12 and 13.

1.2.5. Algorithms for Matching

Another feature available as a part of the SAS IE toolkit is choice of matching algorithm: "all matches," "longest match," or "best match." When a LITI rule is evaluated, the software can assess whether the same span of text has been matched by another concept or rule. Two of the three available matching algorithms use this information to filter out or select among possible matches: the "best match" algorithm and the "longest match" algorithm. In some SAS Text Analytics products, the default algorithm is the third one, "all matches," which returns all the matches after applying the model.

The selection of a matching algorithm is one way you can control the output of your model—for example, to reduce duplicate matches. This choice may determine which matches are returned under the circumstances of overlap or duplication. More details about the three available matching algorithms and how to use them is found in section 13.4.1. The chapters that introduce rules and all the examples up to chapter 12 use the "all matches" algorithm.

1.2.6. Interfaces for Building and Applying Models

Building and applying an IE model can be achieved in two different ways in SAS Text Analytics products: through a GUI or programmatically.

Each SAS Text Analytics product includes a GUI for rule building and testing, which is an iterative process. In the GUI, a data set can be examined, rules can be written, and results of applying the model can be evaluated. Therefore, the GUI environments have been optimized to support this process of model creation and iterative evaluation and improvement.

In each product, the GUI shows the model taxonomy, enables changes to the taxonomy, associates the rule set with the concept in the taxonomy, and shows matches from testing associated with each concept. Tests can be conducted on snippets of text or across all documents loaded into the GUI, and results can then be examined and analyzed. In some SAS Text Analytics products, the metrics of recall and precision are also presented within the GUI context.

If you have created a model in the GUI, it can automatically generate code to apply the model to a new data set. This code is called *score code*, and the process of applying it is often referred to as *scoring*. It enables efficient application of the model to a large amount of data. The score code can be based on DS2 or Cloud Analytics Services (CAS) actions, depending on the product that generates it. Starting with products released in 2019, models can also be exported and applied in an analytic store (ASTORE) format. Score code can be modified, if needed, and applied to a new set of documents or placed in production. One frequent modification to the model parameters in score code is changing the matching algorithm to control the output, as described in section 13.4.

As an alternative to the GUI approach, you can also build and apply IE models programmatically. The process for building a model programmatically is explained in section 5.3.4. You can apply the programmatically built model with the SAS IE procedures or actions, using a SAS programming interface or SAS Studio, as described in section 5.3.5.

This book will focus primarily on the approach to rule building used in the GUIs, but not focus on a particular GUI environment, because the goal is to present information that can be used across all of the GUIs available in SAS Text Analytics products and versions. Where screenshots are shown, the product used will be mentioned, and any relevant differences across products will also be highlighted whenever possible. However, the basics of building and applying rules programmatically are also covered, and the code samples in the supplemental materials online follow this approach (for how to locate these materials, see

About This Book). Therefore, you can quickly reproduce the results presented in the book by simply running the provided code.

1.3. Reasons for Using SAS IE

SAS IE has many benefits over other types of IE approaches. Because it is part of a set of text analytics tools, as well as being integrated into the larger SAS product family, you have the flexibility to combine it with other tools and products, such as statistical or predictive algorithms and machine learning. SAS IE models can be integrated directly into SAS categorization models, used to make more useful topics, or applied independently to create structured data that can be used to populate databases, inform predictive models, or feed into reports such as those available in SAS Visual Analytics.

In addition to being a part of a larger ecosystem of analytics, another benefit of SAS IE is that you can create models right away by creating rules and concepts without requiring large amounts of pre-annotated data for training a model. Furthermore, SAS Text Analytics products provide a set of out-of-the-box concepts that you can leverage immediately, and the GUI enables customization of those rules by adding or removing matches.

If you have annotated data or can create it, you have the option of applying an automated process to generate LITI rules in SAS Text Analytics (starting in 2018 in the programmatic interface and in 2019 in the GUI). You can later edit and cull these rules. Check user documentation for more information about how the algorithms for rule generation work. When building rules, just as with any other model, the amount of knowledge and care given to the creation of the model directly impacts the quality and the usefulness of the model. For this reason, it is not recommended that you rely solely on automated rule generation, but instead combine this method with human understanding, tuning, and testing of the rules to meet your specific goals.

Because rule writing can take time and effort, scientific papers on IE often cite these requirements as drawbacks (Jiang 2012, p.17). However, with the right tools and expertise for building rules, this approach has been proven to be more accurate, robust, and interpretable than typical machine-learning-only or statistical models in a variety of use cases (Chiticariu et al. 2013; Liu et al. 2013; Small and Medsker 2013; Woodie 2018). Other benefits of rule-based systems for IE include readability, maintainability, expressivity, and transparency, as well as the direct transfer of domain and linguistic knowledge into rules (Waltl et al. 2018).

Typical machine-learning models also have drawbacks, such as lack of transparency, limited interpretability, and inability to leverage in-house human expertise. Furthermore, these models require a large amount of manually annotated data for training, development, and testing purposes. In many cases, this data does not come for free, or if it does, then it does not reflect the same type of textual content that may be targeted with the model. In those situations of mismatch between training and target data, the accuracy of the model is lowered even further.

In reality, both defining rules for a complex model and curating annotated (pretagged) data are big jobs. The former simply gives you more control over your model and helps you build up the latter as you go. Therefore, if you want a model that you will reuse repeatedly and perfect over time to be as accurate as possible, then using predefined and custom rules that you define for your specific business needs may be the best path for you.

Another benefit of the SAS IE toolkit is that the NLP work, such as tokenization, stemming, lemmatization, and POS tagging, is done behind the scenes, without users having to build any of those features into their models directly. Users access some of the resulting information inside the syntax of LITI. For example, inflectional variants can be referenced without specifying each variant in rules. A newer feature in SAS Text Analytics products released since 2017 is called *Textual Elements*. Under each parent term, groups of terms, such as misspellings and synonyms, together with inflectional variants, are recognized as a set, which makes easy use of the full set of variants in rules.

As already mentioned, for ease of building, testing, and updating models, as well as taxonomy construction and maintenance, each product that supports the SAS IE toolkit, such as SAS Text Analytics, SAS Contextual Analysis, and SAS Enterprise Content Categorization, includes a GUI. Features, such as syntax highlighting and testing at both the model level and the specific concept level with both test text and documents, facilitate easier experimentation with and maintenance of rules, concepts, and models. In addition to the benefits already mentioned, the GUI also supports componential design. You can abstract pieces of the model for reuse, easier testing, and maintenance through the use of groupings or sets of rules bound together in a single node of the taxonomy or hierarchy.

LITI itself is flexible and scalable: For beginning users and simple tasks, it can be a simple tool; in the hands of an advanced user, it can also be a complex tool for accomplishing complex tasks. For example, a beginning user can easily model a list of keywords to find all of the instances of those words in the data or easily model and find a sequence of elements in text, while a more advanced user can model facts, events, aliases for names, coreference, or grammatical relationships, such as subject-verb-object (SVO) triples.

LITI is powerful but efficient. Rules in LITI are typically short enough to be represented on a single line, and they are human-readable and maintainable. The syntax includes a set of rule types that helps you to target the rule to the type of matching behavior needed, while using only the processing resources required. In this fashion, you have direct control over optimizing the time it takes a model to process data. Furthermore, the set of Boolean and proximity operators included in LITI are designed specifically to capture and extract both very simple and very complex information and relationships from text. LITI also contains additional modifiers and features to allow you to use POS tags to represent tokens, identify other types of placeholder tokens in patterns, mark the exact pieces of text you want returned, and find related matches within the same document.

Because of these benefits, SAS IE can ultimately be used for building precise and powerful models that represent human knowledge and language patterns. These models can be applied to new data and problems either in full or by repurposing pieces of one model in a new one.

The rest of this book focuses on using predefined and custom concepts in isolation and in various types of combinations, but also points out ways where you may be able to leverage existing lists, automatically generated categorization rules, or automatically generated LITI rules to speed your development process. SAS IE, in other words, can help you to solve many business problems in isolation and this book focuses on helping you understand and practice doing so. Once you have gained proficiency in using LITI rules, you will see the many ways you can integrate SAS IE models into the larger context of your analytics operations, as well.

1.4. When You Should Use Other Approaches instead of SAS IE

SAS IE is a powerful way to model patterns in text, to extract information, and to relate different pieces of information to each other. But other tools can also do some of these tasks, and knowing when to select IE instead of another tool is an important part of designing your analytic approach to a problem. The optimal choice will not always be clear, and sometimes experimentation may be required. You may also decide to use SAS IE instead of another option because you are comfortable with the syntax or rule type choices or simply because you like the flexibility of being able to extract or relate information whenever you want to.

Although there are no overarching rules to text analytics, some analytic scenarios lend themselves to one approach over another, and this section will describe some of those situations and mention some of the alternate options to get you started with making these decisions. The most important factor for deciding whether to use IE is what information you want to get as a result of your analysis.

> **Tip:** Pay attention to the output you need from the analysis, because this is a good criterion for deciding which IE approach to leverage.

What if you do not know your text data very well and you already have a predictive model? You want to see whether there is anything valuable in the unstructured text data that could provide some lift for your model. In this case, it may be possible to reach your goals by using either topic modeling or clustering. Topics and clusters create new structured data, like IE does, but because they are unsupervised machine learning tasks, you have no direct control over the data they create. They identify inherent patterns in the data, which may or may not be related to your interests directly. Therefore, it is more difficult to diagnose the cause of the lift of the predictive model. However, the benefit of these approaches is that they are self-driven and do not require subject matter expertise or a predefined target. Either of these strategies may provide sufficient lift for your predictions. Later, if you want even more lift, you might try adding an IE model to this process; see Albright et al. (2013) for a description of this process.

Another scenario that may not lend itself to IE is when you have a set of documents that you want to allocate to various buckets or categories. You have criteria for placing these documents into each category, or you have data that can be used to train such a model. In these circumstances, using SAS categorization will likely be more efficient than IE, because categorization identifies each document as "in" as opposed to "out" of each category that you define. You can also derive categories from topic models. With this approach, there is no overhead for extraction of additional information from the documents. In addition, categorization uses only one type of rule, which may be simpler for some users. However, that rule type is still powerful, and authoring good rules requires some practice. You can categorize documents as a part of your IE model, so if you want to extract data *and* put documents into categories, you should use SAS IE instead or, even better, use a combination of extraction and categorization. The SAS Text Analytics products enable the categorization model to reference rules in the IE model directly. Combining category and concept models is also a good approach if your categorization rules are getting very large and difficult to maintain.

If you want to detect sentiment or attitudes in your data, you should examine the capabilities of SAS Sentiment Analysis. It has great features for automatic, custom, or hybrid methods of creating models. However, it is also possible to leverage SAS IE or SAS categorization for this purpose. SAS IE may be the way to go if you want more detail about the exact words or phrases used to describe the positive or negative position the writer is expressing or to identify the particular feature that is being noted as positive or negative. Otherwise, a categorization approach for document-level sentiment would likely be more efficient.

If you are trying to simply normalize text or do some very mechanical operation to transform text data, then it may be possible to use SAS regular expressions or a language such as Python. SAS IE is probably not the best choice for such situations. However, once you pass the threshold of starting to care about meaning, then SAS IE becomes a relevant option again. Meaning is easier to model with the kinds of tools SAS IE supplies than in regular expressions, which focus on a character-by-character analysis. Types of normalization or transformation that rely on linguistic information, such as sentence boundaries, are easy and quick to do through SAS IE, as well.

If you are trying to do your own foundational NLP, and you want to learn how to find tokens, break sentences, tag words, or the like, then the SAS IE system will not expose those types of tasks. The SAS foundational NLP is mostly hidden from the users to enable users to focus on models for IE or other methods of analysis. That said, you can use SAS IE to expose sentences, generate *n*-grams, or find sets of related items, even triples like SVO.

1.5. Important Terms in the Book

Before continuing, take some time to familiarize yourself with terminology that is important for following the ideas presented in this book. This section explains terms used at SAS, as well as common terms used in the IE field.

1.5.1. Strings versus Tokens

In text processing, *string* means a defined set of sequential characters that may include punctuation but not a new line character. One example of a string is "123 Main Street Apt. 3B."

Note that the term *string* is not the same as *token*. In NLP systems, a *token* is the basic unit of analysis. In SAS, tokens are intended to represent a meaningful unit, identified by taking alphanumeric characters, spaces, punctuation, and special characters, and determining where to draw boundaries between them. Returning to the example just given, the string contains the following tokens:

- 123
- Main
- Street
- Apt.
- 3B
- .

Usually, a token will not contain an internal space, unless it is defined in the system as a *multiword*. A multiword is a set of two or more words that is defined as a token because the combination of the two words means something different than would be expected by the simple meaning of each word, and it functions as a single grammatical unit. An example of a multiword is "high school."

1.5.2. Named Entities and Predefined Concepts

The phrase *named entities* historically refers to one or more words or numeric expressions in sequence that name a single individual or specify an instance of a type in the real world (or an imaginary world). Some of the most common named entities are names of persons, locations, and organizations, as well as currency amounts, dates, times, and percentages. You can learn more about named entities in chapter 2.

The SAS Text Analytics software provides out-of-the-box rule sets for extracting named entities from text. These rule sets are called *predefined concepts*. In this book, the phrase "named entities" describes the generic idea or historical work, and the phrase "predefined concepts" refers to the SAS implementation of this idea. For more about each of the predefined concepts that SAS provides, see chapters 3 and 4.

1.5.3. Parent Forms and Other Variants

In many dictionaries, a single form of a word represents multiple useful words. For example, if you look up the noun "apple," then you will find the singular form "apple," but not the plural form "apples." The form of the word you find in a dictionary is known as the *lemma* or *base form* of the word. Most lemmas have *inflectional variants*, like plural forms for nouns or past tense forms for verbs, that will not be found in the dictionary. These inflectionally related words are considered to be a set in linguistics and in NLP.

Another type of a word set is a proper or accepted spelling as opposed to *spelling variants*. Spelling variants may include incorrect spellings and typos, as well as variants across dialects such as British or American English. Finally, in some linguistic analyses, it is useful to create broader sets of words that may be considered *synonyms* of each other or have some other semantic similarity.

The SAS Text Analytics products can recognize each of these three sets of related word forms and can group them together. The products enable access to the sets through different mechanisms, and you should consult your product documentation for details. In all cases, when showing such sets of forms, the forms are called *terms*. The lemma, properly spelled form, or a user-specified form is called the *parent term* and the other members of the set are the *child terms*.

1.5.4. Found Text and Extracted Match

To be clear when discussing the fundamentals of writing and applying LITI rules, this book uses two sets of terms: *found text* and *extracted match*. LITI rules contain specifications for matching a span of text, which is the *found text*. In some examples, the entire matched span needs to be extracted, but in others it does not. Therefore, a different set of terms is needed for the part that is extracted as the output or result, the *extracted match*. For example, a rule could match the string "Beatles band members" (found text) but return as output only the band name, "Beatles" (extracted match), when it is followed by the string "band members."

1.6. Suggested Reading

To gain more background in the field, consult the following sources in the References list at the end of the book:

- Albright et al. (2013)
- Belamaric Wilsey and Jade (2015)
- Piskorski and Yangarber (2013)
- Sabo (2015)
- Sabo (2017)
- Sarawagi (2007)
- Small and Medsker (2014)

Chapter 2: Fundamentals of Named Entities

2.1. Introduction to Named Entities

One of the easiest ways to get started with information extraction (IE) is by leveraging the SAS Text Analytics predefined concepts, which contain rules for matching what is known in the scientific literature as *named entities*. In this chapter and chapters 3 and 4, you will learn more about the business value that named entities can provide in general and about the SAS predefined concepts specifically. Understanding this information is helpful not only for using the SAS predefined concepts most effectively, but also as a foundation that you can build on for enriching these concepts with custom rules or for creating additional useful concepts that pertain to your business domain.

After reading this chapter, you will be able to do the following:

- Explain which named entities and specific types of numeric expressions are extracted by SAS as predefined concepts to create structured data
- Recognize scenarios in which SAS predefined concepts can be used to solve some of your specific business problems

As you may remember from chapter 1, the phrase "named entity" was first coined in the Message Understanding Conference (MUC-6) in 1995.

> **Remember**: A *named entity* is one or more words or numeric expressions in sequence which name a single individual or specify an instance of a type in the real world (or an imaginary world).

Consider the following example:

> Jim Smith and Ann Jones were pleased with the performance of their new Querkl, which cost only $25.

Pause and think: Can you identify the named entities in the above sentence?

In this example, named entities are "Jim Smith," "Ann Jones," "Querkl," and "$25." You can recognize "Jim Smith" and "Ann Jones" as named entities because they are familiar names for people in English. Furthermore, you can infer from the context that "Querkl," a made-up word, is the proper name of something that is new to Jim and Ann. You also understand that Jim and Ann spent $25 on the Querkl. By understanding these items as named entities, you also understand how to categorize them: "Jim Smith" and "Ann Jones" are the proper names of persons; "Querkl" is the proper name of an object, perhaps a product; and "$25" is an amount of money in United States currency.

It is precisely this process of identification and categorization of named entities that is important in IE because it provides an opportunity to extract structured information from unstructured text. For example, the names "Jim Smith" and "Ann Jones" marked as Person names in a new data set can answer questions about "who" is involved or responsible. There are many types of named entities that can be modeled for IE, including part names, product names, location names, medicine names, dates, times, phone numbers, among others.

How named entities are categorized depends on the purpose for which IE is being performed. Information that is specific and important in a particular context is a good candidate for extraction. Once the text is extracted and categorized as a particular type of named entity, you can perform further analyses and create reports that answer key business questions.

Named entity recognition (NER) is considered to be "the most fundamental task in IE" (Jiang 2012, p. 15). Some of the complex tasks performed in NER include the following:

- Extraction of standard entities
- Resolution of co-reference
- Word sense disambiguation
- Predicate-argument structure for event and relation extraction
- Extraction and normalization of temporal expressions
- Entity linking

Complex tasks like the ones listed above depend on layers of structural and linguistic analysis, which requires natural language processing (NLP) like tokenization, sentence segmentation, and morphosyntactic analysis. By applying NLP behind the scenes, SAS Text Analytics products facilitate today's NER tasks while being flexible and portable across domains and projects, as well as capable of text analysis in various languages.

Once extracted, named entities can contribute to creating structured data out of unstructured text in various possible ways. One way to do this transformation is to count instances of mentions of specific named entities or of particular types of named entities, drawing conclusions about their presence, absence, or frequency. Furthermore, specific named entities can be used as keys to connect to other personal, geospatial, numeric, or timeline data that may exist. Specific business scenarios in which named entities can be leveraged to answer business questions are presented next.

2.2. Business Scenarios

Frequently, it is useful for an organization to know the following kinds of information:

- *When* something occurred
- *Where* it occurred
- *Who* was involved
- *How much* it cost

The types of entities that are often used to find out this information include the following:

- Person
- Location
- Organization
- Date
- Time
- Percent
- Money
- Phone number
- Digital location (URL, IP address, email address, file path, etc.)

To illustrate how these entities can be leveraged, examples of a few specific business scenarios are discussed in the following subsections.

2.2.1. Example: Pinpointing Location Information

When news stories are reported by official news media or through unofficial sources like social media, reporters will often indicate *where* the events are taking place (Location). Extracting Location would be effective for any of these specific situations:

- Intelligence agents can extract the Location entity from news articles when looking for patterns of terrorist attacks or dangerous events. The information can be used to predict potential future events.
- Law enforcement can extract the Location entity from data sources, such as Twitter, to identify areas where unrest is spreading and deploy officers to the corresponding areas. For example, using data from Twitter about riots in London, analysts quickly determined in real time that the riots started in East London at 4 p.m. but later escalated in South London and were spreading to Central London by midnight.
- International organizations can use the Location entity to pinpoint sites where migrants are disappearing or perishing. That information can be used to distribute aid or to put pressure on nations whose actions or policies could be contributing to the problem.

- Health care organizations and government agencies can monitor where people are getting sick from the flu or other viruses to track or mitigate epidemics.

2.2.2. Example: Identifying Supporters and Competitors

Identifying what a particular person has said or who is involved in a particular event can be useful when you want to know whom you should associate with or who your competitors or detractors are. In such cases, extracting the Person or Organization entity that is mentioned may help, as described in these specific situations:

- Political organizations or lobbyists could seek quotes on particular topics and then link them to the person or organization responsible for saying them. This would be an effective way to determine which people to sponsor for public office.
- One manufacturing company extracts the Organization entity from reviews of its products to detect the names of other companies that are mentioned. The company then applies sentiment to determine whether it is favorably or unfavorably compared to its competitors.

2.2.3. Example: Estimating Loss, Gain, and Risk

When taking unstructured text and feeding it into other models, entities can provide structured data to the model so that it can find historical patterns, identify problems, estimate value or losses, and even predict future outcomes with a predictive model. Here are a few specific situations to illustrate this context:

- A bank uses complaints notes and other data sources to identify facts about the problems being reported. The facts include when a transaction or encounter occurred. This approach is a great way to apply Date and Time entities.
- Another large bank analyzes legal documents relating to interactional swaps and captures the parties involved using Organization and Person entities. It also identifies the financial liability involved by applying the Money entity.
- When tracking changes in petroleum rights, one company analyzes the source, target, and operator companies using rules for recognizing Organizations, the percent stake leveraging a Percent entity, and the stake amount by applying the Money entity.
- A patent research company uses a combination of text topics and extracting Money information to determine the estimated value of patent portfolios of various companies.

2.2.4. Example: Detecting Personally Identifiable Information

Personally identifiable information (PII) must often be protected in special ways according to various types of laws. To prevent loss or misuse of such data, NER can be used to detect such data in documents and help in removing or protecting it, as shown in the following examples:

- A human resources organization uses the Person and Location entities to replace PII on resumes with identification numbers to help prevent bias from impacting initial filtering of job candidates.

- A hospital uses Location, Person, Phone, and Digital Location entities to remove PII and anonymize information that is used for research purposes.

2.3. The SAS Approach

Now that you have learned about named entities and seen some examples of how organizations can use them to solve business problems, let's discuss how SAS handles named entities. The SAS approach to named entities is twofold:

- Providing a set of out-of-the-box named entities called *predefined concepts*
- Allowing you to create your own named entities, called *custom concepts*, for use in parallel with the predefined concepts, in combination with the predefined concepts, or in isolation

Each predefined concept is described in detail in chapters 3 and 4, and the processes for creating custom concepts are detailed in chapters 5–10.

Predefined concepts in SAS reflect a predominately rule-based approach generally focused on proper names, as well as common time and numerical expressions. Rule-based systems have been proven to be most reliable and effective for fine-grained and finely tuned projects (Chiticariu, Li, and Reiss 2013). The main drawback to rule-based systems is the time it takes to develop them. At SAS, this drawback has been mitigated by providing out-of-the-box predefined concepts that the SAS linguists have developed and maintained for more than a decade. By using the predefined concepts, you can take advantage of that principled knowledge of specialists across various world languages. SAS linguists and developers are actively researching and exploring innovations in machine learning and hybrid systems. They are regularly adding proven advances, including improvements to predefined concepts, to enhance the breadth and quality of SAS Text Analytics.

> **Remember**: *Predefined concepts* are a set of out-of-the-box standardized concept models for named entities in SAS Text Analytics products.

Starting with SAS Text Analytics Viya releases in 2016, a baseline of seven predefined standardized concept models is provided for the following entities for English:

- Person
- Place (Location)
- Organization
- Date
- Time
- Money
- Percent

Standardization for all other supported languages is ongoing. All supported languages also provide a predefined grammatical pattern to aid in the recognition of multiwords and complex concepts:

- Noun Group

Some languages may also offer additional support for an extended set of predefined concept models, including, for example, the following:

- Measure
- Digital location
- Vehicle

To measure the accuracy of each predefined concept for each support language, SAS linguists have either acquired or created an industry gold standard corpus. The metrics of precision and recall, by predefined concept type, serve to guide development and provide a way for linguists to determine when the models are improving. The corpora are not used as a direct resource to development, so the models do not become tuned to the corpora but are continually aligned with the documented standard. Language models are regularly updated to stay in alignment with the standard and to gain increased accuracy.

2.3.1. Understanding Standard Predefined Concepts

The seven predefined concepts in SAS Text Analytics software were selected to be a standard baseline set from the typical listing of entities covered in NER research. MUC-6 grouped these entities as follows:

- *Enamex* for entity names
  - Person
  - Place
  - Organization

- *Timex* for time expressions
  - Date
  - Time

- *Numex* for numerical expressions
  - Money
  - Percent

These groups are considered the most valuable set of entities to identify in modern IE.

Enamex

The SAS definitions of enamex entities as specified in the predefined concepts include only proper names and not all mentions of things in the world. In other words, mention of "the mountain" (a thing in a class) in the text will not match as Place, but "Mt. Everest" (a particular, named mountain) will. In short, neither common nouns nor pronouns will match any enamex entity without a proper noun.

Aliases for proper names will be a match if they are considered to fit into the same contexts as the true name. For example, a shortened form of a company name will be included, as will a commonly understood nickname for the same company. Aliases include acronyms, nicknames, truncated names, and proper metonyms.

Nickname metonymy occurs when a speaker uses a reference to one entity to actually refer to another entity that is related to the first one. This is commonly done to use a city name to a sports team. For example, "Boston beat Cleveland last week." Both "Boston" and "Cleveland" should be categorized as Organization rather than Place, because the reference is intended to be to the cities' baseball teams, not the cities themselves.

> **Remember**: Predefined concept definitions for Person, Place, and Organization include only proper nouns.

Timex

The SAS definitions of timex entities as specified in the predefined concepts endeavor to capture all explicit answers to the question "when." They do not capture temporal expressions that are too vague to plot on any timeline, or only answer the questions "how long" or "how often." Whenever language indicating a point on a timeline is detected, modifiers that indicate the point is the minimum or maximum of an implicit or explicit range of points are included in the match. Any adjacent information about duration or frequency is also included.

In the interpretation of the text, it is assumed that the reference date is known. In other words, the date tied to "today" or "the date these events occurred" is a known point on a timeline, even if that reference date is not explicit in the text. The granularity of that known point extends only to the full day, not to smaller units that would indicate the reference time of "now." However, "now" may serve as a reference point in relationships with other times if there is a unit of time in the phrase, as in "from now until 1pm," for example.

> **Remember**: Expression definitions for the Date and Time predefined concepts include temporal expressions that can be plotted on a timeline.

Numex

The SAS definitions of numex entities, as specified in the predefined concepts Money and Percent, include an explicit or implied numeric value and a symbol, symbols, or words representing currency or percent. In addition, once these required pieces of information are detected, any modifiers that indicate that the value is a maximum or minimum of a range of values are included within the scope of the match. For example, in the sentence "The children had to score more than 80% on their test to pass," the words "more than" are included in the scope of the percentage match.

> **Remember**: Expression definitions for the Money and Percent predefined concepts include numeric values and specific symbols or keywords.

2.3.2. Understanding Underlying Principles

While the details of how each of the predefined concepts are conceptualized are presented in chapters 3 and 4, some general guiding principles underlie all the concepts and can be used as best practices when you are developing your own extraction rules or standards.

Only Contiguous Matches Are Returned as the Matched String

Any modifiers that appear between two tokens that together comprise a match must be included in the match. For example, "12 big bad million dollars" is one match. You can write rules that match two or more noncontiguous strings as cues in a given context in order to return a match, but that returned match must be one contiguous match string. For example, in the phrase "Washington in the District of Columbia (D.C.)," there are two matches for the Place concept: "Washington" and "District of Columbia (D.C.)," and the second match can be used as context to return the match "Washington" as Place. Compare that with the phrase "a visit to Washington, D.C.," where there is only one contiguous match: "Washington, D.C."

Matches Include Inflected Forms

In languages that have suffixes for cases, definiteness, and other similar grammatical categories, matches reflect all forms of the word, not only the subject form—for example, "České republiky" (of the Czech Republic) and "České republice" (to the Czech Republic), not only "Česká republika" (Czech Republic).

Match Length Is Important

The match is always the longest possible combination of allowed elements. The length also needs to be long enough to capture the entire single individual or instance of a type in the real world.

However, with the special grammatical pattern, Noun Group, the match needs to be short enough to find repeating patterns. Noun Group matches are fed into topic detection, and topics are better if similar expressions for the same thing in the world are counted together. So, the goal is to identify key multiword and complex concepts, but not differentiate on less salient modifiers. For this reason, Noun Group matches are usually only 2 to 3 words long. For example, "one of my three old bank accounts" may not appear in the text more than once, so it is not as useful to count, but "old bank accounts" might appear many times and therefore be more useful for topic detection.

Match Algorithm Is Important

As mentioned in chapter 1, there are several different algorithms that can be used for matching predefined and custom concepts: "all matches," "longest match," and "best match." The choice of algorithm can impact the results you see.

Be aware that the SAS predefined concepts are written to work with the "best match" algorithm, which uses a priority setting to select between competing rules. Overlapping, redundant, or less accurate matches may be seen when you are using predefined concepts with the other matching algorithms. Consult documentation to find out if it is possible to change the match algorithm in your products including score code and, if so, how to do it. See section 13.4.1 for more details about these algorithms and the use of priority settings.

Context Is Important

Leveraging contextual cues in rules can help identify the predefined concept match and type for classification. For example, "Amazon" could be an organization or place; without context, it is impossible to tell which of the two predefined concept types it is. This is especially important for handling ambiguity, when the same name could refer to more than one predefined concept type. If there is no disambiguating context, then a match may not be detected for some predefined concept types. For more information about ambiguity in enamex predefined concepts, see the discussion in chapter 3, and for timex and numex entities, see chapter 4.

2.3.3. Accessing the Predefined Concepts

The SAS predefined concepts are shipped as a set with the SAS Text Analytics products out-of-the-box. To take advantage of this set of concepts, you just need to select that the predefined entities are loaded into your project or model. Consult product documentation for details on how to do so. What to expect as matches with predefined concepts in your project is specified in chapters 3 and 4.

As already mentioned, you can also use these concepts in concert with your own custom concepts, as well as extend them to tune them to your data and or specific purposes. The processes for accomplishing these tasks are addressed in chapters 5–10.

Chapter 3: SAS Predefined Concepts: Enamex

3.1. Introduction to SAS Predefined Concepts

As you will recall from the previous chapter, a *named entity* is one or more words or numeric expressions in sequence which name a single individual or specify an instance of a type in the real world (or an imaginary world).

SAS provides a set of seven predefined entities called *predefined concepts*, spanning the three types of entities described in chapter 2:

- Enamex (Person, Place [Location], Organization), detailed in this chapter
- Timex (Date, Time), detailed in chapter 4
- Numex (Money, Percent), detailed in chapter 4

All fully supported languages also provide a predefined grammatical pattern to aid in the recognition of multiwords and complex concepts:

- Noun group, detailed in chapter 4

Although the rules that are used for the predefined concepts are proprietary and not displayed in the products, you can learn more about the principles and assumptions that form the basis for the rules for each of the predefined concepts in the sections that follow. Knowing what matches are expected for predefined concepts can help you both more accurately predict and modify behavior of the concepts, and more easily identify areas where custom concepts would be most useful for your particular extraction task.

In addition, this information can help you measure the effectiveness of an information extraction system by acting as a standards manual for setting up and annotating a gold standard corpus, as well as for data collection, with all targeted named entities marked in a consistent manner. Measuring the value of information extraction without first defining the targeted entities is like using a yardstick with no numbers or lines. The information in this chapter and in chapter 4 defines the numbers and lines on that yardstick.

Referencing these standards can also be a useful step in troubleshooting matches. It can help you align expectations regarding the existence and disambiguation of matches and their scope in various contexts.

This chapter and chapter 4 are a reference that you can keep coming back to as you work with named entities, whether you are using SAS Text Analytics or some other approach. Because these chapters serve as a set of annotation guidelines for typical named entities, you can use them whether you are using SAS Text Analytics, or implementing your own set of entity rules using other approaches or software. The content is based on extensive research, historical definitions, and best practice guidelines that the SAS linguists have prepared during the development of cross-linguistic standards for predefined concept extraction for more than 30 languages.

In this chapter and chapter 4, matches that meet the definition of each predefined concept type are denoted in square brackets. For example, in the phrase: "the company [SAS]," only "SAS" is an extracted match (for Organization).

3.2. Person

Person is a predefined concept provided by the SAS linguists. Note that the name of this concept in your product may be *nlpPerson* or another similar name. The generic "Person" label is used in this book, because it aligns with industry standard practices and is similar to any concept name used in the SAS Text Analytics products in the past.

Person includes any proper name used to designate a specific individual in the real or in an imaginary world. *Individual* includes any intelligent agent: any real or fictional human, alien, deity, artificial intelligence, or animal.

The matches for Person include two or more of the following:

- First name
- Last name
- Middle name
- Maiden name
- Nickname
- Initials
- Infixes (such as "van", "von", "van der", and "de")
- Suffixes (such as "Jr." or "Sr.")
- Other names specific to particular cultures (for example, Russian patronymic, such as "Alekseevna")
- Title of address

See section 3.2.3 for a discussion of when single-word names are considered Person matches. References with only an initial or initials and no other name must also have a title captured as part of the match—for example, "Mr. T." References to people that are not proper names, as well as common nouns or pronouns are not matches for the Person concept. The match is always the longest possible combination of allowed elements.

Words that are leveraged to identify a potential match for Person include job titles and verbal constructions indicating agents of human-like actions, such as, for example, "exclaim." These markers are not retained in the matched string; they are leveraged only as contextual cues.

> **Remember**: *Person* includes any proper name designating a specific individual in the real or imaginary world.

Special cases that govern whether certain words are included in the match are described in the following sections.

3.2.1. Titles in Person Names

The matches for Person include the following titles of address:

- Common titles
- Familial titles

- Professional titles
- Religious titles
- Military titles
- Royalty titles

In the contexts where a person can be addressed in spoken communication with the title and first and last name, only first name, or only last name, that title is included as part of the tagged match for Person. However, job titles or descriptions are not matches for Person.

Consider the following examples of strings referencing persons:

- Mr. President
- Ms. Jones
- Professor L. Noh
- The Pope
- Queen Elizabeth
- Secretary of Health and Human Services
- Secretary Sylvia Mathews Burwell
- Sylvia Mathews Burwell
- Father M.
- Aunt B
- Sergeant York
- Miss Know-It-All
- Princess Mary of Kent
- King Henry VIII
- The Duke of York
- The President of the United States
- President Lincoln
- CEO of SAS
- The Olympian
- T. said that I should go

Pause and think: Can you identify the Person matches in the above examples?

Matches include only the following:

- [Ms. Jones]
- [Professor L. Noh]
- [Queen Elizabeth]
- [Secretary Sylvia Mathews Burwell]
- [Sylvia Mathews Burwell]
- [Father M.]
- [Aunt B]

- [Sergeant York]
- [Princess Mary of Kent]
- [King Henry VIII]
- [President Lincoln]

Titles like "Secretary of Health and Human Services," "CEO of SAS," "Pope," and "Duke of York" are job or professional titles that can refer to more than one individual throughout history. Such relative references, including phrases such as "Miss Know-It-All," are not specific enough to be considered a match for the Person concept. In addition, only an initial is not enough context for a match to the Person concept.

3.2.2. Suffixes as Part of a Personal Name

Suffixes on names that are part of the specific designation of an individual and not simply related to education or career are included in the match, together with the name or names. Consider the following examples:

- Mary Johns Ph.D.
- John James Jr.
- Frank Sr.
- P. Smith M.D.
- Rob Moore PMP
- S. Matthews III

> **Pause and think**: Can you identify the matches in the examples above?

Matches include the following:

- [John James Jr.]
- [Frank Sr.]
- [S. Matthews III]

Only the first, last names and initials are matched in the following:

- [Mary Johns] Ph.D.
- [P. Smith] M.D.
- [Rob Moore] PMP

The suffixes that follow the last names in these examples are referring to professional designations in the medical and business fields. Therefore, they are not included in the match.

3.2.3. Single-Word Names

Single-word names are included only when the context (person suffixes, job names, birthdays, or other person-related information) indicates a probable match. Consider the following examples:

- Kent exceeded . . .
- Jones, CEO of MyCorp, said . . .
- Lementa, born 1962 . . .
- Gary was nice

Pause and think: Can you identify the matches in the examples above?

Matches include only the following:

- [Jones], CEO of MyCorp, said . . .
- [Lementa], born 1962 . . .

In the remaining examples, the proper nouns are ambiguous because there is not enough context to infer that the reference is to a person. For example, Kent could be a person, company, product, or place name. Similarly, Gary is a common English name for persons but could also refer to a town in Indiana.

3.2.4. Body References

References to a body part, remains, or corpse of a person are not considered a part of the match. Consider the following examples:

- John's body
- The body
- Arms and legs
- The remains of Mr. Smith
- Mimi's singing voice

Pause and think: Can you identify the matches in the examples above?

Matches include only the following:

- [John]'s body
- The remains of [Mr. Smith]
- [Mimi]'s singing voice

Note that the remaining words in the matches above provide reasonably unambiguous context that the proper nouns are referring to persons.

3.2.5. Quotes

Quotes around a descriptive nickname are included within the name match if they appear within or overlap the boundaries of a person's name. Consider the following examples:

- James "the Bully" Holtz
- "James the Bully" Holtz
- James Holtz "The Bully"

> **Pause and think**: Can you identify the matches in the examples above?

Matches include the following:

- [James "the Bully" Holtz]
- ["James the Bully" Holtz]
- [James Holtz] "The Bully"

The nickname is not included in the match for the final example because it does not appear within the boundaries of the person's name.

3.2.6. Locations as Part of Name

Locations that are part of the name are included in the match and not matched separately as Place. But mentions of titles and locations only are not included as matches. In addition, locations named for people are not included as matches to the Person concept.

Consider the following examples:

- Duchess of York
- Grand Duke of Saxe-Weimar-Eisenach William Ernest
- The city of Bismarck
- Princess Anna of Sedgewick
- Fort William

> **Pause and think**: Can you identify the Person matches in the examples above?

Matches include only the following:

- [Grand Duke of Saxe-Weimar-Eisenach William Ernest]
- [Princess Anna of Sedgewick]

The first example is not considered a person match because it is a title that could refer to different people throughout history. In the second example, the title contains a location name, so only the first and last names are parts of the match. In the third and fifth examples, the reference is to a location, even though the place name contains a person name. Therefore, they are not considered matches for Person. In the fourth example, the location is included in the Person match because it helps specify which Princess Anna is being referred to.

3.2.7. Groups of Individuals

Groups of individuals such as national, geographic, religious, or ethnic groups; family or dynasty names; or blended names of two individuals are not a match for Person.

Nonmatches include the following:

- The Kennedy family
- The Joneses
- The Daniel twins
- The House of Hanover
- The Han dynasty
- American
- Frenchwoman
- Bennifer (a blended name of Ben Affleck and Jennifer Garner)

Some groups of individuals match as Organization:

- [Democrats]
- [Girl Scouts]
- [Marines]

See more about organizations in 3.4.

Terms referring to groups of two or more people are not included as matches to the Person concept. However, conjoined or listed names with elision are included as matches. The listed names are considered one single reference if part of the name is elided. The listed names are considered two or more matches if the names on either side of the conjunction are complete.

Matches include the following:

- [Mary and John Smith]
- [John Smith] and [Mark Frank]
- [John, Mary, Jane and Marsha Smith]
- [John Smith], [Mary Smith], and [T. Yokel]

Consider the following examples:

- Latinos
- Muslims
- Republicans
- The Habsburgs
- Brangelina
- Tolbert triplets
- Nicole, Erica, and Jaclyn Dahm
- Barack and Michelle Obama
- Plácido Domingo, José Carreras, and Luciano Pavarotti

Pause and think: Can you identify the matches for the Person concept in the examples on the previous page?

Matches for the Person concept include only the following:

- [Nicole, Erica, and Jaclyn Dahm]
- [Barack and Michelle Obama]
- [Plácido Domingo], [José Carreras], and [Luciano Pavarotti]

The first few examples are referring to ethnic, religious, and political groups of people, as well as family names, conjoined names, and elided names. None of these examples match the Person concept.

3.2.8. Historical Figures, Saints, and Deities

Names of saints and other historical figures are included, unless the context indicates that they appear as a part of the name of another predefined concept type. Proper names for deities are a match, but not references to deities generally, descriptive references, or exclamations.

Consider the following examples:

- George Washington
- George Washington bridge
- St. Frances Cathedral
- St. Frances of Assisi
- God
- God!
- The god
- Jehovah
- Allah
- The Prophet
- our Lord

Pause and think: Can you identify the matches for the Person concept in the examples above?

Matches for the Person concept include only the following:

- [George Washington]
- [St. Frances of Assisi]
- [God]
- [Jehovah]
- [Allah]

The second and third examples are not matches for the Person concept because they are referring to locations, namely a bridge and a cathedral. The sixth example is an exclamation, whereas the remaining nonmatches are not specific enough to refer to one particular deity.

3.2.9. Animals, Fictional Characters, Artificial Intelligence, and Aliens

The proper names of animals, fictional characters, artificial intelligence, and aliens are matches.

Consider the following examples:

- Mr. Ed the talking horse
- Eevee (type of Pokemon creature)
- Time Lord
- E.T.
- Martians
- Vulcans
- Baloo—Mowgli's friend

> **Pause and think**: Can you identify the matches in the examples above?

Matches include only the following:

- [Mr. Ed] the talking horse
- [E.T.]
- [Baloo]—[Mowgli]'s friend

Matches do not include species, such as Eevee, Martians, or Vulcans, because they are groups.

3.2.10. Businesses Named after People

Names of humans, any of which could also be the name of a business, are included as matches to Person unless there is a contextual cue that the name applies to the business, not to the individual. Organization names with embedded person names are not included as matches.

Consider the following examples:

- Dr Kelly Macgroarty
- Steven L. Cox, CPA
- Akram & Associates
- Jaclyn Christie Podiatrists

> **Pause and think**: Can you identify the matches for the Person concept in the examples above?

Matches for the Person concept include only the following:

- [Dr Kelly Macgroarty]
- [Steven L. Cox], CPA

Note that the third and fourth examples are not matches because context, such as "& Associates" and "Podiatrists," identifies a business even though part of the company name may be a person name.

3.2.11. Laws, Diseases, Prizes, and Works of Art

The following situations are not included as matches:

- Laws or legal acts named for people, such as "Dodd-Frank Act"
- Diseases named for people, such as "Alzheimer's"
- Prizes named for people, such as "the Nobel Prize"
- Works of art named for people, such as "The Birth of Venus"

3.3. Place

Place is a predefined concept provided by the SAS linguists. Note that the name of this concept in your product may be *nlpPlace* or another similar name. The generic "Place" label is used in this book, noting that "nlpPlace" and any concepts found in SAS products that have Location within their name are equivalent.

Place includes any proper name or defined expression commonly used to designate a specific site in the real or in an imaginary world, as well as any geo-political entity (GPE). *Site* includes any geographical point or area in physical space, on earth or elsewhere, including imaginary worlds. *GPE* is a composite of the following:

- Population
- Government
- Physical location
- Nation

For example, GPE includes province, state, county, city, town, and others.

> **Remember**: Place includes any proper name or expression designating a specific site or geo-political entity in the real or imaginary world.

In addition to site names and GPE names, matches for Place include location expressions. For example, matches include the following:

- Postal address, crossroads, geographical coordinates expressed as longitude–latitude pairs, or military grid reference system (MGRS) coordinates
- Names of continents
- Regions that are subcontinental, transcontinental, subnational, or transnational
- Nations or countries
- States, provinces, cantons, counties, or district names
- Cities, towns, villages, and hamlets
- Clusters of GPEs that function as political entities
- Airport names and official codes
- Highways, street names, bridge names, and road names
- Street addresses (postal and crossroads)
- Fictional or mythological geographical locations
- Geographical coordinates expressed as longitude–latitude pairs or as MGRS coordinates
- Named geographical features, including mountain ranges and bodies of water
- Park names

Words that are leveraged to indicate a potential match for Place are the following:

- Locative prepositions
- Verbal constructions that indicate nations or governments acting as people
- Words indicating a type of location, like "planet," "nation," and "government"

Special cases that govern whether certain words are included in the match are described in the following sections.

3.3.1. Common Nouns and Determiners

Common nouns may be included in the name if they help clarify the concept or are truly treated in language and by societal conventions as a predefined concept, whether capitalized or not. Determiners like English "a" or "the" may also be included if they are considered a part of the name. For example, the determiner is included in the match of "[Democratic Republic of the Congo]" but not in "the [Southeastern United States]."

Consider the following examples:

- In the river
- The river Seine
- The Amazon River
- The Ruhr valley
- Through the valley
- Mississippi River west bank

- The disputed area of Jordan's West Bank
- The Hague

Matches include only the following:

- The [river Seine]
- The [Amazon River]
- The [Ruhr valley]
- [Mississippi River] west bank
- The disputed area of [Jordan's West Bank]
- [The Hague]

The first and fifth examples do not produce a match because they do not include a proper noun. Note that the determiner is included as part of the match only in the final example.

3.3.2. Subnational Regions and Other Descriptors

Subnational regions are not included when referenced by only compass-point modifiers; generally, there needs to be enough information in the text explicitly that the location could be plotted or an area drawn on a map. Historic modifiers and other descriptors are included only if they are part of the official name.

Consider the following examples:

- South America
- The Southeastern United States
- South Pacific
- The South
- The Southwest region
- The mid-West
- Former Soviet Union
- Former Yugoslav Republic of Macedonia
- Ivory Coast
- The coast of Hawaii
- Eastern North Dakota

Matches include the following:

- [South America]
- The [Southeastern United States]

- [South Pacific]
- Former [Soviet Union]
- [Former Yugoslav Republic of Macedonia]
- [Ivory Coast]
- The coast of [Hawaii]
- Eastern [North Dakota]

Examples like "the South" and "the Southwest region" are not specific enough to be able to be pinpointed on a map, because they could refer to locations in various countries. Note that adjectives such as "former" or nouns such as "coast" are not included in the match when they are a historical or geographical reference, but are included if they are part of the official name of a country.

3.3.3. Street Addresses

Street addresses are included if they contain enough information to identify a specific point on a street or to zero in on a specific building or multi-structure facility with some background information about country and city/town/province as assumed knowledge. For the match to be a Place, it has to be able to be found on a map without guesswork.

Consider the following examples:

- 123 Main Str., Raleigh, NC
- 123 Main
- Empire State Building
- The Bank of America Tower in NYC
- Disney World
- Disneyland Paris
- The Eiffel Tower
- The North Carolina Museum of Art

Pause and think: Can you identify the matches in the examples above?

Matches include the following:

- [123 Main Str., Raleigh, NC]
- [Empire State Building]
- The [Bank of America Tower in NYC]
- [Disney World]
- [Disneyland Paris]
- The [Eiffel Tower]

The remaining two examples are not matches for the Place concept, because the context is not specific enough. The references could be to an organization rather than a place.

3.3.4. Monuments

Monuments that are not aliases for organizations running them are included as matches. All other facilities or buildings are excluded unless they are an airport or they fit the criteria for address.

Consider the following examples:

- The Great Wall of China
- The Eiffel Tower
- Mt. Rushmore
- . . . said the White House
- The Vatican
- The North Carolina Museum of Art

Pause and think: Can you identify the matches for the Place concept in the examples above?

Matches for the Place concept include only the following:

- The [Great Wall of China]
- The [Eiffel Tower]
- [Mt. Rushmore]

The remaining three examples contain matches for the Organization concept.

3.3.5. Celestial Bodies

Names of heavenly bodies and locations are matches so long as the reference is to a specific heavenly body. Consider the following examples:

- Our sun
- The moon's glow
- The smartest person on earth
- A sun like ours
- Any moon will glow
- Waste and earth being trucked
- . . . earth-like
- Welcome to the afterlife
- Earthy old knowledge
- The dead go to heaven or hell or sometime to Limbo
- From here to Pluto

Pause and think: Can you identify the matches in the examples above?

Matches include only the following:

- Our [sun]
- The [moon]'s glow
- The smartest person on [earth]
- The dead go to [heaven] or [hell] or sometime to [Limbo]
- From here to [Pluto]

In the remaining examples, the references are not to specific celestial objects; therefore, no matches are extracted to the Place concept.

3.3.6. Neighborhoods

Names of neighborhoods are included, but generic references to parts of cities or towns are not matches. Consider the following examples:

- The Bronx
- Midland Beach
- Bay Terrace
- Lower Manhattan
- The northernmost borough of NYC
- South NYC

Pause and think: Can you identify the matches in the examples above?

Matches include the following:

- The [Bronx]
- [Midland Beach]
- [Bay Terrace]
- [Lower Manhattan]
- The northernmost borough of [NYC]
- South [NYC]

Note that the cardinal points are not included in the matches in these examples.

3.3.7. Fictional Place Names

Fictional and nonphysical places with names are considered a match so long as the reference is to a specific place. If the reference is generic, it is not a match.

Consider the following examples:

- . . . paradise
- . . . fantasyland
- La La Land

- Oz
- Camelot
- The Garden of Eden
- Tatooine

Pause and think: Can you identify the matches in the examples above?

Matches include only the following:

- [La La Land]
- [Oz]
- [Camelot]
- The [Garden of Eden]
- [Tatooine]

The first two examples are not proper nouns and therefore not matches. The remaining examples are matches because they name specific locations.

3.3.8. Conjoined Location Names

When more than one location name in a row is encountered, they are considered one Place match if the relationship between them is hierarchical and they are adjacent or separated by punctuation or prepositions that establish the hierarchical relationship. They are also considered one Place match if the location names are conjoined or listed with elision. Leading prepositions are not included in the match.

Consider the following examples:

- Dallas, TX
- Frankfurt, Germany
- . . . in Orlando and Miami, Florida
- . . . across the Pacific or Atlantic Oceans
- I went to Dayton, Ohio and then to Columbus
- . . . came from Dayton, Ohio and not from Columbus, Ohio

Pause and think: Can you identify the matches in the examples above?

Matches include the following:

- [Dallas, TX]
- [Frankfurt, Germany]
- . . . in [Orlando and Miami, Florida]
- . . . across [the Pacific or Atlantic Oceans]

- I went to [Dayton, Ohio and then to Columbus]
- . . . came from [Dayton, Ohio] and not from [Columbus, Ohio]

Note that the leading prepositions are not included in the match and that only the final example produces two matches because of intervening text.

3.3.9. Special Cases for Nonmatches

Special cases that are excluded from matches as Place are as follows:

- A city, state, or district name used to refer to a sports team (For example, in the sentence "Boston defeated Cleveland," both "Boston" and "Cleveland" are categorized as Organization rather than Place, because the reference is intended to be to the sports teams, not the cities.)
- Names of artifacts or products or services of organizations, including names of newspapers, websites, and media broadcasts (See section 3.4 for potentially using these names as references to Organizations.)
- Names of purely digital locations, computer memory, websites, or tools, like the Dark Web, the Internet, and Wikipedia
- Location names embedded in person names, organization names, or times
- Names of gulags, forced labor camps, or other similar facilities
- Adjectival forms of location or language names, such as "French cuisine" and "in Japanese"
- Works of art with location names embedded in their names, such as "Washington Crossing the Delaware"
- Names for the people from a location, unless the name also happens to describe the location (For example, "Americans," "Aussies," "the British," "Chinese," and "English" are not matches.)

3.4. Organization

Organization is a predefined concept provided by the SAS linguists. Note that the name of this concept in your product may be *nlpOrganization* or another similar name. The generic "Organization" label is used in this book because it is an industry standard term and reflects previous names used in SAS products for this concept.

Organization means a formally established association. The matches for Organization include the proper names, common aliases, nicknames, or stock ticker symbols of businesses, government units, sports teams, clubs, and formally organized artistic groups. Common types of organizations are as follows:

- Stock exchanges
- Specifically named military organizations, including armies, navies, and special forces
- Paramilitary organizations, governing bodies, and government departments
- Nongeneric names of parts of a government
- Educational organizations

- Commercial organizations
- Entertainment organizations, bands, and performing groups
- Media organizations and conglomerates
- Political parties, advocacy groups, and think tanks
- Professional regulatory and advocacy groups
- Unions (but not names of various job types or categories)
- Charitable organizations and nonprofits
- International regulatory and political bodies
- Religious organizations like denominations or guidance bodies (but not members of a particular religion, unless there is only one guidance body across the whole religion)
- Medical-science organizations and research institutions
- Organizations participating in or facilitating sporting and gaming events
- Official clubs like [Toastmasters International], the [Masons], or [Alcoholics Anonymous]
- Coalitions or alliances of governments
- Multinational organizations

Examples of aliases, nicknames, and pseudonyms include the following:

- [NYPD], an alias for the [New York Police Department]
- [GOP], an alias for the [Republican Party]
- [Big Blue], an alias for [IBM]

Matches also include stock ticker symbols, such as [MSFT] and [CSCO].

The proper names for groups of individuals closely associated with a specific organization are also considered matches. For example, [Girl Scouts] is a proper name associated with [Girl Scouts of America] and [Democrats] is a proper name associated with the [Democratic Party]. Generic names for a type of group or organization, like Latinos, feminists, police, or army, are not considered matches. But a specific proper name is a match; for example, the [Los Angeles Police Department] or [U.S. Congress].

In addition, organization names embedded in locations, such as AT&T Stadium, are not matches for Organization because they are referring to a location.

Remember: *Organization* means the name of a formally established association.

Words that are leveraged to indicate a potential match for Organization include prefixes and suffixes indicative of organizations, verbs associated with businesses or organizations acting like individuals, some prepositions (at, for, with, within, outside of), nouns for associated groups (team, division, chapter, orchestra, club), and facility words as part of the name.

Special cases that govern whether certain words are included in the match are described in the following sections.

3.4.1. Corporate Designators or Suffixes

Corporate designators or suffixes are included in the match. Consider the following examples:

- Akram & Associates Inc.
- Asset Management Partners Ltd.
- Nanoscribe GmbH
- OOO Stellberg

Pause and think: Can you identify the matches in the examples above?

Matches include the following:

- [Akram & Associates Inc.]
- [Asset Management Partners Ltd.]
- [Nanoscribe GmbH]
- [OOO Stellberg]

In all the examples, the various corporate designators are included in the matches.

3.4.2. Determiners before Proper Names

Determiners in front of proper names are included only if they are expected as part of the name. In the example of "The Ohio State University," that university dictates that its name includes "the," so the entire string ([The Ohio State University]) is the match. In contrast, in the text "the United Nations," the determiner is not a part of the match (the [United Nations]).

3.4.3. Facility Names Associated with an Organization

Proper names referring to facilities which are closely associated with an organization that runs or owns the facility are included in the match, even if the facility itself is being referenced in a locative context. One exception is airports, which are not considered organizations.

Consider the following examples:

- Reedy Creek Baptist Church
- WakeMed Cary Hospital
- The Vatican
- The Empire State Building
- The White House
- The Trump Tower
- Westminster Abbey
- Stanford University

- RDU airport
- Disney World

Matches for the Organization concept include only the following:

- [Reedy Creek Baptist Church]
- [WakeMed Cary Hospital]
- The [Vatican]
- The [White House]
- [Westminster Abbey]
- [Stanford University]

Airports and organization names embedded in locations are not matches, which disqualifies the remaining examples from matching for the Organization concept.

3.4.4. Groups of Individuals

Named groups of individuals with a codified and widely accepted set of criteria for membership in the group are included if they are closely associated with a single specific named organization. Consider the following examples:

- Christians
- Muslims
- Jews
- Buddhists
- Boy Scouts of America
- Girl Scouts

Matches include only the following:

- [Boy Scouts of America]
- [Girl Scouts]

The remaining examples denote religious groups and therefore are not matches for Organization.

3.4.5. Aliases

A city, state, or district name is included when it is used to refer to a sports team. This is a common example of *metonymy*, a type of alias.

Consider the following examples:

- Boston vs. Cleveland
- The teams met in Boston
- They won in Cleveland
- The Cleveland uniforms are blue

Pause and think: Can you identify the matches in the examples above?

Matches include only the following:

- [Boston] vs. [Cleveland]
- The [Cleveland] uniforms are blue

When an organization name and an alias are both present, they are considered two separate matches. Consider the following examples:

- The Department of Justice (DOJ)
- Apple (Apple Computers, Inc.) said yesterday . . .
- University of North Carolina–Chapel Hill (UNC-CH)

Pause and think: Can you identify the matches in the examples above?

Matches include the following:

- [The Department of Justice] ([DOJ])
- [Apple] ([Apple Computers, Inc.]) said yesterday
- [University of North Carolina–Chapel Hill] ([UNC-CH])

An organization name or alias that is an explicit reference to a product or brand is included. However, the reverse is not true: References to the products or brands themselves are not automatically matched as organizations. Ambiguous references to products or brands that cannot be discerned from context to be referring to the organization specifically are also not included.

Consider the following examples:

- Coke is the real thing
- Coke tried to buy out the competition
- Honda Civic
- I drive a Lexus
- Apple iPhone
- All iPhones
- . . . on Google
- I Googled that yesterday

- Buy stock in Kleenex
- I need a Kleenex

Matches include the following:

- [Coke] tried to buy out the competition
- [Honda] Civic
- I drive a [Lexus]
- [Apple] iPhone
- . . . on [Google]
- Buy stock in [Kleenex]

The remaining examples are referring to products rather than organizations and are therefore not matches to Organization.

3.4.6. Conjoined Organization Names

Two or more conjoined or listed organization names are considered separate predefined concept matches, even if it looks like they may share elided material. In this case, the shortened name is considered an alias.

Consider the following examples:

- . . . at Cisco and Microsoft Corporation
- Cisco Systems and Apple Inc. are both headquartered in California

Matches include the following:

- . . . at [Cisco] and [Microsoft Corporation]
- [Cisco Systems] and [Apple Inc.] are both headquartered in California

In these examples, although the organization names are conjoined, they are separate matches.

3.4.7. Event Names

Event names are not considered organizations, but the committees and organizations that run the events are. Consider the following examples:

- Super Bowl XXX
- The NFL
- The Olympics

- The Olympic Committee
- China Film Festival

Pause and think: Can you identify the matches for the Organization concept in the examples above?

Matches include only the following:

- The [NFL]
- The [Olympic Committee]

The remaining examples are not matches, because they are names of events.

3.4.8. Special Cases for Nonmatches
Special cases that are excluded from matches as Organization are as follows:
- Organization names that are embedded in location names, such as "the Apple headquarters" and "the SAS campus"
- Industrial sectors and industries or the people or jobs associated with them, such as "accountants," "health insurance," or "the medical profession"
- Works of art with organization names embedded in their names, such as "Campbell's Soup Cans"

3.5. Disambiguation of Matches
Accounting for situations in which one single predefined concept match or pattern could fall into multiple categories is one of the key challenges of named entity recognition. There are ambiguities between enamex entities because many proper nouns could be names of persons, organizations, or locations. Some examples are listed below.

"Duke" could be part of a Person match or an Organization match:

- I met [Stanley Duke]
- We are students at [Duke University]

"Washington" could be referring to a person or place, so it could be part of a Person or Place match:

- [President George Washington] was there
- Our capital is [Washington D.C.]

"Chelsea" could be a part of a Person match, Place match, or Organization match:

- Their daughter is [Chelsea Clinton]
- She was born in [Chelsea]
- He played for [Chelsea club]

Ambiguities are also encountered between enamex and numex entities, as mentioned in chapter 4. In addition, the same text string could be a predefined concept match or not. For example, the acronym "NER" could stand for nucleotide excision repair (nonmatch) or the North-East Railway (Organization).

The SAS predefined concepts account for these types of ambiguity by leveraging contextual cues like common titles, professions, abbreviations, prefixes or suffixes, appositives, and nominal and verbal constructions.

Sometimes it is difficult to distinguish from context whether the reference is to a place or an organization, because of *metonymy*, meaning the use of one term as a stand-in for another. For example, sports teams (organizations) from a particular location are often referred to as that location, as in "Buffalo's win over New York." Similarly, the work of government officials or departments is sometimes referred to by the name of the location, as in "Germany unveils new law." In these and other similar cases, the following predefined concept guidelines offer some direction.

3.5.1. Organization or Place

The following situations describe matches for the Organization concept:

- A city, state, district, or country name used to refer to a sports team or government
- Facilities or buildings that are aliases for organizations running them
- A string containing an Organization followed by a street address or other location (the organization name is a match for the Organization concept)

The following situations describe matches for the Place concept:

- Facilities or buildings that are not aliases for organizations running them
- An airport or location that aligns with the definition of an address match, in that it identifies a place that can be plotted on a map
- An organization name that is embedded in a location name (there are no overlapping matches for two separate predefined concept types, so the entire location name matches only as Place)
- A string containing an Organization followed by a street address or other location (the street address is a match for the Place concept)

Consider the following examples:

- Boston vs. Cleveland
- Croatia beat Slovakia
- The Vatican
- Germany unveils new law
- The White House
- Eiffel Tower
- Westminster Abbey
- Stanford University
- Disney World

- The SAS Executive Briefing Center
- The Apple headquarters
- RDU airport
- Bank of America Branch at 5983 N. Lincoln Avenue in Chicago, IL 60659
- The Macy's on Main Street

Pause and think: Can you identify which of the examples above contain matches for the Organization concept and which ones for Place?

Matches for the Organization concept include the following:

- [Boston] vs. [Cleveland]
- [Croatia] beat [Slovakia]
- The [Vatican]
- [Germany] unveils new law
- The [White House]
- [Westminster Abbey]
- [Stanford University]
- [Bank of America] Branch at 5983 N. Lincoln Avenue in Chicago, IL 60659
- The [Macy's] on Main Street

Matches for the Place concept include the following:

- [Eiffel Tower]
- [Disney World]
- The [SAS Executive Briefing Center]
- The [Apple headquarters]
- [RDU airport]
- Bank of America Branch at [5983 N. Lincoln Avenue in Chicago, IL 60659]
- The Macy's on [Main Street]

3.5.2. Organization or Product

An organization name or alias that is an explicit reference to a product or brand is a match for Organization. However, references to the products or brands themselves and ambiguous references to products or brands that cannot be discerned from context to be referring to the organization specifically are not matches.

Consider the following examples:

- Toyota Highlander
- I drive a Porsche
- Samsung Galaxy
- . . . on Google maps
- Johnson's baby products

- Johnson's babies
- She can't find her Chapstick
- Chapstick® Classic Lip Balm

Pause and think: Can you identify which of the examples above contain matches for the Organization concept?

Matches include the following:

- [Toyota] Highlander
- I drive a [Porsche]
- [Samsung] Galaxy
- … on [Google]
- [Johnson's] baby products
- [Chapstick]® Classic Lip Balm

3.5.3. Organization or Person

Groups of individuals belonging to an organization match as Organization, such as [Democrats], [Girl Scouts], and [Marines]. However, groups of individuals who do not belong to a formally established association are not considered a match for Organization or Person. Thus, for example, members of a particular religion are not considered matching Organization, but members of a particular formally established religious denomination or church may be.

Consider the following examples:

- Christians
- Baptists
- Sunni
- Muslims
- Shia

Pause and think: Can you identify which of the examples above contain matches for the Organization concept?

Matches include the following:

- [Baptists]
- [Sunni]
- [Shia]

Groups of individuals belonging to a particular industrial sector, industry, or job are not considered matches because they are not proper nouns. For example, the job description "financial advisors" is not a match for Person, but "[Bank of America] financial advisors" contains an Organization predefined concept match—the company where that group of individuals works.

Chapter 4: SAS Predefined Concepts: Timex, Numex, and Noun Group

4.1. Introduction to Other SAS Predefined Concepts

As you will recall from chapter 3, SAS provides a set of seven *predefined concepts*, spanning the three types of entities described in chapter 2:

- Enamex (Person, Location, Organization), detailed in chapter 3
- Timex (Date, Time), detailed in sections 4.2 and 4.3
- Numex (Money, Percent), detailed in sections 4.4 and 4.5

This chapter also includes a description of the predefined grammatical pattern, Noun Group, which aids in the recognition of multiwords and complex concepts. This pattern is detailed in section 4.6.

The rules that comprise the predefined concepts are proprietary and not displayed in the products. But, when you learn more about the principles and assumptions that form the basis for the predefined concept rules, as you do in this chapter, you can more accurately identify when you can leverage them and when custom concepts are a better choice.

4.2. Date

Date is a predefined concept provided by the SAS linguists. Note that the name of this concept in your product may be *nlpDate* or another similar name. The generic "Date" label is used in this book because it is an industry standard term and reflects previous names used in SAS products for this concept.

Date matches include patterns that indicate a specific point in time at any granularity from full day to larger amount of time. Matches can also be a range of points with the following:

- Known beginning and ending points
- Known beginning and ending points plus a frequency of units within the range
- Known beginning or ending point and the other point is an explicit date
- Known beginning or ending point plus duration (anchored duration)
- An explicit or strongly implied reference date plus duration (anchored duration)

A *reference date* is either the date that the text was written, or the date that the events in the text occurred. In interpreting a possible Date match, the assumption is that the reference date is known, even if it is not explicitly contained in the text. The granularity of that known point extends only to the full day, not to smaller units of time. However, a word like "now" may serve as a reference point in relationships so long as there is another legitimate time match in the phrase.

The point or points in time modeled by a Date match must be specific enough to be able to be plotted on a timeline. A timeline is a graph of time at any level of specificity:

- Day
- Week
- Month

- Year
- Decade

The smallest unit that can be a Date is a full day.

> **Remember**: *Date* includes expressions of time that can be plotted on a timeline and span at least a full day.

Date matches include formal or informal references to dates, usually composed of a named unit or a numerical value combined with at least some unit of time. Named units include the following names and common expressions for time:

- Days
- Months
- Seasons
- Decade
- Year
- Quarter
- Semester

The match usually encompasses one of the following grammatical categories:

- Noun
- Proper noun
- Noun phrase
- Adjective or adverbial phrase

Note that the match does not encompass clauses or prepositional phrases. The match is as short as possible without losing meaning. Punctuation is considered part of the Date match only if it is a lexical part of the tokens. Some examples include the following:

- [6 Oct.]
- [Aug. 1st]
- [Dec. 31, 2016]
- It increased [last May].

Special cases that govern whether certain words are included in the match are described in the following subsections.

4.2.1 Extended ISO 8601 Format

At least one element of the extended ISO 8601 format, the international standard covering the exchange of date- and time-related data, should be explicit. Units larger than a year are also included. In all cases, at least one point in time should be possible to plot on a timeline from the information given in the text plus the assumption of a known reference date.

Consider the following examples:

- I went home yesterday
- I recently went home to visit my parents
- You stayed at my home Friday
- . . . you stayed at my home for 2 months
- I want to go now
- I have great hopes for the future of my grandchildren

Pause and think: Can you identify the matches in the examples above?

Matches include only the following:

- I went home [yesterday]
- You stayed at my home [Friday]

The remaining examples do not contain enough information to plot on a timeline. The fourth example is not a match because there is not a known reference date for the start or end of the "2 months" period.

4.2.2. Named Dates

Named dates are included unless they are clearly a standalone set or nonspecific reference to a type or class of item, and this can be determined by the immediate context. Consider the following examples:

- We decorate every Christmas
- We decorated for Christmas
- We vacationed as we do every October
- Next year we will vacation in October
- October is my favorite
- Yearly in October, we plan a vacation
- . . . in May last year
- . . . through the Fourth Quarter
- The New Year's Day tradition

Pause and think: Can you identify the matches in the examples above?

Matches include only the following:

- We decorated for [Christmas]
- [Next year] we will vacation in [October]
- [October] is my favorite

- . . . in [May last year]
- . . . through [the Fourth Quarter]

Commonly understood slang or cultural references to dates, as well as references in titles, are included so long as they can be plotted on a timeline with an assumed reference date.

Consider the following examples:

- Wear your Sunday best
- The dog days of summer are here
- During the previous school year
- Next weekend
- "Summer of '69" is one of Bryan Adams' most popular songs

Pause and think: Can you identify the matches in the examples above?

Matches include only the following:

- During the [previous school year]
- [Next weekend]
- "[Summer of '69]" is one of Bryan Adams' most popular songs

The first two examples cannot be plotted on a calendar, so they are not matches for the Date concept.

Common nouns signifying events are excluded from matches unless a date stands for an event. Consider the following examples:

- My birthday
- Her September 2 birthday
- . . . on September 11
- Your wedding
- The June 4 problem

Pause and think: Can you identify the matches in the examples above?

Matches include only the following:

- Her [September 2] birthday
- . . . on [September 11]
- The [June 4] problem

Note that the remaining examples are not matches because they include only common nouns.

4.2.3. Modifiers

Leading or trailing modifiers that bring a more accurate understanding of how to plot the time expression on a timeline are included. This principle applies particularly to modifiers that express that the date is no later than, no earlier than, approximate to, after, or before a given date, or is a specified subset of a given date. However, leading prepositions or phrasal post-modifiers are not generally included unless they help clarify a relationship between multiple points. A vague term like "now" may be part of a range if the other part is a true Date, but not if both are vague.

Consider the following examples:

- On approximately May 1st
- Before the summer of '69
- In the fall of 1992
- In the first 5 days of April
- Less than a year ago
- No less than a year ago
- We travelled most of the week
- We travelled much of last week
- Both now and in the future
- He left after the holiday
- It will get fixed between now and Monday morning

Pause and think: Can you identify the matches in the examples above?

Matches include the following:

- On [approximately May 1st]
- [Before the summer of '69]
- In [the fall of 1992]
- In [the first 5 days of April]
- [Less than a year ago]
- [No less than a year ago]
- We travelled much of [last week]
- It will get fixed [between now and Monday morning]

In the remaining examples, the references to "week" and "holiday" are not specific enough to be plotted on a calendar and therefore are not matches for Date.

4.2.4. Conjoined Dates

Two or more separate date expressions are considered one match for the Date predefined concept if they are adjacent (or separated only by text that relates them) and the relationship is hierarchical. If overlapping or elided material exists between two expressions, then they are related and should always be identified as one match. They are also considered as one match if each point contributes to the understanding of the span of time under discussion, unless there are more than several words of intervening, unrelated material. This applies to range relationships and conjoined dates that could be interpreted as a range, where the ordering of the points is relevant and cannot be reversed without impacting the meaning. In a possessive construction, if both the possessive phrase and the phrase that it modifies are temporal expressions, then they are identified together as a single match. In all these cases, the Date expressions indicate one point in time. Comparative examples are provided in Table 4.1.

Table 4.1. One or More Matches for Date

One Match for Date	Multiple Matches for Date
The test was given [last week on Monday and Wednesday, but not Friday]	The test will be given on [Monday], [Wednesday], [Sunday], and [Tuesday]
[Every Thursday in October]	[Yesterday], [today] and [tomorrow] the stock rose a point

Consider the following examples:

- . . . in March of this year
- We will be on break from July 1-5 this year
- . . . in the fall of 1992
- This year's summer was unusually hot
- My birthday is on August 8 and October 27th is my brother's birthday

Pause and think: Can you identify the matches for Date in the examples above?

Matches include the following:

- . . . in [March of this year]
- We will be on break [from July 1-5 this year]
- . . . in [the fall of 1992]
- [This year's summer] was unusually hot
- My birthday is on [August 8] and [October 27th] is my brother's birthday

Note that the second example produces a single match and the final example produces multiple matches. The former is a range, whereas the latter is a series of separate dates.

4.2.5. Duration

If the time expression is a better answer for the questions "How long" or "How often" rather than "When," it is not a match for Date. However, duration can be included in the Date concept if it is directly adjacent to a Date and helps plotting the Date on a timeline.

Consider the following examples;

- I'm leaving on vacation two weeks from next Tuesday
- In September, we finally went to the show, after a three-month wait for tickets
- Every Tuesday this year, we went to the zoo
- His application was being processed for 10 years and he finally became a citizen on July 4th

Pause and think: Can you identify the matches for Date in the examples above?

Matches of duration that are included in Date include the following:

- I'm leaving on vacation [two weeks from next Tuesday]
- In [September], we finally went to the show . . .
- [Every Tuesday this year], we went to the zoo
- . . . he finally became a citizen on [July 4th]

Portions of the examples above contained references to duration, marked in italics below and not matches for the Date concept:

- . . .after a *three-month* wait for tickets
- His application was being processed for *10 years* . . .

4.2.6. Vague Expressions

Expressions that cannot be plotted on a timeline explicitly because they are underspecified or referring to implicit time are excluded from matches as Date.

Nonmatches include the following:

- For 4 months
- During two entire days
- Every two days
- In recent decades
- In the past
- Now
- For at least the next year or two
- Over the coming months
- A few months ago
- Recently
- The last 4 days of the festival
- On a Tuesday
- Not long ago

Similarly, words like "now," "today," or "tomorrow" are excluded from matches as Date when they have the generic meanings of "these days," "nowadays," or "in the future."

4.3. Time

Time is a predefined concept provided by the SAS linguists. Note that the name of this concept in your product may be *nlpTime* or another similar name. The generic "Time" label is used in this book because it is an industry standard term and reflects previous names used in SAS products for this concept.

Time expressions include patterns that indicate a point in time at any granularity smaller than a full day. Matches can also be a range of points with the following characteristics:

- Known beginning and ending points
- Known beginning and ending points plus a frequency of units within the range
- Known beginning or ending point the other point is an explicit time reference
- Known beginning or ending point plus duration (anchored duration)
- Explicit or strongly implied reference date plus duration (anchored duration)

A *reference date* is either the date that the text was written, or the date that the events in the text occurred. In interpreting a possible Date match, the assumption is that the reference date is known, even if it is not explicitly contained in the text. The granularity of that known point extends only to the full day, not to smaller units of time. However, a word like "now" may serve as a reference point in relationships so long as there is another legitimate time match in the phrase.

The point or points in time must be able to be plotted on a timeline, which is a graph of time at any level of specificity smaller than a full day. The largest unit that can be a Time match is part of a day.

The matches for Time include formal or informal references to times, usually comprising a named unit, or a numerical value combined with at least some unit of time, which may be implicit from context. Named units of time include the following:

- Morning
- Night
- Hour
- Minute
- Second
- Noon
- Midday
- Midnight

The reference could also be a pattern of numbers and punctuation. Punctuation is considered part of the Time match only if it is a lexical part of the tokens. For example, consider the following:

- [5 a.m.]
- [12:00]
- She arrived at [8pm]

Remember: *Time* includes expressions of time that can be plotted on a timeline and are shorter than a full day.

Special cases that govern whether certain words are included in the match are described in the following subsections.

4.3.1. Extended ISO 8601 Format

At least one element of the extended ISO 8601 format, the international standard covering the exchange of date and time-related data, should be explicit enough to plot on a timeline from the information given in the text plus the assumption of a known reference date. Consider the following examples:

- I want to go right now
- He was 15 minutes late
- He will arrive at 2:00
- I leave at 16:00

Pause and think: Can you identify the matches in the examples above?

Matches include the following:

- He will arrive at [2:00]
- I leave at [16:00]

The remaining two examples are not specific enough to plot on a timeline, because there is no known reference point for "now" and "15 minutes late."

4.3.2. Named Times and Time Zones

Time zones, when present, are included in the scope of the match. Names of times are included unless they are clearly a standalone set or nonspecific reference to a type or class of item, and this can be determined by the immediate context. Commonly understood slang or cultural references to time periods, as well as references in titles, are included so long as they can be plotted on a timeline.

Consider the following examples:

- It starts at 8 ET
- She arrives at 1 pm CST
- Rush hour
- We will be done by noon
- It ended at midnight
- Good morning
- He naps every afternoon
- 24-hour gym
- Primetime
- The mail arrives every morning
- The wee hours of the morning
- Happy hour
- The bottom of the hour
- Eleventh hour decision
- At the last minute
- I saw the film "Last night"
- "Minute to win it"
- "60 minutes"
- "Midnight in the Garden of Good and Evil"

Pause and think: Can you identify the matches in the examples above?

Matches include the following:

- It starts at [8 ET]
- She arrives at [1 pm CST]
- [Rush hour]
- We will be done by [noon]
- It ended at [midnight]
- [Primetime]
- [The wee hours of the morning]
- [Happy hour]
- [The bottom of the hour]
- I saw the film "[Last night]"
- "[Midnight] in the Garden of Good and Evil"

Note that cultural references to a specific time of day such as "rush hour" and "happy hour" are included in the matches, but phrases such as "good morning" and "eleventh hour decision" are not, because they cannot be plotted on a timeline.

4.3.3. Modifiers

Leading or trailing modifiers that bring a more accurate understanding of how to plot the time expression on a timeline are included. This principle applies particularly to modifiers that express that the time is no later than, no earlier than, approximate to, after, or before a given time—or are a specified subset of a given time. However, leading prepositions or phrasal post-modifiers are not generally included unless they help clarify a relationship between multiple points. A vague term like "now" may be part of a range if the other part is a true Time, but not if both are vague.

Consider the following examples:

- It may last from a few minutes to a few hours
- At half past three
- From 2:00 onwards
- From now on
- Between 6:00 and 8:00
- From now until 1pm
- It was about 5 hours yesterday afternoon
- By around 5:00

Pause and think: Can you identify the matches in the examples above?

Matches include the following:

- At [half past three]
- From [2:00] onwards
- [Between 6:00 and 8:00]
- [From now until 1pm]
- It was [about 5 hours yesterday afternoon]
- By [around 5:00]

The remaining examples are too vague to be plotted on a timeline.

4.3.4. Conjoined Times

Two or multiple separate Time expressions are considered one match if they are adjacent (or only separated by text that relates them) and the relationship is hierarchical. If overlapping or elided material exists between two entities, then they are related and should always be identified as one match. They are also considered as one match if each point contributes to the understanding of the span of time under discussion, unless there are more than several words of intervening, unrelated material. This applies to range relationships and conjoined times that could be interpreted as a range; in other words, the ordering of the points is relevant and cannot be reversed without impacting the meaning. In a possessive construction, if both the possessive phrase and the phrase that it modifies are temporal expressions, then they are identified together as a single match. In all these cases, the Time expressions indicate one point in time. Some illustrative examples are presented in Table 4.2.

Table 4.2. One or More Matches for Time

One Match for Time	Multiple Matches for Time
We had tests on [Monday at 9:00 AM, at 10:00 AM, and at 11:00 AM]	We had tests on [Monday at 9:00 AM], [Tuesday at 10:00 AM], and [Wednesday at 11:00 AM]
. . . on [Friday morning]	There were doughnuts at the [8:00] meeting [this morning]

Consider the following examples:

- It was about 5 hours yesterday afternoon
- Twelve o'clock January 3, 1984
- He left between 6:00 p.m. and 8:00 p.m.
- After 9PM and before 2AM
- At 5:15 PM on Tuesday and 5 PM on Thursday
- At eleven in the morning

Pause and think: Can you identify the matches in the examples above?

Matches include the following:

- It was [about 5 hours yesterday afternoon]
- [Twelve o'clock January 3, 1984]
- He left [between 6:00 p.m. and 8:00 p.m.]
- [After 9PM and before 2AM]
- At [5:15 PM on Tuesday] and [5 PM on Thursday]
- At [eleven in the morning]

The only example that contains multiple matches is the fifth one because it refers to two distinct times on two different days.

4.3.5. Duration

If the time expression denotes duration and is a better answer for the questions "How long" or "How often" rather than "When," it is not a match for Time. However, duration can be included in the Time predefined concept match if it is directly adjacent to a Time and helps in plotting the Time on a timeline.

Consider the following examples:

- On Monday, we had to wait 20 minutes for the professor
- For 20 minutes last Monday, we waited for the professor
- Two minutes

- 5 hours
- Dinner is from five to six pm tomorrow
- The class is 3-6 pm today

Pause and think: Can you identify the matches for Time in the examples above?

Matches include the following:

- On [Monday], we had to wait 20 minutes for the professor
- Dinner is [from five to six pm tomorrow]
- The class is [3-6 pm today]

Portions of the examples above contained references to duration, marked in italics below, and not matches for the Time concept:

- . . .we had to wait *20 minutes* for the professor
- *Two minutes*
- *5 hours*

4.3.6. Vague Expressions

Like vague expressions of dates, expressions containing time references that cannot be plotted on a timeline explicitly because they are underspecified or referring to implicit time are excluded from Time matches. Some examples of nonmatches include "1 second later" and "a few hours earlier."

4.4. Money

Money is a predefined concept provided by the SAS linguists. Note that the name of this concept in your product may be *nlpMoney* or another similar name using the term "Currency." The generic "Money" label is used in this book.

Money expressions include any explicit or implied numeric value with a monetary denomination or monetary unit symbol. Explicit or implied numeric values can be any of the following:

- Digits
- Number words
- Fractions
- Decimals
- Numeric quantifiers

Numeric quantifiers include determiners and other quantifiers for which a number could be substituted grammatically (implied numeric amount) with the same or very similar meaning: "one," "a," "a few," and so on. Monetary denominations include any official term or abbreviation for currency in any country ("dollar," "quarter," "dime," "peso"), but not slang terms for money or amounts of money ("quid," "bucks," "dough," "clams," "Benjamins," "five-spots," "fivers," "moolah," "greenbacks," "grand," "large").

The match includes the entire string expressing the monetary value: all tokens between the value and denomination or symbol, inclusive within the bounds of a single phrase. For example, matches include the following:

- [One and a half million dollars]
- [$10]
- [0.1 cent]
- [Twenty-something dollars]

If the match of the monetary value and the currency is separated by more than a phrase or short clause, then the matched string may include only the monetary value, and the currency may play the role of context only.

However, generic or implied references to money are not specific enough, so the following examples are not matches:

- There was a lot of pesos on the table
- There were many dollars at risk
- The dollar fell against the yen

> **Remember**: *Money* includes expressions of numeric value with a denomination or monetary unit symbol.

Special cases that govern whether certain words are included in the match are described in the following subsections.

4.4.1. Modifiers

Modifiers that indicate the multiplied value of a unit should be included when the expression remains grammatical and has similar meaning, if such a digit is substituted for the word(s). In other words, some quantifiers may take the place of the numerical value. A minus sign or the words like "minus" and "negative" should be included in the expression.

Consider the following examples:

- There were several 10-dollar bills in my wallet
- There were several bills in my wallet
- A few million dollars fell
- There were no dollars left of my paycheck
- I received a million dollars
- There was minus 15 dollars in the account
- −12 billion dollars

Pause and think: Can you identify the matches in the examples above?

Matches include the following:

- There were [several 10-dollar bills] in my wallet
- [A few million dollars] fell
- There were [no dollars] left of my paycheck
- I received [a million dollars]
- There was [minus 15 dollars] in the account
- [−12 billion dollars]

Modifying words that indicate the approximate value of a number or relative position, as well as verbs and prepositions outside the boundaries of a value and monetary denomination or symbol, are not included. However, modifiers which indicate the value is a maximum or minimum of a range of values (inclusive or exclusive of given value) are included in the match. Some examples of such modifiers include the following:

- Over
- Above
- More than
- Below
- Under
- Less than
- Maximum of

If a modifier occurs in the middle of an expression within the same phrase or sentence as the value and currency marker, then the modifier is included in the match. Consider the following examples:

- Over $5 were lost
- Just under $24 million
- Raised more than five million dollars
- He had barely $6 to his name
- The cost was about $20 too high
- She lost almost 50 dollars in chips
- 12 big bad million dollars
- 11 stinking cents

Pause and think: Can you identify the matches in the examples above?

Matches include the following:

- [Over $5] were lost
- Just [under $24 million]

- Raised [more than five million dollars]
- He had [barely $6] to his name
- The cost was about [$20] too high
- She lost [almost 50 dollars] in chips
- [12 big bad million dollars]
- [11 stinking cents]

Note that in the fifth example, the modifier "about" is not included in the match, because it does not provide any additional information than the sum itself that could be plotted on a number line.

4.4.2. Rates and Ratios

In rate expressions, the unit is included in the matched string.

Ratios of currencies to each other are excluded from Money matches. These ratios do not indicate exact or approximate amounts of money, but only a relationship between types of money.

Consider the following examples:

- $3 per share
- 11 cents/unit
- From highs above 0.7700 on Thursday, AUD/USD has fallen sharply to 0.7500
- US$2-per-day
- USD/CAD has strengthened from lows below 1.2850 to trade above 1.3100
- $12 per person
- NZD/USD has moved from testing 15-month highs at 0.7500 to test the 0.7300 support area

Pause and think: Can you identify the matches in the examples above?

Matches include the following:

- [$3 per share]
- [11 cents/unit]
- [US$2-per-day]
- [$12 per person]

The remaining examples do not produce matches, because the ratios are comparing currencies rather than expressing an amount of money.

4.4.3. Quotes and Parentheses

A quoted or parenthesized number or other information is included in the match when it is in the same phrase with a numerical value and a denomination or monetary unit symbol.

Consider the following examples:

- Above eighty (80) dollars
- 6 "six" cents
- After zero (that means none) dollars in fines

Pause and think: Can you identify the matches in the examples above?

Matches include the following:

- Above [eighty (80) dollars]
- [6 "six" cents]
- After [zero (that means none) dollars] in fines

Note that in all three cases, the information between the amount and currency is included in the match.

4.4.4. Conjoined Expressions

Two or multiple adjacent (or only separated by text that relates them) Money expressions are considered one match if any of the following conditions are satisfied:

- They are hierarchically related
- Overlapping or elided material exists between two entities
- They express a relationship between values in two different currencies or the same value in digits and words
- Their order is relevant and impacts the meaning

In these cases, leading prepositions or modifiers that clarify the relationship between the expressions are included in the match, as shown in the left column of Table 4.3. But if the expressions describe moving from one value to another or if there are more than several intervening, unrelated words, then each point is considered a separate Money match, as shown in the right column of Table 4.3. Money matches that do not have relating or elided material are also considered separate matches when each can stand alone and retains its meaning.

Table 4.3. One or More Matches for Money

One match for Money	Multiple Matches for Money
[Seventeen and then almost eighteen dollars]	I had [$5] and then later [$2] in my wallet
[Nine dollars and ten cents] more	[eleven cents] and [twelve cents]

Consider the following examples:

- We made $700, $1200, and $600 for each of the three jobs
- The cost can be anywhere from $12 through $20
- 5–600 dollars

- Spent 15.6 billion pesos (over US $900 million)
- #26 million ($43.6 million)
- Above eighty (80) dollars
- 6 "six" cents
- $2,000–$3,000 million dollars
- 7–10 dollars

Pause and think: Can you identify the matches in the examples above?

Matches include the following:

- We made [$700], [$1200], and [$600] for each of the three jobs
- The cost can be anywhere [from $12 through $20]
- [5–600 dollars]
- Spent [15.6 billion pesos (over US $900 million])
- [#26 million ($43.6 million])
- Above [eighty (80) dollars]
- [6 "six" cents]
- [$2,000-$3,000 million dollars]
- [7-10 dollars]

Note that the first example contains multiple matches for Money because each can stand alone and retain its meaning. Each of the remaining examples contains a single match.

4.4.5. Approximate Amount

A value + currency adjectival construction or other construction that leaves part of the value open-ended is included, even if the exact amount is not clear, so long as the approximate amount can be inferred. An imprecise value is still counted as a value if it contains a numeric reference.

Consider the following examples:

- He lost the team millions
- Many dollars were lost
- A million-dollar conference party was offered
- The whole budget
- Tens of billions of dollars were donated
- Every dollar I had
- Fortunes were lost
- Many millions of dollars were lost
- All the cash

Pause and think: Can you identify the matches in the examples above?

Matches include the following:

- A [million-dollar] conference party was offered
- [Tens of billions of dollars] were donated
- Many [millions of dollars] were lost

The remaining examples are not matches because an approximate amount cannot be inferred.

4.4.6. Expressions and Metaphors

References to money in standard expressions or metaphors should be analyzed to determine whether there is really an amount of money explicitly stated, and that the meaning has not drifted so far away that it is still valid to acknowledge the value as a Money match. Consider the following examples:

- In for a penny, in for a pound
- Penny whistle
- Penny candy
- A penny for your thoughts
- Penny pincher
- A pretty penny
- A penny saved is a penny earned
- Pennyweight
- On a dime
- A day late and a dollar short
- The almighty dollar
- A dime a dozen
- To nickel and dime someone
- Be two a penny
- Phony as a three-dollar bill
- Feel like a million dollars
- I wouldn't give 2 cents/pennies for that

Pause and think: Can you identify the matches in the examples above?

Matches include the following:

- [A penny] for your thoughts
- [A penny] saved is [a penny] earned
- [A dime a dozen]
- Be [two a penny]

- Feel like [a million dollars]
- I wouldn't give [2 cents/pennies] for that

For the remaining examples, the meaning has drifted from an explicit reference to an amount to a more general metaphorical meaning.

4.5. Percent

Percent is a predefined concept provided by the SAS linguists. Note that the name of this concept in your product may be *nlpPercent* or another similar name. The generic "Percent" label is used in this book because it is an industry standard term and reflects previous names used in SAS products for this concept.

Percent expressions include an explicit or implied numeric amount and a percentage reference. A numeric amount can be expressed with a number, word, or phrase; numeric quantifier; digit; fraction; or decimal. A percentage reference includes words and symbols with the meaning of "percent," including the following:

- Percentage point
- Percentile
- Quantile
- Centile
- Percentile rank
- %

A numeric quantifier includes determiners and other quantifiers for which a number could be substituted grammatically (implied numeric amount) with the same or very similar meaning: "one," "a," "a few," and the like.

The match includes the entire string expressing the percentage value: all tokens between the value and percent reference, inclusive within the bounds of a single phrase. If the match of the numeric amount and the percent marker is separated by more than a phrase or short clause, then the matched string may include only the numeric amount, and the percent marker may play the role of context only. For example, matches include the following:

- [12 percentage points]
- [1 ¾ percent]
- A fixed [106 7/8%]
- [50-something percent]
- [Eighty-eight percent]
- [One and a half percent]
- [10%]
- [.9%]
- A [percentage rate of 0.51]
- The [75th percentile] of the wage distribution

If there is no explicit percentage term within the scope of the same sentence as the numeric value, there is no match for Percent. Compare the preceding matches to the following nonmatches:

- 12 points
- 1.5 times
- About one-third of
- Fees 1 ¾
- A fixed 106 7/8
- Priced at 99 ¼

Similarly, if there is no numeric value or numeric quantifier within the scope of the same phrase or sentence as the percentage term, then there is no match for Percent. If the quantifier cannot be easily substituted for a number without further context, it is too subjective to be a numeric quantifier. Therefore, compare the following matches and nonmatches:

- [A percentage point]
- [Several percentage points] down
- [A few percent] higher
- Up [several tenths of a percent]
- The rate goes up many percentage points
- All percentage discussions

> **Remember**: Percent includes expressions of numeric value with a percent reference.

Special cases that govern whether certain words are included in the match are described in the following subsections.

4.5.1. Acronyms, Initialisms, and Abbreviations

Acronyms and initialisms are not included as matches unless spelled out. However, abbreviations are included. Matches include "[zero annual percentage rate]" and "[6 PCT] higher than last year." Nonmatches include "zero APR."

4.5.2. Modifiers

Modifying words that indicate the approximate value of a number or relative position, as well as verbs and prepositions outside the boundaries of a value and percent reference, are not included. However, modifiers which indicate the value is a maximum or minimum of a range of values (inclusive or exclusive of given value) are included in the match. Some examples of such modifiers include the following:

- Over
- Above
- More than
- Below

- Under
- Less than
- Maximum of

If a modifier occurs in the middle of an expression within the same phrase or sentence as the value and percent reference, then the modifier is included in the match. A minus sign or words like "minus" or "negative" are included in the match.

Consider the following examples:

- At least 5% of the students passed
- About a percent
- It was [over 10%] of what we earned last year
- Up 6 PCT from last year
- Barely 8% over predicted value
- Almost 9/10th of a percent
- One half of one tiny percent difference
- Almost ½ a percent
- Nearly 40 percent of Americans
- At minus 15 percent
- Generated a negative 1% return

Pause and think: Can you identify the matches in the examples above?

Matches include the following:

- [At least 5%] of the students passed
- About [a percent]
- It was [over 10%] of what we earned last year
- Up [6 PCT] from last year
- [Barely 8%] over predicted value
- [Almost 9/10th of a percent]
- [One half of one tiny percent] difference
- [Almost ½ a percent]
- [Nearly 40 percent] of Americans
- At [minus 15 percent]
- Generated a [negative 1%] return

Note that the preposition "about" in the second example is not included in the match because it does not add any additional specification to the percentage amount that could be plotted on a number line.

4.5.3. Quotation Marks and Parentheses

A quoted or parenthesized number or other information is included in the match when it is in the same phrase with a numerical value and a percent reference.

Consider the following examples:

- After zero (that means none) % growth
- Above eighty (80) percent
- Six "6" percent

Pause and think: Can you identify the matches in the examples above?

Matches include the following:

- After [zero (that means none) %] growth
- [Above eighty (80) percent]
- [Six "6" percent]

Note that in all three cases, the information between the amount and percent is included in the match.

4.5.4. Conjoined Expressions

Two or multiple adjacent (or separated only by text that relates them) Percent expressions are considered one match if overlapping or elided material exists between two entities, or if in the context, each point contributes to the understanding of the span of percentage points under discussion (as in ranges or in conjoined expressions that can be interpreted as ranges), as shown in the left column of Table 4.4.

In this case, leading prepositions or modifiers that contribute to clarification of the relationship between two amounts are included in the match. But if the expressions describe moving from one value to another, or if there are more than several intervening, unrelated words, then each point is considered a separate Percent match. Percent matches that do not have relating or elided material are also considered separate matches when each can stand alone and retains its meaning, as shown in the right column of Table 4.4.

Table 4.4. One or More Matches for Percent

One Match for Percent	Multiple Matches for Percent
[5–9%]	[5%], [112%], [18%] or [22%] respectively
[5% through 9%]	The twins got [87%] and [89%] on their tests

Consider the following examples:

- Between 6% and 17% higher than yesterday
- By a factor of maybe 200% or 250%
- Up almost 5–6%

- 20%, 25%, 30% tint pictures
- 11 and then almost 12 percentage points
- Every 10 or 20 mole percent KCl

Pause and think: Can you identify the matches in the examples above?

Matches include the following:

- [Between 6% and 17%] higher than yesterday
- By a factor of maybe [200%] or [250%]
- Up [almost 5–6%]
- [20%], [25%], [30%] tint pictures
- [11 and then almost 12 percentage points]
- Every [10 or 20 mole percent] KCl

The second and fourth examples contain multiple matches in each example because each of the matches can stand alone and meaning is not lost. The remaining examples contain one match per example.

4.5.5. Multiword Expressions

Multiword expressions that include percent references, such as "percent growth," "percent yield," or "percent margin," and are used in the proximity of numeric values are included as matches in some languages, but not in others; in any case, they should be treated consistently. In the context of broader mathematical or other values or representations, only the percent reference and numeric value it describes are considered a match for Percent.

Consider the following examples:

- By a 35 percent growth
- With 85 percent yield in a gas recycle
- $5.2 \pm 5.4\%$
- Standard deviation is 2.3% of the mean of 4.4

Pause and think: Can you identify the potential matches in the examples above?

Potential matches include the following:

- By a [35 percent] growth
- By a [35 percent growth]
- With [85 percent] yield in a gas recycle
- With [85 percent yield] in a gas recycle
- $5.2 \pm [5.4\%]$
- Standard deviation is [2.3%] of the mean of 4.4

The first and second examples contain two possible spans for the matches, depending on how multiword expressions are treated. In the SAS predefined concepts, the narrower match has been implemented.

4.5.6. Fractions and Ratios

Derivative or related mathematical items, like fractions, ratios, or other parts-per-N expressions, where the percentage relationship is not explicit, are not included as matches.

Nonmatches include the following:

- 5 out of 10 children
- 2/5 of the pieces of fruit are oranges
- The amount of orange juice concentrate is 1/5 of the total liquid
- The presence of two molar proportions
- 2‰ (per mille)

4.5.7. Special Cases for Nonmatches

The percent symbol, when used in the encoding of characters, as a modulus, or as substitution for a white space character as in a path or URL, is not considered a match, even if it is adjacent to a number.

Nonmatches include the following:

- Fran%c3%a7ois
- http://www.edg.com/true&width=80%&height=80%
- http://call.co/app/?q=php20%

4.6. Noun Group

Noun Group consists of a head noun and closely tied modifiers: nominal modifiers, most adjectival modifiers, and some adverbial modifiers. A head noun can be only a common noun, not a pronoun, number, proper noun, or another predefined concept type.

This approach differs from the way that a noun phrase is defined in grammatical theories, natural language processing, and text analytics systems, which have different purposes for noun phrase identification. The goal for Noun Group matches in the SAS processing approach is to identify complex concepts that consist of multiple words or tokens, which can then be used for topic generation and other text analytics tasks. Therefore, unlike noun phrases, Noun Groups do not include pre-determiners, determiners, numerical determiners (quantifiers), or negation adverbials, whether they are words, phrases, or clauses. In some languages, like English, post-head modifiers are also excluded. Furthermore, a bare head noun is not a Noun Group match. For example, only parts of the noun phrases in the following sentence are matches for Noun Group:

The dog's [speedy recovery] from the five [long days] spent wandering was due to a [kind-hearted old lady], who found him at the [main gate] of her community.

Special constraints that govern whether certain words are included in the Noun Group match serve to prevent the match from becoming too specific (too long) to be useful. Different languages vary in their use of these constraints, but in general, Noun Group matches have no more than two or three modifiers of different part-of-speech tag types. In addition, they do not include conjunctions.

Modifiers joined with conjunctions, as well as conjoined nouns, are not combined into a conjoined phrase.

Consider the following examples:

- Boys and girls
- The five unruly boys and girls
- Cookies and milk
- Very delicious cookies and milk
- Bangers and mash
- Large but fixed amount of money
- Her considered and well-articulated opinion

Pause and think: Can you identify the potential matches in the examples above?

Matches include the following:

- The five [unruly boys] and girls
- Very [delicious cookies] and milk
- Her considered and [well-articulated opinion]
- Large but [fixed amount] of money

The first, third, and fifth examples do not contain modifiers to the nouns and therefore do not produce Noun Group matches.

4.7. Disambiguation of Matches

Accounting for situations in which one single predefined concept match or pattern could fall into multiple categories is one of the key challenges of named entity recognition. Ambiguities between enamex entities were detailed in chapter 3, but there are also ambiguities between enamex and numex entities. Some examples are included below.

"May" can be part of a person's name or a date:

- [Prime minister Theresa May] arrived yesterday.
- It happened in [May] this year.

"April" can be part of a person's first name, an organization name, or a date:

- [Mayor April O'Neil] was elected last Monday.
- He works at [April Group].
- In [April], she went to a conference.

In addition, the same text string could be a predefined concept match or not. Consider the following sentence (from https://www.bbc.com/sport/cricket/47273785):

Adil Rashid claimed 2-21, Chris Woakes 2-28 and . . .

The numbers in this sentence could be referring to dates in the month of February in the context of, for example, claiming days off from work. In this context, the numbers should be extracted as dates. However, the sentence above comes from a sports context, and in this case extracting dates would be inaccurate, because the rest of the sentence includes "Mark Wood 2-35." The numbers are referring to cricket players' statistics and are not timex entities. Similarly, in European data sources, soccer scores are often represented in a format that may match a time, such as "4:10." It would be inappropriate to extract the final score of a soccer match as a time.

The SAS predefined concepts account for these types of ambiguity by leveraging contextual cues. To give a simple example, when a personal title is encountered in front of a proper noun, it is likely that the proper noun is a person, as in the example "Ms. May." If, on the other hand, there is a numeral before or after "May," then it is more likely to be a date, as in "May 5, 2017."

4.8. Supplementing Predefined Concepts

The information about named entities in this chapter may have inspired you to think about augmenting the set of provided concepts with applications specific to your own area of interest. You may have realized that there is information that would be useful to extract but that is not matched in the predefined concepts. To assist you with those tasks, the focus of the next several chapters is creating your own custom concepts using some of the same best practices that are reflected in the predefined concepts.

Chapter 5: Fundamentals of Creating Custom Concepts

5.1. Introduction to Custom Concepts

In chapters 2–4, you learned that, for the purposes of information extraction, you can leverage the predefined concepts. This chapter will introduce you to the fundamentals of custom concepts and writing your own rules. Why might you want to create your own concepts and rules?

Perhaps you have information in your documents that you want to extract but that is not covered by the predefined set of named entities. For example, maybe you want to extract names of medicines, treatment options, vehicle parts, body parts, grocery items, and the like. One way to extract custom information is by relying on automated approaches, such as statistical or machine learning models. Some drawbacks of these models include difficulties in optimization and in explanation of results. Instead, by writing custom IE rules, you can take a deterministic approach with increased control over the quality and interpretability of your results.

After reading this chapter, you will be able to do the following tasks:

- Recognize the required and optional parts of LITI rules, including elements, modifiers and punctuation
- Use best practices for concept naming and referencing
- Troubleshoot common rule-writing errors for all rule types

5.2. LITI Rule Fundamentals

This chapter focuses on concepts and rules for information extraction using LITI syntax. LITI is an acronym for *language interpretation for textual information*. It is a proprietary programming language for extracting specific pieces of information or relationships between specific pieces of information from text. SAS documentation already provides the basics of writing LITI rules. Building on that information, this chapter and the next five chapters provide technical details on required and optional elements of each rule type, usage through examples, and information about run-time complexity and computational cost, as well as pitfalls, guidelines, and tips on writing rules with LITI syntax.

The types of rules that you can write in LITI include the following:

- Concept rule types, detailed in chapters 6 and 7
  - CLASSIFIER
  - CONCEPT
  - C_CONCEPT
  - CONCEPT_RULE
- Fact rule types, detailed in chapter 8
  - SEQUENCE
  - PREDICATE_RULE
- Filter rule types, detailed in chapter 9
  - REMOVE_ITEM
  - NO_BREAK
- REGEX rule type, detailed in chapter 10

The final section of this chapter includes troubleshooting tips that apply to all the rule types. Each subsequent chapter will highlight any troubleshooting tips specific to the rule types presented in that chapter.

In the examples in chapters 6–11, the matching algorithm that is assumed is "all matches," meaning each rule that defines content found in the text returns a match. Furthermore, the project setting is "case insensitive matching," unless otherwise noted. For more information on project settings and other matching algorithms and their uses, see chapter 12. Unless otherwise noted, the data used in examples is constructed from the authors' experiences to resemble real business data.

5.2.1. Required Parts of LITI Rules

As shown in Figure 5.1, each LITI rule has at least 3 parts:

- A *declaration of the rule type*, which is written in ALL CAPS
- A *colon*, which is the separator between the rule type declaration and the rule definition
- A *rule definition*, which varies according to the rule type

Figure 5.1. Simple LITI Rule Example

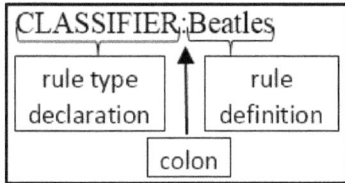

In Figure 5.1, the rule type is CLASSIFIER, which is the most basic type of rule in the LITI syntax. The rule definition specifies that the string "Beatles" is extracted when it is found in the text. The rule type declaration and rule definition are separated by a colon.

5.2.2. Optional Parts of LITI Rules

Although all rule types in the LITI syntax include the sections listed above, it is also possible to write more complicated rules using a section called the *output declaration*. This rule section holds information between two colons after the *rule type* and before the *rule definition* that specifies how the rule output should appear. For example, there are some rule types that allow for extra information or commands to be placed between two colons. These rule types include the following elements:

- CLASSIFIER, for the coreference command
- SEQUENCE and PREDICATE_RULE, for extraction label declaration

The extraction label declaration lists the user-defined extraction labels that will be used in the rule definition. Figure 5.2 shows a more complex example.

Figure 5.2. Complex LITI Rule Example

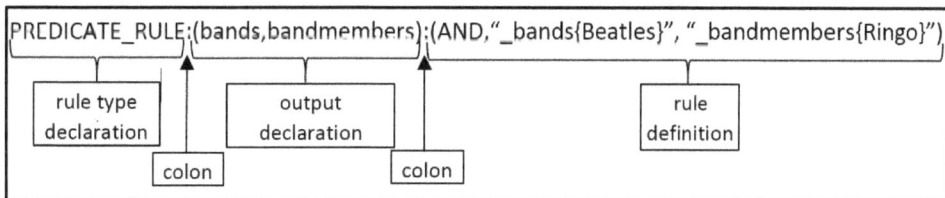

The rule shown in Figure 5.2 extracts the string "Beatles" as an extracted match for the "bands" extraction label and extracts the string "Ringo" as an extracted match for the "bandmembers" extraction label. The rule returns the two strings, as well as the text between them, as one extracted match.

The extraction labels are enclosed in parentheses and separated from each other by a comma. Similar to what appears in Figure 5.1, where the colon is a separator between the two parts of the rule, in this example two colons separate the three sections: rule type declaration, output declaration, and rule definition. Note that the output declaration section of the rule can include not only an extraction label declaration, but also a concept name declaration (in programmatic rule-writing) or coreference command (in the CLASSIFIER rule type).

5.2.3. Rule Definition

Rule definitions may include the following components:

- Elements
- Modifiers
- Punctuation

Rule *elements* are the essential parts of the rule definition that can stand alone, be modified, and define arguments. They represent some piece of text that may be found in a document. Table 5.1 describes possible rule elements.

Table 5.1. Elements in Rule Definitions

Elements	Description	Examples	Rule Types
String	One or more literal alphabetic, numeric, or alphanumeric characters without newlines	Rolling Stones band \c (for comma) \#	All – comma (in CLASSIFIER) and hash characters must be escaped
Concept name	Can be predefined or custom name; represent a set of rules	nlpPerson bandMembers	All except CLASSIFIER and REGEX
Part-of-speech tag and special tags	A part-of-speech or special tag preceded by a colon; represent the set of all words filling a given role in context	:ADV :CONJ :N :sep (for punctuation)	All except CLASSIFIER and REGEX
Word symbol	Represents a single token, including single punctuation marks in some contexts	_w	All except CLASSIFIER and REGEX
Cap symbol	Represents any single token, which begins with an uppercase letter	_cap	All except CLASSIFIER and REGEX
Regular expression	Special expression combining strings and operators in a PERL-like syntax* that represent a span of text	[Bb]and(:?'s)?[ ] music	Only REGEX

*To learn more about PERL syntax, consult chapter 10, which focuses on regular expressions.

Rule *modifiers* are used to modify or relate the elements to each other in some way. Provided in Table 5.2 are examples for the contexts in which modifiers are used. The modifiers themselves are shaded gray.

Table 5.2. Modifiers in Rule Definitions

Modifiers	Description	Examples	Rule Types
Comment character	Marks the remainder of a line as a comment to be ignored in processing; #	# This is a comment Tip: To match # as a literal, escape it like this \#	All except REGEX; but you can put # before a REGEX rule
Morphological expansion symbol	Add to the end of a string when you want to match inflectional variations; @, @N, @V, @A	go@ = go, going, goes, gone bottle@N = bottle, bottles	All except CLASSIFIER and REGEX
Extraction label	Precede with _c and enclose an element or series of elements in curly braces to mark as the section of the match to extract; _c{}	The following rule: C_CONCEPT:said _c{_cap _cap} on dayOfWeek can produce the result: Jane Wu	C_CONCEPT CONCEPT_RULE REMOVE_ITEM NO_BREAK
User-defined extraction label	Precede with underscore and any word and enclose an element or series of elements in curly braces to mark the section of the match to target in fact rules; ties label to extracted match; _name{}	The following rule: SEQUENCE:(name, day):said _name{_cap _cap} on _day{dayOfWeek } Can produce the result: name=Jane Wu day=Tuesday	SEQUENCE PREDICATE_RULE
Coreference symbol	For tying extracted matches together and enabling additional matches based	See the rule sections for the rule types for examples of use of: _ref{}, >, _P{} and _F{}	C_CONCEPT CONCEPT_RULE

Modifiers	Description	Examples	Rule Types
	upon preceding or successive text		
Argument	Any element or set of elements inside explicit quotations and governed by an operator or marked with an extraction label	CONCEPT_RULE:(OR, "_c{love@V}", "_c{like@V}", "_c{enjoy@V} driving")	CONCEPT_RULE SEQUENCE PREDICATE_RULE
Operator	Used to combine arguments in Boolean and proximity relationships	CONCEPT_RULE:(SENT, (DIST_5, "broken", "_c{partVehicle}"))	CONCEPT_RULE PREDICATE_RULE

Punctuation, such as backslashes, colons, commas, quotation marks, and different types of brackets are also used to separate or relate the elements and their modifiers to each other. Please refer to your product documentation for how different punctuation is used in each rule type.

White space is not explicitly encoded as part of a rule, except for REGEX rules. In all other rule types, for languages in which white space is used for tokenization, white space is used to separate elements from one another. In general, do not put two elements together without white space intervening when you are working with such languages.

> **Tip**: Do not put two rule elements together in a rule definition without white space intervening in languages in which white space is used to delimit tokens or words.

Now that you are familiar with the terminology for parts of the rule definition, you can see some of the parts combined in Figure 5.3, which is an example PREDICATE_RULE type. This example rule is the same as the one in Figure 5.2, but with detailed labels for parts of the rule definition.

Figure 5.3. PREDICATE_RULE Example

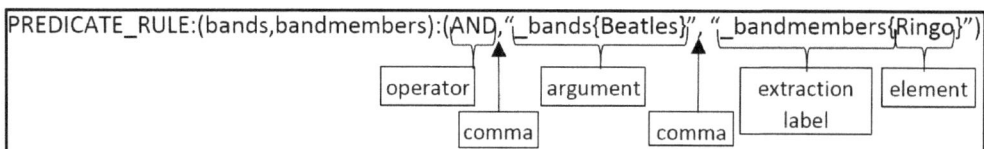

Notice in Figure 5.3 that there are two arguments of the operator "AND" and they are separated by commas. Each argument is enclosed in quotation marks and consists of an extraction label and an element enclosed in curly brackets.

There are two ways to write LITI rules: in the graphical user interface (GUI) and programmatically. The discussion of custom rules in this and following chapters applies to both approaches. However, if you choose to write rules programmatically, you need to be aware of a few additional rule conventions, which are detailed in section 5.3.4.

5.3. Custom Concept Fundamentals

A *concept* is a grouping of one or more LITI rules. Each concept has a name, and the name can be used to reference its group of rules from other concepts.

Sometimes a concept can contain a long list of rules, so it is recommended that you use the comment character and a descriptive comment to break up the list into different sections for ease of maintenance. For example, take a long list of rules of painkiller drug names in a concept named drugTypeA. As shown in the excerpt below, the comment character and a short description separates different types of painkiller drugs in the list.

```
#Over the counter
CLASSIFIER:aleve
CLASSIFIER:tylenol
CLASSIFIER:ibuprofen
CLASSIFIER:advil
CLASSIFIER:motrin
#Prescription
CLASSIFIER:vicodin
CLASSIFIER:percocet
CLASSIFIER:oxycontin
```

In this book, some of the example rules are too long to be represented on a single line; therefore, long rules are wrapped. However, in the SAS Text Analytics products, each LITI rule is always constrained to one line. Any new line interrupting a LITI rule causes compilation errors.

> **Tip**: Make sure each LITI rule is constrained to one line.

5.3.1. Best Practices for Naming Custom Concepts

Because concept names can be used in the same positions in LITI rules as strings are, it is important that you follow some guidelines for naming the concepts so that you can distinguish them from strings and other rule elements.

Avoid naming concepts with a single word that may occur in your text. For an example and explanation of this best practice, see section 6.3.1.

In addition, it is recommended that concept names use "camel" case without spaces between words and start with a lowercase letter. Some example concept names that follow these guidelines include "lossAmount," "posSentiment," and "loanOrigin."

In English projects in products released starting in 2017, you can also use numbers and underscores in the name, but if you want to name the concept with a leading underscore, make sure you follow it with an alphabetic character, not a number. In addition, if you want to use a leading or trailing underscore, balance it with an underscore on the other end of the concept name. Be careful not to include "_Q" anywhere in a concept name, because the name will not work properly.

For projects in English before 2017 and in other languages in products released before the summer of 2019, the recommendation is to use only ASCII letters in concept names. For products released after this date, the guidelines just given can be applied across all supported languages. Additionally, all alphabetic characters may be used.

Consider the following concept names:

- _Companies1
- Companies1_
- manufacturers
- companyList
- _Quarter_
- COMPANY_LIST
- mylist
- _234123_
- the1stQuarter
- _1stQuarter_

Pause and think: Which of the concept names above follow the suggested guidelines?

As you may have realized, only the concept names companyList and the1stQuarter follow the guidelines, because they are not a single word that could appear in the text, they do not have unbalanced underscores or underscores followed by a number or Q, and they are written in camel case. Although COMPANY_LIST and mylist could also be used as concept names, it would be easier to distinguish them from other rule elements if their casing were more distinctive and consistent.

To summarize, adhere to the following guidelines about concept naming to prevent loss of extracted matches or unintended matches:

- Avoid naming concepts with a single word that may occur in the text.
- Use only ASCII letters in product releases before 2017 for English and before 2019 for other languages.
- Use all letters, numbers, and underscore in product releases after 2017 for English and after 2019 for other languages, so long as you follow these guidelines:

  ○ Do not use _Q anywhere in the name.

  ○ If you use an underscore as the first character, use a letter for the second character and an underscore for the final character.

Another best practice in naming concepts is that names should be descriptive of the content you will be extracting with the rules in a given concept. For example, if you are extracting information about a vehicle part, then name the concept that contains those rules something like "vehiclePart." If you are extracting something grammatical, include the grammatical element in the name. For example, use "posAdj" for extracting positive adjectives. You should make the name long enough to be descriptive and informative, but short enough to be easily typed in new rules without introducing errors. Concept names are case-sensitive and must be consistently spelled whenever they are used in rules.

> **Tip**: When naming your concept, use "camel" case with no spaces between words. Make the concept name singular if you will be extracting one instance of the item that you define in each rule within the concept. Pay attention to case and consistency when referencing concepts in rules.

5.3.2. Best Practices for Referencing Custom Concepts

As mentioned in chapter 1, the taxonomy for your project contains concepts that are sets of rules. Each of those sets of rules can be referenced in another concept. To do so, include the referenced concept's name as an element in a rule in another concept. In this way, concepts are like code objects, so it is good to treat each one as a component of a whole. This approach follows a common way to build things in general. For example, vehicles, houses, and watches are all made up of a set of parts that are made for a specific purpose. Your concepts should work the same way.

Concept names with simpler rules will be used in the rules of more complex concepts, and the readability of such rules depends on how well you name and design each concept. Also, your ability to test and determine quality of a concept depends on how well your design reflects the types of data you will process with the model. Use singular names, for example, when extracting one item with the rules in your concept, because this way you will be able to read the more complex rules more accurately. This means that, if you are extracting a part name, then use the concept name "vehiclePart," not "vehicleParts."

5.3.3. Concepts versus CONCEPT and CONCEPT_RULE Rule Types

It is important to distinguish between concepts as groupings of rules, and the CONCEPT and CONCEPT_RULE rule types. A *concept* is represented by a node in the taxonomy tree. It can contain one or more rules of any type, including but not limited to CONCEPT and CONCEPT_RULE. This meaning is represented in the phrase "concept rules" in the title of this book. When concepts are mentioned in general, the word "concept" is written in lowercase letters.

The *CONCEPT rule type* refers to a rule that starts with the declaration "CONCEPT:" and a *CONCEPT_RULE type* refers to a rule that starts with the declaration "CONCEPT_RULE:". When the rule types are mentioned, the word "CONCEPT" is written in all-caps so that these types can be easily distinguished from concepts in general.

An additional phrase that you will encounter in some versions of the SAS software and documentation is "Concepts node." This phrase is referring to the pipeline node, which contains the predefined and custom concepts and their rules—in other words, the concept model. You can see the relationship between the concept model, the concepts themselves, and the rules in Figure 5.4.

Figure 5.4. Concept Model, Concepts, and Rules

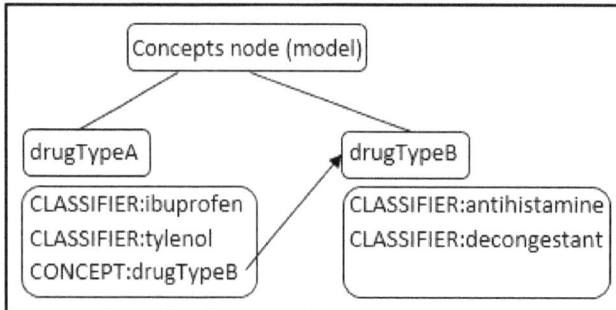

The concept drugTypeB has two CLASSIFIER rules. The concept drugTypeA has two CLASSIFIER rules and a CONCEPT rule referencing the concept drugTypeB. Because of that CONCEPT rule, extracted matches for the concept drugTypeB will also be extracted matches for the concept named drugTypeA.

> **Remember**: In this book, "concept" refers to a node in a taxonomy that contains LITI rules, not an idea in general.
>
> In this book, references to rule types (e.g., CONCEPT, CONCEPT_RULE) will always be in all capital letters, as in the rule type declaration itself.
>
> SAS documentation and products may refer to a "Concepts node," meaning a node within a pipeline that houses the model; this book will always refer to a "Concepts node" as a concepts model to avoid confusion.

5.3.4. Programmatic Rule Writing and Model Compilation

If you are writing custom concept rules programmatically, rather than using the GUI in products such as SAS Contextual Analysis or SAS Visual Text Analytics, you should know about additional requirements regarding the underlying configuration syntax. When you write rules in the GUI, it interprets the syntax of each rule and converts it to the underlying configuration syntax.

In this underlying syntax, a rule type declaration is followed by a required output declaration for every rule. The output declaration must contain the concept name with which the rule is associated. This concept name precedes any extraction label declaration (in fact rule types) or coreference command (in the CLASSIFIER rule type). Be careful not to put an additional colon between these two parts of the output declaration section. See the examples immediately below.

```
CLASSIFIER:musicBand:Rolling Stones
PREDICATE_RULE:musicBand(bands,bandMembers):(AND, "_bands{Beatles}",
"_bandMembers{Ringo}")
```

In addition to the rule type declaration, there are two additional declaration types: ENABLE and CASE_INSENSITIVE_MATCH. You need to explicitly call out with the ENABLE declaration each concept that is enabled, which allows the given concept to provide output from the model. Any concept that is in the model, but not enabled, may still find text spans, but will only pass extracted matches along to referencing concepts, not provide output from the model. In the example below, the concept named musicBand is enabled.

```
ENABLE:musicBand
```

The CASE_INSENSITIVE_MATCH declaration specifies that any string in any rule in that concept should be interpreted in a case-insensitive manner, extending the possible matches to both uppercase and lowercase alphabetic characters. All concepts are case-sensitive by default.

```
CASE_INSENSITIVE_MATCH:musicBand
```

Putting all these pieces together in a configuration file is shown in the following example.

```
ENABLE:musicBand
CASE_INSENSITIVE_MATCH:musicBand
CLASSIFIER:musicBand:Beatles
CLASSIFIER:musicBand:Rolling Stones
PREDICATE_RULE:musicBand(bands,bandMembers):(AND, "_bands{Beatles}",
"_bandMembers{Ringo}")
```

This configuration file, saved in a .txt format, is also provided as part of a larger code example in the supplementary materials for this chapter, accessible online as mentioned in About This Book.

The underlying configuration syntax just explained is used by DS2 code or Cloud Action Services (CAS) actions in the SAS Text Analytics Rule Development action set for compiling an IE model.

There are several ways to compile a model containing custom concepts. The supplementary materials for this chapter contain two such examples. The first one uses macros and DS2 code to compile the configuration file (in text format) into a concepts model binary file and then to apply it to score a data set. The other example uses the INFILE statement in data step to build a data set from the same configuration file. This data set can then be used to compile the model binary file with the compileConcept CAS action and apply it with the applyConcept CAS action.

As an alternative to using the INFILE statement with a text file or macros, you can also write the content of the configuration file as a SAS data set, using datalines. As in the example with the INFILE statement, you can then compile the data set can into a model binary file by using the compileConcept action. This method is used for the supplementary materials in the examples for the remainder of the book.

Another method to compile the model is to write the rules from the configuration file into a CAS table that can be used to compile the model binary file with the use of compileConcept. This approach requires that each rule have a ruleId and that the rule itself be enclosed in single quotes. Reference the example below.

```
data sascas1.concept_rule;
   length rule $ 200;
   ruleId=1;
   rule='CASE_INSENSITIVE_MATCH:musicBand';
   output;

   ruleId=2;
   rule='ENABLE:musicBand';
   output;

   ruleId=3;
   rule='CLASSIFIER:musicBand:Beatles';
   output;

   ruleId=4;
   rule='CLASSIFIER:musicBand:Rolling Stones';
   output;

   ruleId=5;
   rule=' PREDICATE_RULE:musicBand(bands,bandMembers):(AND,
"_bands{Beatles}", "_bandMembers{Ringo}")';
   output;

run;
```

Note that the remaining chapters of this book present the examples in the format of the rules used in the product GUIs. The programmatic format is used in supplemental materials so that the code can be run "out of the box" in DS2 code or with CAS actions.

5.3.5. Programmatic Model Application

Once your model has been built, you can use the SAS IE procedures or CAS actions in the Text Analytics Rule Score action set to run the model against a data set, using a SAS programming interface or SAS Studio. This method may work best when you are stringing together many different SAS analytic and visualization processes. Sample code for applying a SAS IE model by using both DS2 and CAS actions is provided in the supplementary materials for this chapter.

SAS Enterprise Content Categorization Server offers application of models using Java, Python, C#, and Perl. The Java and Python client interfaces are bundled as part of the server download, whereas the other types are standalone bundles.

5.4. Troubleshooting All Rule Types

Now that you are familiar with the required and optional parts of the different rule types, you can make sure that you avoid unexpected matches by following some general troubleshooting tips. There is no tracing mechanism in the LITI matcher that will tell you which rules or concepts match a particular string of text, so you will need to design your taxonomy, name your concepts, and write your rules and comments with this in mind.

This section is intended to help you identify why your model may be extracting spans that you did not intend or failing to extract spans as you expected. The pitfalls presented in this section are common to all the rule types. But you should also consult the troubleshooting sections specific to each rule type for additional errors to guard against.

Some of the possible reasons for unexpected matches include the following:

- General syntax errors
- Comments
- Misspellings or typographical errors
- Tokenization mismatch
- Filtered or removed matches

Syntax errors that are possible for all rule types include failing to use all-caps for the rule type or misspelling the name of the type. Be sure that you have a colon after the rule type and after any special section—that is, before the main rule definition. For example, the PREDICATE_RULE type, as shown in Figure 5.2, has a label declaration section between the rule type and the rule definition; there should be a colon both before and after such a section.

You can comment out a line or a part of a line by using the hash character (#); however, if you intend to match the hash character as part of the rule definition, you must escape it with a backslash like so: \#. See the rules below that match hashtags expressing positive sentiment.

```
#Hashtags
CLASSIFIER:\#bestproducts
CLASSIFIER:\#bestgifts
```

These rules could be applied to the following input documents:

1. I don't normally use hashtags, but I love my new phone! #bestproducts
2. Thanks for my new phone! #bestgifts

Pause and think: Assuming the rules above are in the posSentiment concept, can you predict the extracted matches for the input document above?

The extracted matches are shown in Figure 5.5.

Figure 5.5. Extracted Matches

Doc ID	Concept	Matched Text
1	posSentiment	#bestproducts
2	posSentiment	#bestgifts

You can see that there is no match for "hashtags" because "#Hashtags" is just a comment. The extracted matches for both CLASSIFIER rules include the hashtag symbol because it was escaped with a backslash in the rules.

Misspellings can occur either in the rule or in the text. If the spelling is not exactly the same in both the text and the rule, then there will be no match. Also, beware of mistyping concept names, because concept names are always case-sensitive.

Another common cause of missing matches is that the rule contains a part of a token instead of the entire token. You can review what a token is in section 1.5.1. For example, consider the following rule aiming to capture a unit of measurement.

```
CLASSIFIER:ft
```

An input document that this rule could be applied to is as follows:

It was a 3ft drop to the bottom of the hill.

> **Pause and think:** Assuming the rule above, can you predict whether a match will be extracted from the input document above?

If the rule contains only letters, but the input text contains an alphanumeric token, as in the example just shown, there will be no match. The rule will not match "ft" because the "3" is also a part of that alphanumeric token.

Note that the Measure predefined concept will see this token as a measurement, matching the full token "3ft" from the text because it contains a REGEX rule that captures the entire alphanumeric string.

One issue that you might observe is extracted matches without obvious rules aligning with the match. This can happen if you are using a predefined concept or other concept created by SAS. In this case, the rules may be hidden but operating in the background. You are given the opportunity to modify the behavior of such concepts through the addition of rules that contribute extracted matches or the addition of rules that filter extracted matches, or both.

Another issue that you might observe is that expected matches may be missing. In addition to the errors just explained that cause a rule not to match properly, there may be effects of rule-specific pitfalls, which will be covered in the following chapters. The primary one that you should be aware of, when you are using the "all matches" algorithm, is filtering done by global rule types, such as the filter rule types addressed in chapter 9.

The other reasons that extracted matches may be missing involve the alternate matching algorithm. If you are missing matches and your algorithm is set to either "best match" or "longest match," then try resetting your project to "all matches" and testing your rule again to see if this is the problem. If so, look at section 13.4.1 for advice on working through the issue, using your chosen match algorithm.

Chapter 6: Concept Rule Types

6.1. Introduction to the Concept Rule Types

In chapter 5, you learned about four groupings of LITI rule types:

- Concept rule types (including CLASSIFIER, CONCEPT, C_CONCEPT, and CONCEPT_RULE)
- Fact rule types (including SEQUENCE and PREDICATE_RULE)
- Filter rule types (including REMOVE_ITEM and NO_BREAK)
- REGEX rule type

Each one of these rule types is described briefly in the SAS Text Analytics product documentation. But it is often difficult to grasp the full power of each rule type in the context of a project. Therefore, the current chapter focuses on three of the concept types in the first group above: CLASSIFIER, CONCEPT, and C_CONCEPT rules. These rule types are used when you need to extract one contiguous string of information.

In this chapter, you will find basic and advanced uses for each of these three concept rule types, with examples. You should focus first on mastering the basic use cases and then extend your knowledge to the more advanced use cases.

To aid with troubleshooting unexpected behavior, each rule type section includes a checklist of possible errors specific to that rule type. To help you make the most out of each rule type in your models, this chapter also contains best practices for using that rule type. Finally, the requirements and optional elements for each rule type are summarized at the end of each section so you can keep coming back to that section as a quick reference when you are building your models.

After reading this chapter, you will be able to do the following tasks:

- Use the LITI syntax to write efficient and effective CLASSIFIER, CONCEPT, and C_CONCEPT types of rules
- Avoid common pitfalls and use best practices to create better rule sets
- Troubleshoot common rule-writing errors

6.2. CLASSIFIER Rule Type

CLASSIFIER rules match literal strings that represent a token or sequence of tokens. The full span of text found by the rule is returned as the extracted match in the output.

6.2.1. Basic Use

The basic syntax is as follows:

```
CLASSIFIER:token
CLASSIFIER:token token
```

This rule type specifies to extract the token, which can contain any character sequence, consisting of letters, numbers, and punctuation, as well as multiple tokens separated by spaces. So the following examples are valid rules:

```
CLASSIFIER:Mets
CLASSIFIER:Red Sox!
CLASSIFIER:2-3 teams including the Astros
```

Consider applying the rules above to the following input documents:

1. I like the Mets but she roots for the Red Sox!
2. They love 2-3 teams including the Astros.

You can try this and other examples in this chapter yourself with the code provided in the supplemental materials for the book (for instructions on downloading the supplemental materials, see About this Book).

> **Pause and think**: Assuming that the rules above are in a concept named baseballTeams, can you predict the extracted matches for the input documents above?

The extracted matches are presented in Figure 6.1.

Figure 6.1. Extracted Matches for the baseballTeams Concept

Doc ID	Concept	Match Text
1	baseballTeams	Mets
1	baseballTeams	Red Sox!
2	baseballTeams	2-3 teams including the Astros

Be careful not to include commas in the definition portion of the rule, because commas have a special role in CLASSIFIER rules as cues for the information field (see section 6.2.3 for details). If you want to include a comma in your extracted match, use the special escape sequence "\c". For example, see the following instance:

```
CLASSIFIER:The Red Sox \c Inc.
```

This rule would match "The Red Sox, Inc." but not "The Red Sox Inc." (without the comma) or "The Red Sox, Inc" (without a trailing period on the abbreviation).

Many rule-based information extraction (IE) systems take advantage of dictionaries or lists of specialized terms to be extracted. The SAS IE system performs the same task through the CLASSIFIER rule type.

6.2.2. Advanced Use: Coreference Command

A special form of the CLASSIFIER rule type includes a section in square brackets between the rule type and the rule definition. This special section is the *coreference command*, which can enable you to extract a match when an alias is used to refer to a string that is referenced with a full name in the same document. To capture co-occurrence of the terms, you can define the coreference in a CLASSIFIER rule.

The basic syntax is as follows:

```
CLASSIFIER:[coref=our company]:SAS Institute
```

You can read this rule this way: When the terms "SAS Institute" and "our company" appear in the input document, "our company" should be a match in the same concept as "SAS Institute." If only "SAS Institute" appears in the document, it is still extracted as a match, but if "our company" appears without "SAS Institute," it is not extracted as a match for that concept. The prerequisite for the coref part of the rule definition to produce a match is that the primary rule definition is found in the text. This approach adds an if-then condition to the match logic.

Consider the following examples. Assume each numbered item is a separate observation in the input data set:

1. SAS Institute is a great company. Our company has a recreation center and health care center for employees.
2. Our company has won many awards.
3. SAS Institute was founded in 1976.

> **Pause and think**: Assuming that the rule above is in a concept named bestEmployer, can you predict the matches with the input documents above?

The scoring output matches are in Figure 6.2; note that the document ID associated with each match aligns with the number before the input document where the match was found.

Figure 6.2. Extracted Matches for the bestEmployer Concept

Doc ID	Concept	Match Text	Canonical Form
1	bestEmployer	SAS Institute	SAS Institute
1	bestEmployer	Our company	SAS Institute
3	bestEmployer	SAS Institute	SAS Institute

In the user interface of some SAS Text Analytics products, the canonical form is visible in the terms list in parsing. For example, Figure 6.3, a view of SAS Visual Text Analytics, shows that "sas institute" is the lemma (parent or canonical form) for "our company" in those instances where they both appear in the same input document. To review what a lemma is, consult section 1.5.3.

To get the same output in your SAS Visual Text Analytics product, you need a project with a Concepts node and a Parsing node after it. First, open the Concepts node and create a new concept named "bestEmployer." Put the rule above into the rule editor window, and run your entire pipeline. Then, open the Parsing node and expand the term "sas institute" in the Term column.

Figure 6.3: SAS Visual Text Analytics Output of CLASSIFIER Rules with the Coreference Command

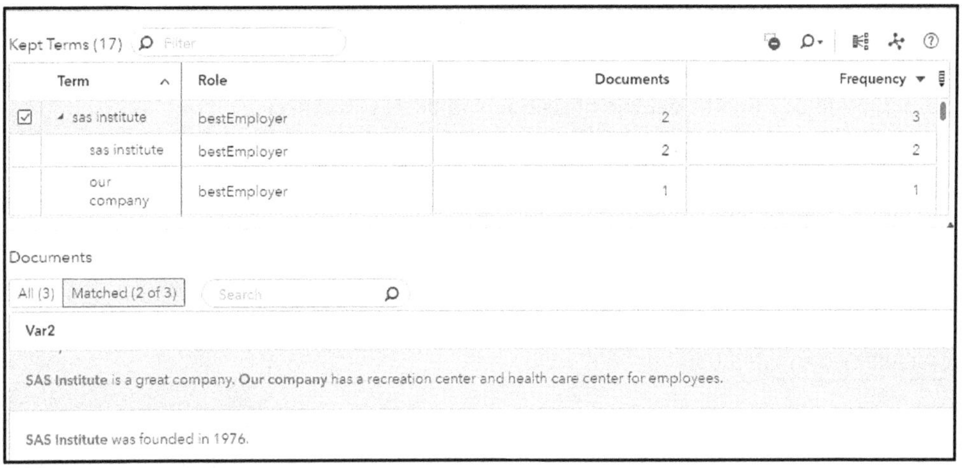

As shown in Figure 6.3, company name aliases are a good reason for using the coreference capability. In relatively short documents or with less ambiguous aliases, all instances of the alias in the document that mentions the full company name at least once are probably also referring to that company. Note that you cannot use this rule type with more than two aliases per rule.

This command is not the best way to handle resolution of pronouns, such as "we" or "our," because pronouns are not always tied to one noun. The recommended best practice in those cases is to use C_CONCEPT and CONCEPT_RULE types instead. Read more about these rule types in section 6.4 and in chapter 7, respectively.

The best time to use the coreference command in a CLASSIFIER rule is in cases where you may want term or phrase A to always be associated with term or phrase B that is present in the text. However, if term or phrase B is not in the text and you still want to extract term or phrase A and associate it with term or phrase B, use the information field feature instead. This feature of the CLASSIFIER rule type is described in section 6.2.3.

6.2.3. Advanced Use: Information Field

Another special form of the CLASSIFIER rule includes a comma in the rule definition, which signifies the beginning of the *information field*. Some versions of the SAS Text Analytics products can use this information field as a means for specifying the lemma of the match. The lemma acts as an umbrella term under which various forms of the same matched term are aggregated. For example, in SAS Visual Text Analytics, the information field allows you to set up a parent-child relationship between two terms or sets of terms in contexts where the child term (or set of terms) appears in the text, but the parent does not necessarily appear. In this sense, the information field is similar to the coreference command. The difference is that the parent term or terms are not required to be in the text when you use the information field, but the parent term must be matched in the text for a rule with the coreference command to be applied.

However, in some software versions, the information field is not displayed or provided as output, and in others this information is lost if the concept containing the CLASSIFIER rule is referenced by another concept. Therefore, you should use this option with caution and always consult the documentation for your specific product and version before using this feature. Before using the information field in the design of your model, you should build a brief test to confirm the outputs of scoring will be as you expect.

The basic syntax is as follows:

```
CLASSIFIER:token,information field
```

Two rule examples follow:

```
CLASSIFIER:United States,USA
CLASSIFIER:U.S.,USA
```

Remember that, with the coreference command, both spans of text in the rule must be found in the input text. With the information field, only the span of text in the rule definition (appearing before the comma) must be found in the input text.

Consider the following input text documents. As before, each numbered item is a separate row in the input data set:

1. I live in the United States.
2. The U.S. is their home country.
3. They chanted: USA! USA!

Pause and think: Assuming that the rules above are in a concept named usAlias, can you predict the matches for the input documents above?

Assuming the rules and input documents above, the matches are in Figure 6.4.

Figure 6.4. Extracted Matches for the usAlias Concept

Doc ID	Concept	Match Text	Canonical Form
1	usAlias	United States	USA
2	usAlias	U.S.	USA

Notice that only the first two input documents produce a match. The third one does not, because there is no rule definition that matches the term "USA"—It is mentioned only in the information field of the two rules. In short, the information field does not extract matches; it only adds a canonical form to the already extracted match.

In software versions that support using the information field, when both rules are processed with the input text, the two matches will be aggregated in the terms list in the parsing node under the lemma "usa" and will contain the role of the concept name, in this case usAlias. The lemma is displayed in the Canonical Form column in Figure 6.4.

An example from SAS Visual Text Analytics is provided in Figure 6.5. To replicate this result, create the concept usAlias, containing the rules above in a Concepts node. Make sure a Parsing node follows in your pipeline. Then run the pipeline, open the Parsing node, and expand the term "usa" with the role usAlias.

Figure 6.5. SAS Visual Text Analytics Output of CLASSIFIER Rules with the Information Field

Term		Role	Documents	Frequency
usa		PN	4	4
◢ usa		usAlias	13	14
u.s.		usAlias	4	4
united states		usAlias	9	10

In Figure 6.5, note that the term "usa" as a proper noun is separate from the term "usa" as the lemma of the usAlias concept. This example illustrates that the term in the information field of the rules above is not being matched in the rules. The information field term or terms do not need to be present in the document for the rules to produce matches and for the matches to be aggregated.

The term or terms in the information field unify the extracted matches like a parent. As the figure illustrates, this observation includes the frequency of the different aliases. This behavior is especially useful with text processing of terms that may have different forms in the text but are not in the dictionary and therefore not automatically grouped together by the software.

6.2.4. Troubleshooting

Even though CLASSIFIER rules in their basic form are relatively simple to write, you may discover that a particular rule is not matching as you expected. Potential causes for this could be one of the pitfalls outlined in section 5.4—namely, general syntax errors, comments, misspelling/mistyping, tokenization mismatch, or filtered matches. In addition, there are also errors that you can check for that are specific to the CLASSIFIER rule type, such as the following:

- White space
- Comma use in CLASSIFIER rules
- Syntax error

In a CLASSIFIER rule type, white space is reduced to a separator for a list of elements and not counted as an element itself. You cannot specify, for example, that you want to match the tokens "blue," space character, space character, and "dinosaur" in sequence. For that type of specific character matching, you need to use the REGEX rule type. However, if you want to match two adjacent tokens in text, you can eliminate the white space between the elements.

For example, if you want to match the string "Go!" and you want to match these two tokens side-by-side, then the rule will work the same way if you define it as either of these rules:

```
CLASSIFIER:Go!
CLASSIFIER:Go !
```

Remember that a comma signifies an advanced use (information field) of the CLASSIFIER rule type. So, a CLASSIFIER rule containing a comma will not match a comma in the text. To match a comma in the text, replace the comma in the CLASSIFIER rule with "\c" instead. The other character that must be escaped to match literally is the hash "#," because it acts as a comment marker. Comment the hash when you want to match it, like so: \#.

In addition to checking for common syntax errors that are possible with any rule types, if you are writing the advanced CLASSIFIER rules, then check for proper use of square braces, colon, and equal sign.

6.2.5. Best Practices

The best time to use CLASSIFIER rules is when you have a list of tokens or token sequences that you either want to extract or want to use as context for extraction. You cannot use CLASSIFIER rules to reference elements other than tokens, such as part-of-speech (POS) tags, other concepts, or regular expressions.

The benefit of using CLASSIFIER rules is that they are relatively low-cost computationally and simple to generate from lists. However, because they can result in many individual rules, perhaps thousands, they can be difficult to maintain. One way to improve maintainability is to group smaller sets of CLASSIFIER rules into concepts that can then be referenced by other rules but are still short enough to review for comprehensiveness and to troubleshoot for errors. For an example, see section 6.3.1. The CLASSIFIER rule type is useful for beginners and for the fundamental rules of a project, but be careful not to over-rely on it when a smaller set of patterns would be easier to maintain.

Always test that each rule matches as you would expect. Be especially careful with the advanced uses of CLASSIFIER rules. In addition, consult your product-specific documentation before using the information field, to confirm that the behavior you need is supported.

6.2.6. Summary

Requirements for a CLASSIFIER include the following:

- A rule type declaration in all-caps and followed by a colon
- A token or sequence of tokens to match literally (a comma or a hash character must be escaped with backslash)

Allowed options for the rule type include the following:

- Comments using the "#" modifier
- Coreference command
- Information field (which is set off by a comma from the string to be extracted)

6.3. CONCEPT Rule Type

When a CLASSIFIER rule cannot do everything that you need, consider the use of a CONCEPT rule instead. CONCEPT rules return the entire found text as the extracted match just as CLASSIFIER rules do. The rule can include tokens, punctuation, references to POS tags, and references to other concepts, as well as special elements used to identify any token (_w), capitalized word (_cap), or modifiers (listed in Table 5.2).

6.3.1. Basic Use

The basic syntax is one element (from the ones listed in Table 5.1), such as a string, POS tag, or concept name, following the rule type declaration and colon. Regular expressions in the rule definition are not allowed for this rule type.

```
CONCEPT:element
```

Referencing Other Concepts

The most basic use of a CONCEPT rule type is to refer to another concept, pulling the matches from that other concept into the one containing the CONCEPT rule type. For example, you can combine two lists of strings by referencing two other concepts that each contain lists of CLASSIFIER rules, without repeating all the possible combinations.

Consider a concept named targetCity containing these rules:

```
CONCEPT:capitalCity
CONCEPT:companyCity
```

The first rule references the concept named capitalCity, which contains a series of classifier rules defining matches for capital cities in the United States:

```
CLASSIFIER:Nashville
CLASSIFIER:Raleigh
CLASSIFIER:Springfield
```

The second one references the concept named companyCity, which contains a series of classifier rules defining the set of cities where your company has offices:

```
CLASSIFIER:Memphis
CLASSIFIER:Charlotte
```

There are many reasons for keeping two or more different lists of city names, as in this example. Some reasons may be for organizational purposes or for ease of maintenance. For example, having separate lists for each state or each country of interest will provide shorter lists. Redundancy does not matter much, and the flexibility gained by having separate lists will offset the drawback of having the same item appear in multiple lists. In addition, different lists may come from different sources or represent different subcategories of a larger category.

Assume here that your marketing department is building a model to use for finding mentions of particular cities involved in a promotional offer. They leverage the two lists already available to create the concept targetCity.

Consider the following input text document:

Best Health Systems Inc is headquartered in Nashville, TN with local offices in Memphis, TN, Raleigh, NC, Charlotte, NC, New York, NY and Springfield, IL.

Pause and think: Assuming the model above and settings that allow for the examination of the matches from all three concepts (capitalCity, companyCity, and targetCity), can you predict the output for the document above?

Assuming the model and input document above, as well as the "all matches" algorithm, the matches are listed in Figure 6.6.

Figure 6.6. Extracted Matches for the targetCity, companyCity, and capitalCity Concepts

Doc ID	Concept	Match Text
1	targetCity	Nashville
1	capitalCity	Nashville
1	companyCity	Memphis
1	targetCity	Memphis
1	capitalCity	Raleigh
1	targetCity	Raleigh
1	companyCity	Charlotte
1	targetCity	Charlotte
1	capitalCity	Springfield
1	targetCity	Springfield

There are no matches for "New York," because there are no rule definitions for that string. All of the matches in the output represent pairs of matches for each of the defined strings: Each pair contains one match for the concept, with the CLASSIFIER rule containing that string, and a second match for the concept with the CONCEPT rule. As you may remember from section 1.4, some concepts can be marked as *helper concepts* in some products so that they do not contribute to the final result set directly, but only through other concepts that reference them. Using this approach and designating the capitalCity and companyCity concepts as helper concepts can eliminate one of the sets of duplicate matches shown in Figure 6.6. To learn more about the role that helper concepts play in IE models, see section 13.3.2.

Because a concept name can contain letters, numbers, and underscores, and therefore can look like a regular word token, it is important to name concepts using strings that would not be encountered in the text. In this way, you can avoid inadvertently matching the name as a string literal. To illustrate, consider the following example project. Despite the suggested best practice, one concept is named "protein," containing the following rules:

```
CLASSIFIER:keratin
CLASSIFIER:collagen
```

Another concept is named macroMolecule and contains rules defining types of macromolecules:

```
CONCEPT:protein
CONCEPT:lipid
CONCEPT:nucleic acid
```

Now consider the following input sentence:

Collagen works in conjunction with another important protein, keratin.

Pause and think: Taking into consideration the concepts and input document above, can you predict the output?

The rules in the protein concept will return matches for "collagen" and "keratin," which are expected. These two matches will also be returned to the macroMolecule concept, which is expected as well. However, what may be unexpected is that a match for the string "protein" is also returned to the macroMolecule concept. If you had intended to reference only the concept named "protein," not the literal string "protein," then the resulting match may be surprising. To avoid this situation, always name concepts as different from string literals you may find in the data.

Referencing POS Tags

In the CONCEPT rule type, you can also write grammatical rules by using POS tags and special tags such as ":sep," ":digit," and ":time." These rules are all preceded by a colon and are case-sensitive:

```
CONCEPT::A
CONCEPT::N
```

The first rule will match any adjective in the input document, whereas the second rule will match any noun. Note that because the rule type declaration ends in a colon and the POS tag begins with one, there are two colons next to each other when a POS tag or special tag is the first element in a rule.

The list of POS and special tags that can be used in CONCEPT rules is available in your product documentation. The tags may be different in different versions of the software, so you should always consult the documentation for the appropriate version.

In addition, exercise caution when using POS tags, because it is possible that the tag you think a particular word may have is not the same as the tag assigned to that word by the software in the context in which it appears. Always test your expectations with a small sample of text. Keep in mind that the same word can have different POS assignments (if that is a possibility for your language) in different contexts. In your tests, ensure that the grammatical structure of your sample text is parallel to the structure of the data that you want to process.

One example in which POS tags are useful is if your goal is to extract all proper nouns from a text as part of data exploration. For this purpose, you could have a concept named properNoun, containing the following rule:

```
CONCEPT::PN
```

Consider the following input document:

> The company Best Health Systems Inc is headquartered in Nashville, TN.

> **Pause and think**: Assuming the rule and input document above, can you predict the output?

Assuming the rule and input document above, the matches are outlined in Figure 6.7.

Figure 6.7. Extracted Matches for the properNoun Concept

Doc ID	Concept	Match Text
1	properNoun	Best
1	properNoun	Health
1	properNoun	Systems
1	properNoun	Inc
1	properNoun	Nashville
1	properNoun	TN

The next exploratory step may be to write a rule containing a sequence of several POS tags. Using sequences of elements in CONCEPT rules is discussed in sections 6.3.2 and 6.3.3.

Referencing Special Elements and Modifiers

In CONCEPT rules, you can also use special elements, such as _w and _cap, as well as modifiers such as the expansion symbol @. See the example rule here:

```
CONCEPT: _w
```

This rule extracts every token in a corpus. It is useful for creating a unigram model.

> **Tip**: Although _w is called a "word symbol," it actually represents any token in the text. This means that it will match single punctuation, as well as any word.

The expansion modifiers, when used after a lemma, allow matches of inflectional variants in the same POS class of a particular word, on the basis of the variants in the underlying dictionary. To review what a lemma is, consult section 1.5.3. Here is one example:

```
CONCEPT:part@N
```

You can read this rule as follows: Expand the matches to any entries in the underlying dictionary that stem to the word "part" and have the POS "noun." This rule will match any instances in the text of the words "part" or "parts," because each of these variants is listed in the dictionary as a singular and plural noun, respectively. However, be cautious in interpreting this rule. It does not mean that the words with the POS tag of ":N" will be located, but only the strings "part" and "parts." Each of these strings may also be tagged as verbs in the input text. In that case, the rule above will match them as well.

Another example of a rule containing the expansion symbol is as follows:

```
CONCEPT:part@V
```

This rule will match any instances in the text of the words "part," "parts," "parted," or "parting," no matter which role the words are actually playing in the document itself. The reason for this behavior is that the rule is expanded in the background during compilation of the model based on the dictionary, but the POS tag for the word in the text is not known at that time. The run-time processing of data has not begun.

> **Tip:** When you are using the expansion modifiers, such as @N, @V, and @A, the variants are generated in accordance with the POS tags in the underlying dictionary. Any of the variants are then matched as strings in the text, regardless of the role that the words are playing in the input text.

6.3.2. Advanced Use: Combination of Various Elements

A more complex example of a CONCEPT type of rule combines various elements to extract longer matches. This rule type is useful for matching text using patterned sequences of elements. For example, you can capture "an important decision" and "a valuable resource" with a sequence of the POS tags: determiner adjective noun. The syntax is several elements separated by a space, where each element may be any item in Table 5.1 except regular expression.

```
CONCEPT:element1 element2 … elementN
```

One example is to combine references to concept names with strings and punctuation. For example, if you know that a city name that you want to extract will always be followed by a comma and a string signifying a U.S. state, then you can write the following rule in a concept named modelCity:

```
CONCEPT:capitalCity, usState
```

In this example, the concept named usState contains the following rules:

```
CLASSIFIER:TN
CLASSIFIER:NC
```

As before, the concept named capitalCity contains the following rules:

```
CLASSIFIER:Nashville
CLASSIFIER:Raleigh
CLASSIFIER:Springfield
```

Consider the following input document.

> Best Health Systems Inc is headquartered in Nashville, TN with local offices in Memphis, TN, Raleigh, NC, Charlotte, NC, New York, NY and Springfield, IL.

Pause and think: Taking into consideration the concepts and input document above, can you predict the output if the "all matches" algorithm is specified?

The matches for the concepts and input document above are presented in Figure 6.8.

Figure 6.8. Extracted Matches for the capitalCity, modelCity, and usState Concepts

Doc ID	Concept	Match Text
1	capitalCity	Nashville
1	modelCity	Nashville, TN
1	usState	TN
1	usState	TN
1	capitalCity	Raleigh
1	modelCity	Raleigh, NC
1	usState	NC
1	usState	NC
1	capitalCity	Springfield

The other cities in the input document do not match, because no rules have been written to capture those city names.

6.3.3. Advanced Use: Combination of Elements and Modifiers

Consider the following rule, which combines a concept rule reference and POS tags, as well as the expansion modifier @:

```
CONCEPT:partName be@ :V
```

You can read this rule this way: When a match from the partName concept is followed by any form of "be" that is in the dictionary and then by any token with the POS tag of "verb," extract the entire match to the concept where this rule appears. This concept could be named, for example, reportedIssue. The concept referenced in the rule definition, partName, includes the following rules:

```
CLASSIFIER:damper frame
CLASSIFIER:damper wheel
CLASSIFIER:thumb piece
CLASSIFIER:rubber foot
CLASSIFIER:dashboard
CLASSIFIER:coil spring
```

Some input documents that this very simple model could be applied to are as follows:

1. Some of the issues that I noticed are that the damper frame is twisted, the damper wheel was installed wrong, and the thumb piece was blown.
2. The rubber foot is broken.
3. I saw that the dashboard is fractured and the coil spring was worn.
4. The thumb pieces were broken.
5. The dashboard must have been cracked previously.

Pause and think: Assuming the model above, can you predict the matches for only the reportedIssue concept with the documents above?

Assuming the partName concept is marked as a helper concept, the rule matches for the reportedIssue concept with the input documents above are in Figure 6.9.

Figure 6.9. Extracted Matches for the reportedIssue Concept

Doc ID	Concept	Match Text
1	reportedIssue	damper frame is twisted
1	reportedIssue	damper wheel was installed
1	reportedIssue	thumb piece was blown
2	reportedIssue	rubber foot is broken
3	reportedIssue	dashboard is fractured
3	reportedIssue	coil spring was worn

Note that there are no matches for the fourth input document, because the concept partName did not return a match for "thumb pieces." The rule in the partName concept was written to match the string "thumb piece," and the document contains "thumb pieces." To extract this additional match, you can add an additional CLASSIFIER rule to account for the string or change the existing rule as follows:

```
CONCEPT:thumb piece@
```

There are also no matches for the fifth input document because the string "must have been" does not match "be@" in the rule. In this example, the grammatical structure of the sentence did not match the grammatical structure of the rule in the reportedIssue concept.

6.3.4. Troubleshooting

If you discover that a particular rule is not matching as you expected, potential causes for this could be one of the pitfalls outlined in section 5.4—namely, general syntax errors, comments, misspelling/mistyping, tokenization mismatch, or filtered matches. In addition, there are also errors that you can check for that are specific to the CONCEPT rule type, such as the following:

- White space
- Misspelling/mistyping
- Tagging mismatch
- Expansion mismatch
- Concept references
- Predefined concept references
- Cyclic dependencies

White space is reduced in a CONCEPT rule to a separator for a list of tokens and not counted as a token itself. You cannot specify, for example, that you want to match the tokens "blue," space character, space character, and "dinosaur" in sequence in this rule type. For doing that type of specific sequence matching, you need to use the REGEX rule type.

Misspelling can occur either in the rule or in the text. For the CONCEPT rule type, beware of mistyping concept names, because concept names are case-sensitive.

It is possible that the POS tag you think a particular word may have is not the tag assigned to that word by the software in that particular context. The best way to prevent this error is to test your expectations with targeted examples in context, before applying the rule to a sample of documents that is like the data you will process with the model. Also, be aware that the best natural language processing system will make errors in POS tagging even in perfectly grammatical text. Take that error rate into account as you design your model.

In addition, it is possible that the POS tag is misspelled or does not exist. Different languages, versions, and products may use different POS tags. Consult your product documentation for lists of acceptable tags for rule-building. The spelling and case of the tags in the rules must be exactly as documented. Because writing a rule with a nonexistent tag like ":abc" is not a syntax error, but a logical error, the syntax checking protocols will not catch it as an error, but there will not be any matches.

Another potential error when you are writing rules that contain a POS tag is forgetting to include the colon before specifying the tag. Without the colon, the system considers the rule to refer to a concept by that name or a string match, which may produce unexpected or no results. Syntax checking protocols will not return an error in this case.

When using the expansion symbols (e.g., @, @N, @V, @A), note that the expansion includes only related dictionary forms, not any misspellings that may have been identified by the misspelling algorithm or other variants associated with that lemma through use of a synonym list. To review what a lemma is, consult chapter 1. Also, remember that the forms of the words are looked up before processing, and when matching happens, the associated POS assignment of the word in the text is not considered. You can work around this issue, if you want to, using a CONCEPT_RULE type of rule; see chapter 7 for more information. Examining your output from rules that contain expansion symbols is recommended.

Note that if the word before the @ is looked up and not found in the dictionary, then the word is treated as an unknown word, and only that specific string up to the @ sign will be matched without variants. No error is generated in this situation. Another common type of error is accidentally adding an @ modifier to a CLASSIFIER rule without changing the rule type to CONCEPT. Because the CLASSIFIER rule will treat the characters literally, you will likely see no matches to that rule.

Referencing concepts by name without ensuring that you have used the correct name, including both case and spelling accuracy, can also reduce the number of expected matches. If you reference predefined concepts, be sure that they are loaded into your project, and always check the names, because they may be different across different products.

Any rule that can reference a concept and returns matches (e.g., not REMOVE_ITEM or NO_BREAK) has the capacity to participate in a cyclic dependency error. A cyclic dependency is when two or more concepts refer to each other in a circle of concept references. For example, if the concept myConceptA has rules that reference myConceptB, and myConceptB has rules that reference myConceptA, there is a cycle of references between them. This type of error will prevent your whole project from compiling. This error is another reason to test your project often as you are adding concepts and rules. In this way, you will know that the latest rules added to the model created the cyclic dependency. Another strategy to use to avoid this error is careful design for your taxonomy and model. Refer to chapter 12 to learn more about taxonomy design best practices.

6.3.5. Best Practices

Use a CONCEPT rule when a CLASSIFIER rule does not have enough power to capture the types of patterns and combinations that you need to model in your rule. A CONCEPT rule is the best choice when you need access to elements other than the literal token, or series of literal tokens, and still want to extract the found span of text in its entirety.

The benefits of using a CONCEPT rule include a powerful ability to match both literal tokens and a variety of other pattern types, such as a series of POS tags or intervening tokens. The syntax of the rule is otherwise very straightforward because each element of the rule must be found in the text in order to match. The rule type should be used frequently in most models. However, do not use a CONCEPT rule when you are extracting only a literal token, or set of literal tokens, because using many CONCEPT rules instead of CLASSIFIER rules for this purpose will have a negative impact on the performance of your model.

Test your rules frequently while building to ensure that each rule is doing what you expect. In particular, it is easy to misspell or mistype concept names and tag names, so be sure your rule is working on a snippet of data before testing a set of documents. Also, do not expect POS tagging to be 100% accurate. Instead, use testing to determine how accurate your rule needs to be, and either swap out your use of POS tag with another method after using the tag for exploration, or build into your rules compensation for tagging errors.

Coreference symbols may be used in CONCEPT rules but are not recommended. Instead, for better syntax checking and consistency of using the _c{} extraction label, use a

C_CONCEPT rule when writing rules with coreference. See section 6.4 for more information on the C_CONCEPT rule type.

When naming your concepts, be sure to follow all the naming conventions introduced in section 5.3.1 (or create your own standard guidelines while still adhering to the name requirements). Keep your model logical, with clear and well-designed names, to save time when testing, troubleshooting, and maintaining your models.

6.3.6. Summary

Requirements for a CONCEPT include the following:

- A rule type declaration in all caps and followed by a colon
- One or more elements

Types of elements allowed include the following:

- A token or sequence of tokens to match literally ("#" character must still be escaped for a literal match to occur)
- A reference to another concept name or a series of concept names, including predefined concepts
- A POS or special tag preceded by a colon
- A word symbol (_w), representing any single token
- A cap symbol (_cap), representing any capitalized word

Allowed options for the rule type include the following:

- Comments using the "#" modifier
- Morphological expansion symbols, including @, @N, @V, and @A

6.4. C_CONCEPT Rule Type

The benefits of the C_CONCEPT rule type include the ability to control the portion of the found text that is extracted as a match and returned as output, allowing for fine-grained specification of the structured data that your rules will create. Also, coreference matching is available and compatible with C_CONCEPT rules.

In the two rule types described in the previous sections, the found text was the same as the extracted match. However, sometimes you need to specify context that determines whether the text should be extracted, especially when the match itself is ambiguous. In this case, the found text is not the same as the extracted match, and you should use the C_CONCEPT rule type.

6.4.1. Basic Use

The basic syntax is as follows:

```
C_CONCEPT:_c{element} element
C_CONCEPT:element _c{element}
```

Note that only the part between the curly braces is the extracted match. You can also use additional elements on either side of the braces and use multiple elements inside the braces.

For example, the following rules use strings of text to extract the various contexts in which "Congo" is referring to a country name as opposed to the name of a river:

```
C_CONCEPT:republic of the _c{Congo}
C_CONCEPT:_c{Congo}, republic of the
C_CONCEPT:the _c{Congo} republic
C_CONCEPT:west _c{Congo}
C_CONCEPT:former French _c{Congo}
```

In each of the rules above, only the string "Congo" is extracted as a match, but only if preceded or followed by the specified strings, which disambiguate the string as a country name.

Consider the following input documents:

1. Africa :: CONGO, REPUBLIC OF THE. Flag Description . . .
2. The Democratic Republic of the Congo (DRC) is located in central sub-Saharan Africa . . .
3. The Republic of the Congo (French: République du Congo), also known as the Congo Republic, West Congo, the former French Congo . . .

> **Pause and think**: Assuming that the rules above are in a concept named africanCountry, can you predict the matches from the input documents above?

The matches for the rules and input documents above are in Figure 6.10.

Figure 6.10. Extracted Matches for the africanCountry Concept

Doc ID	Concept	Match Text
1	africanCountry	CONGO
2	africanCountry	Congo
3	africanCountry	Congo
3	africanCountry	Congo
3	africanCountry	Congo
3	africanCountry	Congo

Note that, although the last four matches come from the same document, each match is from a different context: the first one from "republic of the Congo," the second from "the Congo republic," the third one from "West Congo," and the fourth one from "former French Congo."

C_CONCEPT rules can also include other types of elements, such as POS tags, special symbols such as _w or _cap, or names of other concepts. For example, in a project requiring extraction of adjectives that appear in front of the names of certain famous hotels, the rule below takes into consideration the context of the hotel name being mentioned, but extracts only the adjectives as matches. In this example, the rule is in a concept named hotelDescriptor:

```
C_CONCEPT:_c{:A} hotelName
```

The hotelName concept, referenced here, contains CLASSIFIER rules that match certain hotel names. Because only the adjectives need to be extracted, the hotelName is a helper concept.

```
CLASSIFIER:Four Seasons hotel
CLASSIFIER:Taj Mahal Palace hotel
CLASSIFIER:Plaza Hotel
```

Consider the following input documents:

1. The renowned Four Seasons hotel . . .
2. The famous Taj Mahal Palace hotel . . .
3. The owners of the famed Plaza Hotel . . .

Pause and think: Assuming that the rule above is in a concept named hotelDescriptor, can you predict the matches for the input documents above?

The matches for the hotelDescriptor concept with the input documents above are in Figure 6.11.

Figure 6.11. Extracted Matches for the hotelDescriptor Concept

Doc ID	Concept	Match Text
1	hotelDescriptor	renowned
2	hotelDescriptor	famous
3	hotelDescriptor	famed

Alternatively, the rule above could be rewritten to extract only the names of the hotels if the project required their extraction after certain adjectives. The list of adjectives could be specified with CLASSIFIER rules in one or more concepts named, for example, positiveAdjective or negativeAdjective. One rule that could extract only the hotel name when it follows an adjective in the positiveAdjective concept could be written as follows:

```
C_CONCEPT:positiveAdjective _c{hotelName}
```

6.4.2. Advanced Use: Multiple Strings as Matches

In all the examples in the previous section, the match that was returned corresponded to one element in the rule definition. Advanced C_CONCEPT rule uses can return multiple elements in the match string and use more than two elements for specifying the context.

For example, in a project containing U.S. customers' addresses, a company may want to extract only the city and state of the address. The project contains a concept named firstLineAddress, with rules that define the first line of the address, such as "123 Main Str." or "4004 Oak Blvd Ste #300." Some of the rules in this concept are included here:

```
CONCEPT:anyDigit _cap Str.
CONCEPT:anyDigit _cap St poundDigit
CONCEPT:anyDigit _cap Ave NE
CONCEPT:anyDigit _cap Ave SW
CONCEPT:anyDigit _cap _cap Ste poundDigit
CONCEPT:anyDigit _cap _cap Dr.
```

The rules above leverage the anyDigit and poundDigit helper concepts. You can read more about helper concepts in section 15.2. The anyDigit concept contains a REGEX rule that captures one or more adjacent digits. You can learn more about REGEX rules in chapter 10.

```
REGEX:[0-9]+
```

The poundDigit helper concept contains a REGEX rule that matches one or more digits following the pound sign:

```
REGEX:\#[0-9]+
```

In addition, the model contains the helper concept customerCity, which includes CLASSIFIER rules of city names.

```
CLASSIFIER:Lansing
CLASSIFIER:Boston
CLASSIFIER:Rockford
CLASSIFIER:Cary
```

The helper concept customerState contains CLASSIFIER rules of two-letter state codes:

```
CLASSIFIER:MI
CLASSIFIER:MA
CLASSIFIER:NC
```

The concept customerCityState has a C_CONCEPT rule that extracts the city and state of the customer's address on the basis of expectations that the match to the firstLineAddress will be followed by a comma (modeled as any punctuation by use of the ":sep" tag), and then the match to the customerCity concept, another comma, and finally a match to the customerState concept:

```
C_CONCEPT:firstLineAddress :sep _c{customerCity :sep customerState}
```

Consider the following input documents:

1. 1300 Center Str., Lansing, MI 48906
2. 256 E St #1, Boston, MA 02127
3. 8200 Peachtree Ave NE, Rockford, MI 49341
4. 100 SAS Campus Dr., Cary NC 27513

> **Pause and think**: Assuming the model described above, can you predict the matches for the customerCityState concept on the basis of the input documents above?

The matches for the customerCityState concept is in Figure 6.12.

Figure 6.12. Extracted Matches for the customerCityState Concept

Doc ID	Concept	Match Text
1	customerCityState	Lansing, MI
2	customerCityState	Boston, MA
3	customerCityState	Rockford, MI

Note that there is no match for the fourth document because there is no comma between the city and state. In all the other cases, the comma is present and extracted as part of the match because in the rule definition, the second ":sep" tag is inside the curly braces.

6.4.3. Advanced Use: Coreference

The C_CONCEPT rule type can also be used for coreference, which applies to any situation in which you need to tie variant references to a standard reference. For example, coreference often applies to the use of pronouns in language, where the pronouns refer to some other noun in the text. In comparison with the CLASSIFIER rule type approach to coreference, the C_CONCEPT rule type has the benefit of being able to use elements other than strings in the rule definition.

For example, imagine that you are trying to extract drug side effects from medical notes explaining patients' complaints. You may have rules that extract patients' reactions, such as "severe pain," in a statement such as "Patient reported severe pain." You could do so with a C_CONCEPT rule such as the following one, in a concept named, for example, sideEffect:

```
C_CONCEPT:patient _c{:V :A :N}
```

With the example sentence above as input, the rule would return a match for "reported severe pain." But in some cases, the medical notes may use pronouns to refer to the patient. Several examples follow:

1. The patient stated that she had severe reactions to the medicine.
2. Patient complained that he experienced painful headaches.

Because the patients' reported reactions do not follow the word "patient," the rule above would not produce any matches. In these cases, it may be useful to resolve the pronouns "she" and "he" in a rule such as the following one in a concept named patientReport:

```
C_CONCEPT: _c{patient} :V that _ref{:PRO}
```

In both documents above, "patient" and the pronouns "she" and "he" would be matches in patientReport. Now, in the sideEffect concept an additional rule can be written that includes cases in which a pronoun is referring to the patient, by referencing the patientReport concept:

```
C_CONCEPT:patientReport _c{:V :A :N}
```

Consider the following input documents, adapted from the Vaccine Adverse Event Reporting System 2016 data (https://vaers.hhs.gov/):

1. The patient claimed that she had abdominal pain and vomiting for 3 months after vaccination.
2. On 14 Oct 2016, same day after the vaccination, the patient reported that he has red bumps on both arms (Rash papular).
3. Patient reports that she had excruciating pain in the back of her head.
4. On the same day, the patient complained that she had swelling at the base of her shoulder.

Pause and think: Assuming the model described above, can you predict the matches for the input documents above?

The matches to the sideEffect concept for the input documents above are in Figure 6.13.

Figure 6.13. Extracted Matches for the sideEffect Concept

Doc ID	Concept	Match Text
1	sideEffect	had abdominal pain
2	sideEffect	has red bumps
3	sideEffect	had excruciating pain

Note that in the first three cases, the concept named patientReport is identifying the pronouns "she" and "he" and passing them as matches to the concept sideEffect. However, not all notes about patient side effects are written in the same pattern of verb, followed by adjective and noun, as demonstrated by the fourth input document. In this case, although there would be a match for "patient" and "she" in the concept patientReport, there would be no match for the sideEffect concept. To capture this type of sentence structure, another C_CONCEPT rule could be defined in the sideEffect concept. An example is provided here:

```
C_CONCEPT:patientReport _c{:V :N}
```

Because of this rule, the fourth document would also produce a match if the model is rerun.

If the data has even more variability in how symptoms are described, then more rules would be required. This example illustrates that the best time to use the C_CONCEPT rule type for modeling coreference is when the sentence structure is somewhat predictable, without many different variations of patterns. Otherwise, a better choice may be the CONCEPT_RULE type, as described in chapter 7.

6.4.4. Troubleshooting

If you discover that a particular rule is not matching as you expected, potential causes for this could be one of the pitfalls outlined in section 5.4—namely, general syntax errors, comments, misspelling/mistyping, tokenization mismatch, or filtered matches. In addition, there are also errors that you can check for that are specific to the C_CONCEPT rule type, such as the following:

- White space
- Syntax errors
- Missing extraction label
- Tagging mismatch
- Expansion mismatch
- Concept references
- Predefined concept references
- Cyclic dependencies

In C_CONCEPT rule types, white space is reduced to a separator for a list of elements and not counted as an element itself. You cannot specify how many white space characters or what type can appear between elements. For specifying white space characters in your match, you need to use a REGEX rule type. In short, white space works the same way in this rule type as in the CLASSIFIER and CONCEPT rule types.

Another error in C_CONCEPT rules includes forgetting the extraction label and its curly braces or putting it on the wrong element or elements. In the C_CONCEPT rule, there may only be a single extraction label used, _c{}.

It is possible that the POS tag you think a particular word may have is not the tag assigned to that word by the software in that particular context. The best way to prevent this error is to test your expectations with targeted examples in context, before applying the rule to a sample of documents that is like the data you will process with the model.

In addition, it is possible that the POS tag is misspelled or does not exist. Different languages, versions, and products may use different POS tags. Consult your product documentation for lists of acceptable tags for rule-building. The spelling and case of the tags in the rules must be exactly as documented. Because writing a rule with a nonexistent tag like ":abc" is not a syntax error, but a logical error, the syntax checking protocols will not catch it as an error, but there will not be any of the expected matches.

Another potential error when you are writing rules that contain a POS tag is forgetting to include the colon before specifying the tag. Without the colon, the system considers the rule to refer to a concept by that name or a string match, which may produce unexpected or no results. Syntax checking protocols will not return an error in this case.

When using the expansion symbols (e.g., @, @N, @V, @A), note that the expansion includes only related dictionary forms, not any misspellings that may have been identified by the misspelling algorithm or other variants associated with that lemma through use of a synonym list. To review what a lemma is, consult chapter 1. Also, remember that the forms of the words are looked up before processing, and when matching happens, the associated POS assignment of the word in the text is not considered. You can work around this issue, if you want to, using a CONCEPT_RULE; see chapter 7 for more information. Examining your output from rules that contain expansion symbols is recommended.

Referencing concepts by name without ensuring that you have used the correct name, including both case and spelling accuracy, can also reduce the number of expected matches. If you reference predefined concepts, be sure that they are loaded into your project, and always check the names because they may be different across different products.

Any rule that can reference a concept and returns matches (e.g., not REMOVE_ITEM or NO_BREAK) has the capacity to participate in a cyclic dependency error. A cyclic dependency is when two or more concepts refer to each other in a circle of concept references. For example, if the concept myConceptA has rules that reference myConceptB, and myConceptB has rules that reference myConceptA, then there is a cycle of references between them. This type of error will prevent your whole project from compiling. This error is another reason to test your project often as you are adding concepts and rules. In this way, you will know that the latest rules added to the model created the cyclic dependency. Another strategy to use to avoid this error is careful design for your taxonomy and model. Refer to chapter 13 to learn more about taxonomy design best practices.

6.4.5. Best Practices

The C_CONCEPT rule type should be used when you want context to constrain or trigger a match, but the context itself should not be part of the extracted match. Like the other rule types described in this chapter, this rule type lists each piece of the rule in the order in which it should appear in the text. Therefore, its syntax is as simple as a CONCEPT rule plus the addition of the _c{} extraction label. This rule type is fundamental to most good models, but should be used only after you fully understand the application and purpose of the _c{} extraction label.

Be sure that when you are using this rule, all the elements that you specify appear in order in the targeted text. Ensure this through frequent testing of sample data from the data sources that you will be processing, using your model. The more different types of documents you have in your source data, the more complex your model will probably have to be to model the increased variation. People use language differently, depending on their purposes: writing an email, writing a report, creating a form, preparing a presentation, and so forth. Be aware of these sources of variation in your data, and if the variation is too extreme, consider winnowing down the data you will process with your model, or develop multiple models (perhaps with shared concepts) for different data sources. See section 12.2 for a further discussion of understanding your data.

A key best practice for all rules and rule types is to comment your rules or sections of rules with the intent of the rule, special considerations, decisions, and any other information that will make assessing or editing the rule later more efficient. Because C_CONCEPT rules do not return the whole match, this practice is even more important with this rule type and with the more complex ones that follow this chapter. Commented lines should start with the hash symbol, like so:

```
# The rule below extracts the city and state of the customer's
# address when the match to the firstLineAddress is followed by a
# comma and then the match to the customerCity concept, another
# comma and finally a match to the customerState concept.

C_CONCEPT:firstLineAddress :sep _c{customerCity :sep customerState}
```

As you design your project and your rules, keep in mind that as you identify the pieces you need, keeping those pieces meaningful and naming them with useful names will help you trace through your project later. You will be able to diagnose problems more easily because your assumptions will be clear either through the project design and concept names, through comments, or through both. Also, make concepts only as large as they need to be; smaller concepts with fewer rules are easier to troubleshoot and to understand than very large concepts with many rules.

Tip: Use comments to allow you to assess and edit rules more efficiently.

When you are using coreference symbols, be sure that you are using the correct one. Generally, you will want to use only the _ref{} modifier, because it matches only what you specify in your rule. However, if you have very short documents that stay focused on one topic or person, you may be able to use _F{}, which matches what you specify plus every instance of the coreferences for the rest of the document after your initial match. Least recommended is _P{}, which matches what you specify and any preceding matches.

6.4.5. Summary

Requirements for a C_CONCEPT include the following:

- A rule type declaration in all-caps and followed by a colon
- The extraction label, _c{}, with one or more elements to be extracted specified between the curly braces
- At least one element outside of the curly braces

Types of elements allowed include the following:

- A token or sequence of tokens to match (# character must still be escaped for a literal match to occur)
- A reference to another concept name, including predefined concepts
- A POS or special tag preceded by a colon
- A word symbol (_w), representing any single token
- A cap symbol (_cap), representing any capitalized word

Allowed options for the rule type include the following:

- Comments using the # modifier
- Coreference symbols, including _ref{}, _P{}, or _F{}
- Morphological expansion symbols, including @, @N, @V, and @A

Chapter 7: CONCEPT_RULE Type

7.1. Introduction to the CONCEPT_RULE Type

In chapter 6, you learned about three of the concept rule types: CLASSIFIER, CONCEPT, and C_CONCEPT. The focus of chapter 7 is the fourth rule type in this group: CONCEPT_RULE.

This rule type is unique among the concept rule types because it enables the use of operators that specify the distance that your elements can be from one another and still trigger a match. These operators include standard Boolean operators, such as AND, OR, and NOT, and special proximity operators, such as SENT, which constrains a match to within a single sentence. Notice that all the operators are in uppercase, which is a requirement for their use in rules. Table 7.1 and chapter 11 describes the types of operators allowed in a CONCEPT_RULE and provides details about how they work and how to select the right one. In addition, advanced use examples in the following sections may help you understand specific applications of these operators.

The CONCEPT_RULE rule type should be used more sparingly than other rule types. In addition, adding a CONCEPT_RULE should trigger additional careful testing of your model.

After reading this chapter, you will be able to do the following tasks:

- Use the LITI syntax to write efficient and effective CONCEPT_RULE type of rules
- Avoid common pitfalls and use best practices to create better rule sets
- Troubleshoot common rule-writing errors

7.2. Basic Use

A CONCEPT or C_CONCEPT rule may not do everything you need if the context in your text is not predictable or the distance between elements is far. In that case, you may want to use a CONCEPT_RULE instead.

The basic syntax of the rule definition is each operator enclosed within parentheses with its arguments in a comma-separated list. Each argument is one or more elements enclosed within double quotation marks. As in C_CONCEPT rules, the _c{} extraction label encloses in curly braces the element, or elements, whose match should be extracted. The following template shows the structure of this rule, with "OPERATOR" and "element" as placeholders:

```
CONCEPT_RULE:(OPERATOR, "element1", "_c{element2}")
CONCEPT_RULE:(OPERATOR, "_c{element1 element2}", "element3")
```

For example, the following rule finds a date in the same sentence as a percentage and extracts the match for the date. This rule might be useful in business or news documents to extract the dates on which some stock price or revenue target changed by some percentage:

```
CONCEPT_RULE:(SENT, "_c{nlpDate}", "nlpPercent")
```

This rule contains the rule type in all-caps, followed by a colon. Then, within parentheses, the SENT operator is listed along with its arguments in a comma-separated list. Each of the two arguments is enclosed in double quotation marks. The nlpDate element is marked with the _c{} extraction label, so the nlpDate span of text is extracted if there is a match.

> **Remember**: Whenever an operator is used in a rule, the operator is always enclosed in parentheses in a comma-separated list with its arguments.

As another example situation, imagine that you are an executive at a large bank and you want to use some data found online to figure out how much cash other banks are offering to customers as an incentive to open a new account. The data for this example is modified from customer complaints to the U.S. Consumer Financial Protection Bureau (https://www.consumerfinance.gov/data-research/consumer-complaints/).

Consider the following input documents:

1. I opened an account using the $300.00 bonus offer promotion.
2. I opened a Premier Everyday Checking account on March 31, 2017 online and was told that I am eligible to receive a $250.00 bonus once I complete a set of activities within 60 days of opening the account.
3. They promised to pay $400.00 to the new users of an opened VIP account package.

> **Pause and think**: Considering the input documents, can you write a CONCEPT_RULE to extract the promotion amount near the mention, event, or action of opening an account?

One way to extract matches for the amount associated with a promotion is to use the following rule in a concept named, for example, promotionAmount:

```
CONCEPT_RULE:(DIST_18, "_c{nlpMoney}", "open@ _w account")
```

This rule contains the DIST_n operator with the value of 18 as the number of tokens away that the match can occur. Otherwise, the syntax is the same as in the first example, except that there is more than one element in the second argument; in fact, there are three elements: open@, _w, and account. Because of the placement of the extraction label around the nlpMoney concept, this rule would extract the currency value associated with the new account.

The matches with the above input documents are in Figure 7.1.

Figure 7.1. Extracted Matches for the promotionAmount Concept

Doc ID	Concept	Match Text
1	promotionAmount	$300.00
2	promotionAmount	$250.00
3	promotionAmount	$400.00

As you further investigate the real data available from the U.S. Consumer Financial Protection Bureau, you observe that another amount is sometimes mentioned alongside the promotion amount, and that is the amount used to open the bank account. To remove those matches from the promotionAmount concept, you can create another concept that specifies the context within which the amount used for opening the account is encountered and then remove those matches from matches to the above concept. This is a more complex approach and involves the REMOVE_ITEM filtering rule type, discussed in chapter 9.

A third scenario illustrating the basic use of operators in a CONCEPT_RULE involves the operator DIST_n with a value of 0 for *n*, which can be used to match a token and its part of speech (POS) at run-time. In this example, the information technology (IT) department of a company wants to extract information from reports about equipment issues and outages. In the text data, there are mentions of the token "monitor" with two different parts of speech: a noun referring to the computer peripheral, and a verb referring to the action of observing a situation. A rule needs to capture only the instances referring to the part so that these instances can be routed to the IT department that handles computer peripherals. This rule is in the concept partIssue.

```
CONCEPT_RULE:(DIST_0, "_c{monitor@}", ":N")
```

Consider the following input documents:

1. ITS continues to monitor the issue.
2. The monitors were flickering.

> **Pause and think**: Considering these input documents, can you predict the matches for the partIssue concept?

The token "monitor" in the first document is a verb, whereas "monitors" in the second document is a noun. Because the rule allows for the nouns "monitor" or "monitors" to be matched by using the @ morphological expansion symbol, a match is returned only for the second document.

Note that you can use the same operators in a CONCEPT_RULE type of rule as in the PREDICATE_RULE type, which is discussed in chapter 8. Some of the same CONCEPT_RULE goals described above and in the advanced sections that follow can be achieved with PREDICATE_RULE rules, but because the latter are more computationally expensive, using the CONCEPT_RULE type, if possible, is recommended. The PREDICATE_RULE type should be reserved for scenarios in which the CONCEPT_RULE cannot achieve the same results.

7.3. Advanced Use: Multiple and Embedded Operators

What makes the CONCEPT_RULE type very powerful is the ability to embed an operator and its arguments as an argument of another operator. This nesting of operators allows for interactions between the types of operators to help you specify the exact conditions under which the meaning in the text will be a match for the desired information.

> **Remember**: You can embed an operator and its arguments as an argument of another operator.

Using this technique of embedded operators, you can do many things to control how the text is interpreted by the rule. One of the most common patterns in rule-writing involves limiting matches to within a sentence, with each argument of SENT being a list of arguments under an OR operator:

```
CONCEPT_RULE:(SENT, (OR, "element1", "element2"), (OR, "_c{element3
element4}", "_c{element5}"))
```

Note that, in the rule template above, the operators are filled in, but the elements are just placeholders. You can plug in your own elements to use the rule in the software.

It is very important that if the _c{} extraction label encloses all or part of an argument of an OR operator, all the other child arguments of that operator must also include the extraction label. Some SAS Text Analytics products do not give a compilation warning in this situation, but matches will not work properly without all of the necessary _c{} labels. In all other contexts, only one or more consecutive elements in the same argument may have the _c{} label, because for each rule match, only one match string can be extracted by a match on this type of rule.

> **Tip**: If the _c{} extraction label encloses all or part of an argument of an OR operator, all the other child arguments of that operator must also include the extraction label.

Recall that one of the rules in section 7.2 finds specific currency amounts near information about opening an account. During testing, you may discover that you need to constrain this rule further with a third argument to capture the context of the bonus payment. You can handle this situation by adding under the DIST_n operator a third argument that lists the possibilities under an OR operator, as shown in the rule below. You can also move the extraction label to these elements, if you want to know how often the offer is a bonus versus a promotion:

```
CONCEPT_RULE:(DIST_18, "nlpMoney", "open@ _w _w account", (OR,
"_c{bonus}", "_c{promotion}"))
```

This more advanced rule contains (as shown in bold) a new set of parentheses, enclosing the new operator OR with its arguments, after the second argument of DIST_n, "open@ _w account."

You can read the new rule this way: First match the existence of one of the following: the strings "bonus" or "promotion," the predefined concept nlpMoney, or the string in the second argument. Then scan 18 tokens in either direction to find matches for the remaining arguments. Because of the placement of the extraction label, the match returned is now either the string "bonus" or the string "promotion."

Consider the following input documents, modified from the U.S. Consumer Financial Protection Bureau data:

1. Open a checking account and earn $300.00 promotion.
2. To receive the $300.00 bonus, you must open an interest account and set up and receive 10 Qualifying Direct Deposits . . .
3. I opened an express account with the promotion of $300.00 for premier checking and $200.00 for premier savings accounts.
4. I said I was interested in opening the savings account as well preferably at the 1.49 % rate but if not then 1.34 % rate. Also, I was told that if I were to answer a few questions related to my finances, they will give me a $25.00 gift card.
5. I met with the manager at my local branch and signed up for a promotion that would give me $1000.00 bonus after opening a savings account . . .

> **Pause and think**: Assuming that the rule above is in a concept named promotionStrategy, can you predict the matches for the input documents above?

The matches in the input documents above are listed in Figure 7.2.

Figure 7.2. Extracted Matches for the promotionStrategy Concept

Doc ID	Concept	Match Text
1	promotionStrategy	promotion
2	promotionStrategy	bonus
3	promotionStrategy	promotion
5	promotionStrategy	promotion
5	promotionStrategy	bonus

Note that there are no matches for the fourth document, because it does not contain either "bonus" or "promotion." But even if "gift card" were added to the rule as an additional argument of the OR operator, the distance between the amount and the match to the second argument would be too great for a match to be produced using this rule. The rule could additionally be modified by increasing the distance to 45 for example, and then the string "gift card" would be extracted as a match.

Another common pattern in advanced CONCEPT_RULE rules is use of the SENT operator to bound the scope of DIST_n, ORD, or ORDDIST_n to within a single sentence:

```
CONCEPT_RULE:(SENT, (DIST_4, "_c{element1}", "element2", "element3"))
```

This rule template extracts the first element, if all three elements are found within a distance of four tokens of each other in the same sentence. As above, elements in this rule template are placeholders for you to substitute with your own content before using in the software.

Caution should be exercised with the AND operator. This operator can be very useful when applied to short documents. However, for mid-sized or long documents, an AND operator that is not bounded by another operator may match in situations you do not expect. In those cases, the use of SENT, DIST_n, or SENT_n instead of AND will usually give you the more targeted behavior you are looking for.

> **Tip**: The AND operator is most useful for short documents. For longer documents, use an operator with more restricted scope, such as SENT, DIST_n or SENT_n. Do not embed AND under one of these operators.

7.4. Advanced Use: Negation Using NOT

The CONCEPT_RULE type is the first type of LITI rule covered so far that can accomplish some types of negation and filtering of matches on its own. In other words, you can use this rule type to specify both what you want to find, and what should not be present within a given scope of the matched elements.

There are two operators that help you specify what to exclude from matching: the NOT operator and the UNLESS operator. This section will describe the behavior of NOT and provide a few examples of when this approach could be useful.

The NOT operator specifies along with other criteria for a match what should *not* be found in the document. It must be one of the arguments of an AND operator. In other words, as one argument of the AND operator, you specify what you want to find in the document, and as another argument you specify the NOT operator and its argument.

For example, perhaps you want to find documents that mention aircraft, but not catch documents that talk about American football, because you are collecting information for a report on the use of airspace over American cities. In this way, you can eliminate documents about the New York Jets, which would otherwise be false positives in your result set. Here is how you might write that rule:

```
CONCEPT_RULE:(AND, "_c{aircraftConcept}", (NOT, "footballConcept"))
```

This rule references two other concepts not shown in detail here: aircraftConcept, defined with keywords that describe different types of aircraft, and footballConcept, populated with keywords that are common football-specific terms. The rule aims to return matches for aircraftConcept only if the document does not discuss football, in accordance with the terms defined in footballConcept.

Some of the rules in aircraftConcept include the following:

```
CLASSIFIER:aircraft
CLASSIFIER:jet@
```

Some of the rules in footballConcept include the following:

```
CONCEPT_RULE:(SENT, "_c{fly@V}", "ball@N")
CLASSIFIER:the Jets, New York Jets
```

Keep in mind that the NOT operator always has document-level scope, so it cannot be limited to a sentence by putting an operator like SENT in front of it in the structure of the rule. Therefore, a rule like the one below will not limit the scope of NOT to the sentence because SENT is not able to control the matches to NOT. You will not get the results that the structure of the rule implies; therefore, this is an error:

```
ERROR -> CONCEPT_RULE:(SENT, (AND, "_c{aircraftConcept}", (NOT,
"footballConcept")))
```

Tip: The NOT operator has document-level scope and cannot be limited, for example to a sentence, by putting another operator higher in the structure of the rule.

A similar type of example would include extracting instances of weapons mentioned in text, but not wanting to extract matches on documents that were discussing video games. This might be the focus of government analysts tracking the purchase and ownership of weapons in online forums. Using NOT is a way of filtering out matches, assuming you are certain that the filtered items are ones you do not want. Here is an example rule:

```
CONCEPT_RULE:(AND, (OR, "_c{firearmsList}", "_c{amunitionList}",
"_c{bombList}"), (NOT, "videoGameTerm"))
```

This rule references four other concepts not shown in detail here that have been defined in a variety of ways and used to separate out different types of weapons references in order to use them in different combinations within the model. For example, no large-scale weapons (like tanks) are represented, but those usually used by individuals are included. The goal of this rule is to find mentions of such weapons, but not in the context of a document that has terms commonly used when describing or discussing video games.

Just as with AND, you must be careful when using NOT, because both have document-level scope. This means they may not behave as you want if your documents are very long. If you are familiar with SAS Categorization models, then you may be tempted to try using the operators NOTINDIST or NOTINSENT to get around this limitation on NOT. These operators are not supported in LITI rules; they will result in a compilation error.

Another type of example for using the NOT operator involves the use of a key phrase or marker to indicate a specific document type. For example, if you want to find all person names in the documents, but you know that the document collection includes a form used for registering voters, and you want to exclude those documents from matching, then you can build a rule like the one here:

```
CONCEPT_RULE:(AND, "_c{nlpPerson}", (NOT, "Voter Registration Form"),
(NOT, "Voter ID Number"))
```

This rule will match on person names, but not in any documents that contain the phrase "Voter Registration Form" or "Voter ID Number." If either of the phrases under a NOT operator is present, then it is enough to block the match to nlpPerson from appearing as a match to the concept where this rule is written. You cannot easily specify that both items are required to eliminate the match, unless you build another concept to reference in this rule, and that other concept requires both phrases in order to match.

7.5. Advanced Use: Negation Using UNLESS

Another way to exclude matches that you do not want is to use the UNLESS operator. This operator has some specific limitations that you should know. First, it takes just two arguments, where the second one is one of the following operators: AND, SENT, DIST_n, ORD, and ORDDIST_n. Each of these operators may take two or more arguments. The UNLESS operator blocks a match if the first argument appears between the arguments under the later operator.

Let us use the example of tracking specific events. You have a basic rule that you want to find situations where a particular sports team wins a game. This rule, for example in a concept named trackingWins, says that when a match to the baseballTeam concept is followed by "win" or its variants, you want to extract the date that occurs in the same sentence:

```
CONCEPT_RULE:(SENT, (ORD, "baseballTeam", "win@"), "_c{nlpDate}")
```

The baseballTeam concept includes the following rules:

```
CLASSIFIER:Cleveland Indians
CLASSIFIER:Indians
```

Because the definitions in the baseballTeam concept include references to the Cleveland Indians baseball team, the rule in the trackingWins concept outputs matches in sentences like the following. Note that highlighted tokens signify matches for each of the arguments, which are required in order for the rule to return a match for the _c{} label:

1. Brantley singled two home runs on the first pitch of his first at-bat and Carlos Carrasco worked out of a bases-loaded jam in the sixth inning, leading the Cleveland Indians to a 3-2 win in their chilly home opener over the Kansas City Royals on Friday.
2. It wasn't pretty, but the Cleveland Indians found a way to win the first home series of 2018 with a wild 3-1 win over the Kansas City Royals on Sunday.
3. Coming into the season, the Indians were expected to win somewhere near 100 games this year, win the division convincingly, and contend for a World Series title.

The matches returned to the trackingWins concept due to the _c{} label are listed in Figure 7.3.

Figure 7.3. Extracted Matches for the trackingWins Concept

Doc ID	Concept	Match Text
1	trackingWins	this season
1	trackingWins	on Friday
2	trackingWins	of 2018
2	trackingWins	on Sunday
3	trackingWins	this year

Note: Because of how the nlpDate concept is predefined, matches include both "on Friday" and "Friday," as well as "on Sunday" and "Sunday." You can use postprocessing code to retain the most specific date for each document ID. Alternatively, the near-duplicate matches can be cleaned up by using a REMOVE_ITEM rule that removes the match containing a preposition if the same match but without a preposition that has been found already. See chapter 9 for more information about this rule type:

```
REMOVE_ITEM:(ALIGNED, "_c{nlpDate}", "_w nlpDate")
```

You are doing some postprocessing on this data to get the results aligned with the news article date and interpreting the results, but hits like the third document are throwing your statistics off. It is a false positive match, because it references wins that have not yet happened. You are counting more wins than the team actually has. You can remove the hypothetical wins while retaining matches for confirmed wins by using the UNLESS operator:

```
CONCEPT_RULE:(UNLESS, "expect@", (SENT, (ORD, "myTeam", "win@"),
"_c{nlpDate}"))
```

This rule allows matches only if a form of the word "expect" does not occur between the two arguments of the SENT operator. This modification using UNLESS will exclude the third sentence above from matching the rule.

Another restriction on the UNLESS rule is more of a safety recommendation, and therefore has exceptions. The recommendation is to use a reference to a concept with UNLESS only if that concept contains only CLASSIFIER or REGEX rules.

Tip: When you are using UNLESS and the first argument is a concept name, that concept should contain only CLASSIFIER or REGEX rules.

In another example, perhaps you have a rule by which you want to find mentions of your product or service with positive adjectives, like "happy," "useful," "best," and the like. You can use UNLESS to help you exclude situations in which that adjective is modified with negation adverbs like "not" and "never." For example, see the following rule:

```
CONCEPT_RULE:(UNLESS, "negList", (DIST_7, "custServiceRep",
"_c{posAdj}"))
```

The project containing this rule in a concept named posMention also includes three other concepts that are partially shown below: negList, a list of negative adverbs as CLASSIFIER rules; custServiceRep, a list of terms that describe customer service representatives in an airline; and posAdj, a list of positive adjectives that may be used to describe the quality of the customer service by the representative.

The concept negList contains the following rule:

```
CLASSIFIER:not
```

The concept custServiceRep contains the following rules:

```
CONCEPT:attendant@
CONCEPT:agent@
CLASSIFIER:help desk
CLASSIFIER:personnel
```

The concept posAdj contains the following rules:

```
CLASSIFIER:helpful
CLASSIFIER:kind
```

Consider the following input documents, which simulate airline feedback data.

1. The ladies at the help desk were not helpful at all.
2. Some rather unpleasant personnel were rude or not helpful.
3. The attendants were kind but not helpful.
4. There was one agent in particular, Mr. Jim Wilsey, who was very helpful.
5. In any event, one of the flight attendants was extremely helpful and apologetic.

> **Pause and think**: Assuming the input documents above, can you predict the matches for the posMention concept?

The matches are represented in Figure 7.4.

Figure 7.4. Extracted Matches for the posMention Concept

Doc ID	Concept	Match Text
3	posMention	Kind
5	posMention	helpful

Note that there are no matches for the first and second documents because the "not" in these sentences is a match for the negList concept and prevents matches to the posMention concept through the UNLESS operator. The "helpful" match in the third document is also filtered by UNLESS, but the "kind" match to the posAdj concept is passed on to the posMention concept. The fourth document has no matches because the distance is greater than 7 tokens between "agent" from the custServiceRep concept and "helpful" from the posAdj concept.

7.6. Advanced Use: Coreference and Aliases

The coreference symbol _ref{} can be used in CONCEPT_RULE rules to tie a reference back to a lemma (canonical form). See chapter 1 for an explanation of lemmas. This approach can be useful when you are trying to establish relationships between items, where some of the relationships may involve pronouns, common nouns, or aliases. For example, perhaps you want to find each reference to a company, whether the full name is used or not. You may want to do so to tie other information that you find back to the company in your analysis. You may start with a rule like the following:

```
CONCEPT_RULE:(AND, "_c{SAS Institute}", (OR, "_ref{SAS}","_ref{they}",
"_ref{company}"))
```

In this rule, the _c{} extraction label encloses the string element "SAS Institute." The string elements "SAS," "they," and "company" are also considered to be company references in this rule. All of the arguments of the OR operator are marked with a _ref{} symbol. This shows that they are the references that should be tied to the primary return string, marked with the _c{} label. In other words, this rule says that if you find a match for "SAS Institute," then also look anywhere in the document for any of the possible defined coreferents, and link them to the canonical form returned by the _c{} label.

Consider the following input document:

> I work for SAS Institute. SAS is a large private software company. They make software for various business purposes centered around the idea of analytics. The company puts customers first and has recently celebrated their 40th anniversary.

Pause and think: Assuming the rule above is in a concept named sasAlias, can you predict the matches with the input document above?

The matches for the sasAlias concept containing the above rule with the input document are in Figure 7.5.

Figure 7.5. Extracted Matches for the sasAlias Concept

Doc ID	Concept	Match Text	Canonical Form
1	sasAlias	SAS Institute	SAS Institute
1	sasAlias	SAS	SAS Institute
1	sasAlias	SAS	SAS Institute
1	sasAlias	company	SAS Institute
1	sasAlias	They	SAS Institute
1	sasAlias	company	SAS Institute

Alert! The coreference functionality works properly only in a subset of the SAS Text Analytics products. To use it, you should confirm that you have the output shown in Figures 7.6 and 7.7.

Figure 7.6 shows the relationship between the highlighted word in the text and the canonical form elsewhere in the text. This information is used during the rule-building process to confirm that the correct results are found by a particular rule or concept. In Figure 7.6, the highlighted word is "company" and the pop-up window shows that it is connected to the canonical form of "SAS Institute."

Figure 7.6. Canonical Form Representation in SAS Enterprise Content Categorization

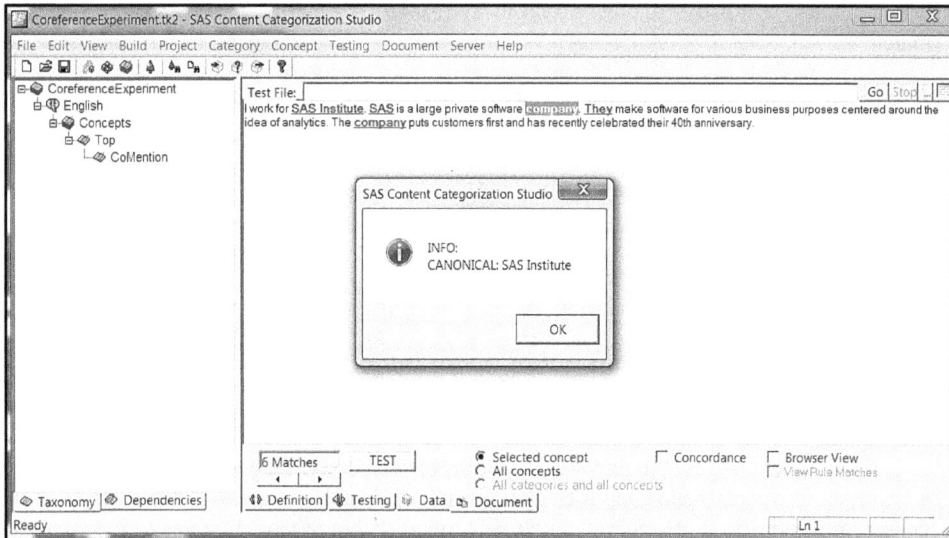

Figure 7.7 shows matches in the scoring output in SAS Studio that includes the relationship between the coreference matches in the term column and the canonical form in the canonical_form column. Note that, based on the offsets, the first and second matches overlap. The concept name is evident in the name column. This information is accessible in a production context when you are scoring many documents with a completed model.

Figure 7.7. Canonical Form Representation in SAS Studio

Total rows: 6 Total columns: 7

	document_id	name	full_path	start_offset ▲	end_offset	term	canonical_form
1	1	sasAlias	Top/sasAlias	11	23	SAS Institute	SAS Institute
2	1	sasAlias	Top/sasAlias	11	13	SAS	SAS Institute
3	1	sasAlias	Top/sasAlias	26	28	SAS	SAS Institute
4	1	sasAlias	Top/sasAlias	58	64	company	SAS Institute
5	1	sasAlias	Top/sasAlias	67	70	They	SAS Institute
6	1	sasAlias	Top/sasAlias	159	165	company	SAS Institute

In the rule that extracted the strings shown above, matches to the coreference terms may appear anywhere in the document because of the AND operator. If you want to control this matching behavior more closely, use a different operator. For example, use of ORD will limit the coreference matches to after the first match of the primary reference. ORDDIST_n will limit the matches to some distance from the primary reference. SENT and ORD used together will restrict the scope of the match to within the bounds of the same sentence as the primary reference match, but require the primary reference to occur first. To illustrate, the following rule is very similar to the previous rule, except that it limits the order and distance of the matches:

```
CONCEPT_RULE:(ORDDIST_15, "_c{SAS Institute}", (OR, "_ref{SAS}",
"_ref{they}", "_ref{company}"))
```

The matches for this rule are similar to the matches shown above, with one difference. The last match on "company" is now too far away from the primary reference, so it no longer matches.

Assuming that this rule is in the concept named sasAlias, the matches for the input text in the previous example are in Figure 7.8.

Figure 7.8. Extracted Matches for the sasAlias Concept

Doc ID	Concept	Match Text	Canonical Form
1	sasAlias	SAS Institute	SAS Institute
1	sasAlias	SAS	SAS Institute
1	sasAlias	Company	SAS Institute
1	sasAlias	They	SAS Institute

In general, unless the documents are very short or the coreference variants are not ambiguous, a best practice recommendation is to start with the ORDDIST operator. For a very conservative approach, use SENT with ORD together, but always first verify the approach with your data.

Table 7.1 summarizes the behavior you can expect from each operator that may be used in this type of rule.

Table 7.1. Behavior of Operators

Operator	Behavior
AND	Matches any occurrence of primary reference and matches any coreference, whether it follows or precedes the primary reference in the document. It ties all coreference instances to the first primary reference found in the document, not the closest one.
ORD	Matches any occurrence of primary reference and then matches any coreference that follows the first primary reference match. It ties all coreference instances to the first primary reference found in the document, not the closest one.
SENT	Matches only when the primary reference and the coreference occur in the same sentence but does not require the primary reference to come first. Govern with the ORD operator to require the primary reference to be matched first.
DIST_n	Matches only when the primary reference and the coreference occur within a specified number of tokens from each other but does not require the primary reference to come first. Use ORDDIST instead to require the primary reference to be matched first.
SENT_n	Matches only when the primary reference and the coreference occur within the specified number of sentences but does not require the primary reference to come first. Govern with the ORD operator to require the primary reference to be matched first.

Operator	Behavior
PARA	Matches only when the primary reference and the coreference occur in the same paragraph but does not require the primary reference to come first. Govern with the ORD operator to require the primary reference to be matched first.
ORDDIST_n	Matches any occurrence of the primary reference, then matches any coreference that both follows the first primary reference match, and appears within the specified number of tokens of that match. After the maximum match distance is reached, a match must first be a primary reference to trigger more coreference matches again.

Note that rules that result in coreference or canonical form matches must be at the top level of the model to generate such information in the output. In other words, the concept that houses them will not pass along this information to any calling concept. Keep this in mind when you design your models, and consider using multiple models, if necessary.

7.7. Troubleshooting

If you discover that a rule is not matching as you expected, potential causes for this could be one of the pitfalls outlined in section 5.4—namely, general syntax errors, comments, misspelling/mistyping, tokenization mismatch, or filtered matches. In addition, there are also errors that you can check for that are specific to the CONCEPT_RULE type of rule, such as the following:

- White space
- Syntax errors
- Missing extraction label
- Extra extraction label
- Tagging mismatch
- Expansion mismatch
- Concept references
- Predefined concept references
- Using nonexistent operators
- Logical error with operators
- Cyclic dependencies

White space in a CONCEPT_RULE is not very important because of the use of the parentheses, commas, and double quotation marks to set off pieces of the rule. However, within an argument (double quotation marks), white space is a separator for a list of elements and not counted as an element itself.

One of the common syntax errors that is specific to CONCEPT_RULE is forgetting the extraction labels or curly braces in the extraction label, or misplacing them: The braces must always be inside the double quotation marks defining an argument. Remember also that the operators and arguments inside a set of parentheses are a comma-separated list. Do not forget the commas. Finally, parentheses and quotation marks must come in pairs.

In the CONCEPT_RULE rule, there can be only a single extraction label: _c{}. However, do not forget that, if you have marked all or part of an argument of an OR operator with the _c{} label, then you will also have to place the label somewhere on all of the sister arguments under the same OR, as well. Otherwise, you will not see the matching behavior that you expect. If you use multiple _c{} extraction labels in any other context, your rule will compile but will not match anything.

It is possible that the POS tag you think a particular word may have is not the tag assigned to that word by the software in that particular context. The best way to prevent this error is to test your expectations with targeted examples in context, before applying the rule to a sample of documents that is like the data you will process with the model.

In addition, it is possible that the POS tag is misspelled or does not exist. Different languages, versions and products may use different POS tags. Consult your product documentation for lists of acceptable tags for rule-building. The spelling and case of the tags in the rules must be exactly as documented. Because writing a rule with a nonexistent tag like ":abc" is not a syntax error but a logical error, the syntax checking protocols will not catch it as an error, but there will not be any of the expected matches.

Another potential error when you are writing rules that contain a POS tag is forgetting to include the colon before specifying the tag. Without the colon, the system considers the rule to refer to a concept by that name or a string match, which may produce unexpected or no results. Syntax checking protocols will not return an error in this case.

When using the expansion symbols (e.g., @, @N, @V, @A), note that the expansion includes only related dictionary forms, not any misspellings that may have been identified by the misspelling algorithm or other variants associated with that lemma through use of a synonym list. To review what a lemma is, consult chapter 1. Also, remember that the forms of the words are looked up before processing, and when matching happens, the associated POS assignment of the word in the text is not considered. You can work around this issue, if you want to, using a CONCEPT_RULE; see section 7.2 for more information. Examining your output from rules that contain expansion symbols is recommended.

Referencing concepts by name without ensuring that you have used the correct name, including both case and spelling accuracy, can also reduce the number of expected matches. If you reference predefined concepts, be sure that they are loaded into your project, and always check the names because they may be different across different products.

Even though the form of a CONCEPT_RULE looks similar to rules used in SAS Categorization, there are some important differences. If you are used to writing categorization rules, you may make special types of errors in LITI rules. For example, you cannot use the following symbols in LITI rules:

- * as a wildcard match on beginning or end of a word
- ^ to tie match to beginning of a document
- $ to tie a match the end of the document
- _L to match a literal string
- _C to specify case-sensitivity

Another difference is that, in categorization rules, you do not need the _c{} extraction label, because you are not extracting anything; the rule either matches or does not. In a CONCEPT_RULE, the _c{} extraction label is required for the output that should be extracted. Finally, there are operators that you can use in categorization rules that are <u>not available in LITI,</u> including the following: NOTIN, NOTINSENT, NOTINPAR, NOTINDIST, START_n, PARPOS_n, PAR, MAXSENT_n, MAXPAR_n, MAXOC_n, MINOC_n, MIN_n, and END_n.

Any rule that can reference a concept and returns matches (e.g., not REMOVE_ITEM or NO_BREAK) has the capacity to participate in a cyclic dependency error. A cyclic dependency is when two or more concepts refer to each other in a circle of concept references. For example, if the concept myConceptA has rules that reference myConceptB, and myConceptB has rules that reference myConceptA, there is a cycle of references between them. This type of error will prevent your whole project from compiling. This is another reason to test your project often as you are adding concepts and rules. This way you will know that the latest rules added to the model created the cyclic dependency. Another strategy to use to avoid this error is careful design for your taxonomy and model. Refer to chapter 13 to learn more about taxonomy design best practices.

If you have checked all the above and are still having problems with your rules, then you should look at the logic defined by your combination of operators. A full understanding of operators is recommended if you are combining them together in a single rule. Consult chapter 11 to learn more about operators and how they interact. If you need more help with troubleshooting this rule type, see the discussion of match algorithms in section 13.4.1.

Finally, if you can use a simpler rule type to extract the information that you are trying to extract with a CONCEPT_RULE type of rule, always use the simpler rule type instead. Although the CONCEPT_RULE type is very powerful, it can be more difficult to maintain and troubleshoot in larger models. If you use it, make sure you use it correctly.

7.8. Best Practices

The best time to use a CONCEPT_RULE is when you have some complexity in the elements' relationship to one another. Then it is useful to be able to specify the relationship between the elements, using a combination of operators. Another reason to use a CONCEPT_RULE is that you have more distance between targeted textual elements, such that predicting the intervening text is tricky or impossible.

Because the CONCEPT_RULE type is very versatile, some beginners are tempted to do most of the extraction that is possible with the previously discussed rule types, using only CONCEPT_RULE rules. However, because of the higher complexity level of this rule, it is not recommended to take such a "shortcut" in larger projects. One reason is that the computational load may be higher, which will mean the project will run more slowly. The second reason is that CONCEPT_RULE rules will be more difficult to read, so more comments will be needed to remember and record what each rule is intended to do. The result is that the project will be somewhat more difficult to maintain than if the beginner rule-writer had used more easily read rules instead.

Beginners should avoid this rule type, if possible, until some experience with the matching process is gained through practice of building and testing the simpler rule types. Table 7.2 contains some examples of situations in which you may try to use a CONCEPT_RULE when you should be using a different rule type.

Table 7.2. Examples of Situations in Which CONCEPT_RULE Should Not Be Used

Situation	Suggested resolution
List of items	Instead of a list of arguments under an OR operator, use a series of CLASSIFIER or CONCEPT rules.
Predictable context	Instead of using DIST_n, use :sep, or _w in C_CONCEPT.
Return multiple matched elements	Use CONCEPT rule, if possible, or use SEQUENCE rule type or, if that fails, use PREDICATE_RULE type.

Another best practice is to try to reference concepts containing simpler rule types, such as CLASSIFIER, CONCEPT or C_CONCEPT, in CONCEPT_RULE rules. Avoid other rule types, such as REGEX, unless they are necessary. Additionally, avoid stacking CONCEPT_RULES, so that one CONCEPT_RULE references another, which references another, creating layers. However, this may also sometimes be necessary to achieve certain goals. In short, keep rule types simple in concepts that are referenced in other rules, when possible.

> **Tip**: Whenever possible, use simpler rule types for concepts that are referenced in other concepts higher in the taxonomy.

Build rules that are generalized to capture different types of patterns, while keeping them specific to the type of meaning they target. In other words, try to do only one task with each rule that you build; do not combine multiple tasks together into a single rule, unless that single rule is doing a specific and describable task itself with the pieces. For example, if you have a rule that targets finding a piece of information, like blood pressure, when it occurs in a context with person names, you should keep that as a separate rule from a rule that targets blood pressure, but in the context of drug names. This approach is recommended for the purposes of testing and maintainability. Even though the information you are finding and extracting in each situation is the same, the strategy, test data, and the types of language patterns will be different.

Keep in mind that CONCEPT_RULE rules have a lot of power, but that also means that they can sometimes match in contexts that you had no intention of matching. A powerful, general rule can be useful for some purposes, but if the rule leads to matches in the wrong type of situations, then it may need to be constrained further. A typical example is when you are finding dates, such as with the rule here:

```
CONCEPT_RULE:(SENT, (ORD, "_c{MonthName}", (OR, ":digit", ":NUM")))
```

This rule is intended to capture any month name like "January," followed in the same sentence by a reference to a number. This approach may seem good and bring good results back in your initial tests. However, if you do not realize that this rule really assumes that the month name will always be referencing a month, then you may find yourself matching the wrong thing in situations where what you assume is the month could actually be a person name (June, April) or a regular word at the beginning of a sentence (May). In these cases, you should probably keep those ambiguous names separate from the unambiguous ones and put them only into more constrained rules. This strategy assumes that you are trying to maximize precision, as well as recall, in your testing.

> **Tip**: To maximize precision, as well as recall, keep rules with ambiguous elements separate from rules with unambiguous elements.

Another key best practice for complex rules like CONCEPT_RULES is to build and test the pieces first and then combine them into the complex rule. You can compare the results you get with the pieces with the results you get with the full rule to verify that the rule is doing what you intend. For more information on good testing practices, see chapter 14.

A key best practice for all rules and rule types is to comment your rules or sections of rules with the intent of the rule, special considerations, decisions, and any other information that will make assessing or editing the rule later more efficient. Commented lines look like this:

```
# This rule should find a product name in the context of a marker
# that shows a positive assessment and return the marker -> put this
# marker into new data column called Positives in post-processing.
CONCEPT_RULE:(UNLESS, "negList", (DIST_5, "myProducts", "_c{PosAdj}"))
```

When you design your project and your rules, keep in mind that as you identify the pieces that you need, keeping those pieces meaningful and naming them useful names will help you to trace through your project later. You will be able to diagnose problems more easily because your assumptions will be clear either through the project design and concept names, or through comments, or both. Also, make concepts only as large as they need to be; smaller concepts with fewer rules are easier to troubleshoot and to understand than very large concepts with numerous rules. See chapter 13 for more information on designing projects.

7.9. Summary

Requirements for a CONCEPT_RULE include the following:

- A rule type declaration in all-caps and followed by a colon
- One or more Boolean or proximity operators, in a comma-separated list with arguments enclosed in parentheses
- Each argument comprises one or more elements enclosed in double quotation marks
- One _c{} extraction label on an element or multiple elements within the same argument that indicates what information to extract (If under an OR operator, put the _c{} extraction label somewhere in each of the arguments under the OR operator, otherwise use the _c{} operator only once per rule)

Types of elements allowed include the following:

- A string, a token, or sequence of tokens to match literally ("#" character must still be escaped for a literal match to occur)
- A reference to another concept name, including predefined concepts
- A POS or special tag preceded by a colon
- A word symbol (_w), representing any single token
- A cap symbol (_cap), representing any capitalized word

Allowed options for the rule type include the following:

- Comments using the "#" modifier
- Coreference symbols, including _ref{}, _P{}, and _F{}
- Morphological expansion symbols, including @, @N, @A, and @V

Chapter 8: Fact Rule Types

8.1. Introduction to Fact Rule Types

In chapter 5, you learned about four groupings of LITI rule types:

- Concept rule types (including CLASSIFIER, CONCEPT, C_CONCEPT and CONCEPT_RULE)
- Fact rule types (including SEQUENCE and PREDICATE_RULE)
- Filter rule types (including REMOVE_ITEM and NO_BREAK)
- REGEX rule type

The SEQUENCE and PREDICATE_RULE types of rules are grouped together because they are used for extracting *facts*. Fact matches involve identifying multiple items in a relationship, as well as identifying events or slots within a template structure. For example, some types of relationships between items are listed in Table 8.1.

Table 8.1. Fact Matching Relationships, Slots, and Examples

Relationship	Slots	Example
X is a type of Y.	X, Y	Cash back is a type of promotion.
X was born in Y.	X, Y	The CEO was born in Texas.

Relationship	Slots	Example
X can cause the allergic reactions of A, B, or C.	X, A, B, C	A vaccine can cause the allergic reactions of itchy skin, difficulty breathing, and a reduction in blood pressure.

The relationships shown in the table include a "typeOf" relationship between "cash back" and "promotion," a "bornIn" relationship between "CEO" and "Texas," and a "causeReaction" relationship between "vaccines" and various types of reactions or symptoms. These are just examples to help you start thinking of all the things you can model with fact rule types. In these sentences, there is an explicit mention of the relationship, but in some cases the relationship might be indicated more subtly or even implied by context. You can still build fact rules to capture these contexts effectively in many cases.

A template structure is just a more complex form of this two-way relationship. In other words, the relationship between multiple things can be modeled together. Types of events or template structures that a fact rule can be used for are listed in Table 8.2.

Table 8.2. Templates, Slots, and Examples for Fact Rules

Template	Slots	Example
Payment event type happened on Y date for Z amount.	Y, Z	The bill was paid on 12.12.2012 for $12.
A marriage event occurred with these attributes: • Location = A • Date = B • Bride = C • Groom = D • Number of people attending = E	A, B, C, D, E	Mary Smith married John Brown on August 11, 2018, in Little Rock, AR with 150 people in attendance.
A verb type has been found with the following slots: • Subject = A • Direct object = B • Time adverb = C	A, B, C	The tenants caused damages to the sewer pipes yesterday.

An event is usually modeled as a set of slots to be filled or left empty, depending on the specificity of the information about the event in the text. For example, as shown in Table 8.2, a marriage event could include all the slots listed, but the text might not contain information about the number of people attending. All the other slots might be filled by information in the text, in which case you would have an event template with an incomplete instantiation. This might still be useful, because it results in a similar situation to when there are missing values in structured data. Even though some data points are missing, the ones that are known can still be useful.

Both relationships and events can be modeled with the use of fact rule types in the SAS IE toolkit by leveraging either or both of the two rule types illustrated in this chapter. But keep in mind that fact rules produce intrinsically different results than concept rules: For example, when considering output tables, remember that fact rule matches are found in the factOut table, whereas concept rule matches are found in the conceptOut table.

Although these rule types are described briefly in the SAS Text Analytics product documentation, there are intricacies of usage that you need to know to use them effectively and efficiently. This chapter will extend your understanding of the SEQUENCE and PREDICATE_RULE through tips, potential pitfalls, and examples that show both basic and advanced uses of each. The requirements and optional elements for each rule type are summarized at the end of each section so that you can keep coming back to that section as a quick reference when you are building your models.

After reading this chapter, you will be able to do the following tasks:

- Use the LITI syntax to write efficient and effective SEQUENCE and PREDICATE_RULE types of rules
- Understand how the output of fact rules is different from the output of concept rule types
- Avoid common pitfalls and use best practices to create better rule sets
- Troubleshoot common rule-writing errors

8.2. SEQUENCE Rule Type

The SEQUENCE rule type works like the C_CONCEPT type except that it enables you to extract more than one part of the match. When you have ordered elements and need to extract more than one matched element, use a SEQUENCE rule type to model the fact and the surrounding context. The SEQUENCE rule type is designed to exploit the inherent sequential order of elements in text while focusing its attention on matching facts and extracting multiple arguments.

8.2.1. Basic Use

The basic syntax comprises a rule with three sections:

- Rule type declaration
- Label declaration
- Rule definition

Between each of the three sections is a colon. The label declaration section includes one or more user-defined extraction labels in a comma-separated list enclosed in parentheses. The rule definition contains two or more elements marked for extraction with the label, or labels, and zero or more additional elements. Here is the basic rule syntax:

```
SEQUENCE:(label1, label2):_label1{element1} _label2{element2}
SEQUENCE:(label1, label2):elementA _label1{element1} elementB
_label2{element2} elementC
```

For descriptive convenience, some of the elements have been labeled with numbers; others, with letters. You can read the first rule this way: If element1 and element2 are both in the text in sequential order, extract element1 as a match to label1 and extract element2 as a match to label2 in the concept in which this rule is written. In addition, the entire span of text between element1 and element2 is returned as a match to provide insight into the context of the matches.

You can read the second rule this way: If element1 and element2 are both in the text in the sequential context specified by elementA, elementB, and elementC, then extract element1 as a match to the label named label1 and extract element2 as match to the label named label2 in the concept in which this rule is written. In this example, there are 5 total elements, two of which are marked as targets for extraction with user-defined extraction labels. Again, note that the entire span of text between element1 and element2 is extracted as an additional match.

In some SAS Text Analytics products, you can append additional tokens onto the beginning and end of the extracted match bounded by the two matches with labels. This approach provides you even more context through a bigger window of content. Creating output with three sections (preceding context, extracted match, and following context) is called *concordancing*.

Notice that in the label declaration section of the rule, the labels are listed within parentheses separated by a comma, but in the rule definition, each of the extraction labels is directly preceded by a single underscore and followed by curly braces surrounding the elements to be matched. This is similar to the _c{} extraction label in other rule types, but keep in mind that you cannot name the label "c," because it is reserved by the system. It is recommended to also avoid the following names: "Q," "F," "P," and "ref," although these names might not cause any problems in fact rules.

The names of extraction labels must start with a letter, followed by any series of letters, underscores, or digits. Note that, in some older products, using an uppercase letter in an extraction label name could cause compilation errors.

> **Remember**: Extraction label names must start with a letter, followed by any series of letters, underscores, or digits.

Here is an example rule used to find problems in vehicles in a concept named reportedDefect:

```
SEQUENCE:(part, mal):_part{engine} is _w _mal{overheating}
```

The extraction labels in this rule are "part" and "mal" (malfunction). For matches to be extracted to these labels, those matches must be in the same order in the text as in the rule definition and include the word "is" and another token between them.

Consider the following input documents.

1. The engine is quickly overheating whenever the water pump does not engage.
2. Because the engine is always overheating, the thermostat also quit working.

> **Pause and think**: Assuming the rule and input documents above, can you predict the output?

Fact rule matches are usually returned in a different output table or format in the graphical user interface (GUI) than concept rule matches. This is due to the extra information that fact matches create. For example, the extracted matches for the reportedDefect concept and the input document above include the following: the token "engine" for the label "part" and the token "overheating" for the label "mal," as well as the entire span of text between these two matches in each of the input documents, as shown in Figure 8.1.

Figure 8.1. Extracted Matches for the reportedDefect Concept

Doc ID	Concept	Extraction Label	Extracted Match
1	reportedDefect		engine is quickly overheating
1	reportedDefect	mal	overheating
1	reportedDefect	part	engine
2	reportedDefect		engine is always overheating
2	reportedDefect	mal	overheating
2	reportedDefect	part	engine

In this example, the literal strings ("engine" and "overheating") that are explicitly defined in the rule are assigned as matches to the extraction labels ("part" and "mal") when the fact is found. This rule works well for counting occurrences of specific strings. Note that the string between the first and last match is also returned for both documents, providing context. In fact matches, there is always at least one match per defined extraction label, plus one extra match to show the span between the first extracted string and the last extracted string.

Although at least one extraction label is required in the SEQUENCE rule type, it is recommended to specify two or more extraction labels because the intended use of this rule type is to model a relationship among multiple extracted matches. If you want to specify a single label, a C_CONCEPT rule type is more appropriate because it is less computationally expensive. You can read more about C_CONCEPT rules in section 6.4. However, an exception to the guideline is when you need to match multiple pieces of text with the same label in the same rule definition. This is not possible with a C_CONCEPT rule type.

Returning to the previous example, if more than one match should be extracted for the "part" label, then a single extraction label can be used to capture all the parts mentioned:

```
SEQUENCE:(part):The _part{engine}, _part{transmission}, and
_part{suspension} have been replaced
```

Consider the following input documents:

1. The engine, transmission, and suspension have been replaced.
2. The engine and transmission have been replaced.

> **Pause and think**: Assuming that the rule above is in a concept named replacedPart, can you predict the matches for the input documents above?

The matches for the replacedPart concept and the input document above are shown in Figure 8.2.

Figure 8.2. Extracted Matches for the replacedPart Concept

Doc ID	Concept	Extraction Label	Extracted Match
1	replacedPart		engine, transmission, and suspension
1	replacedPart	part	suspension
1	replacedPart	part	transmission
1	replacedPart	part	engine

Note that there are four matches for the first document: three matches for the label "part" and one match that extracts the text between the first and last of the three matches. There are no matches for the second document, because only two of the three required elements are found in the text.

The basic use of the SEQUENCE rule is useful in highly structured text, where the extracted matches and context are very predictable. In the next section, you will see how to extend the usefulness of this rule type by generalizing and replacing string literals with other elements.

8.2.2. Advanced Use with Other Elements

To capture a sequence of unknown terms or a larger set of previously defined terms, you can replace each string with another element such as a part-of-speech (POS) tag or a concept name. For example, the rule from the previous section could be rewritten by replacing the strings with "_w," which represents any single token, including any word that has not been previously specified in any rules or has not been previously extracted. Using "_w" is a good strategy for exploring your data and finding unknown part names or abbreviations.

```
SEQUENCE:(part):The _part{_w}, _part{_w}, and _part{_w} have been
replaced
```

In this rule, any words found in sequence in the context specified would be extracted as matches to the part argument. If this rule were to replace the previous one in that same concept named replacedPart, and the input sentences were the same as before, the output would also be the same. However, if the input text included different words, whereas the former rule would extract no matches, this modified rule would extract the new automotive parts.

Consider the following input documents:

1. The engine, transmission, and suspension have been replaced.
2. The windshield, wipers, and mirrors have been replaced.

> **Pause and think**: Assuming that the rule above is in a concept named replacedPart, can you predict the matches with the input documents above?

The matches for the replacedPart concept with the above documents as input are represented in Figure 8.3.

Figure 8.3. Extracted Matches for the replacedPart Concept

Doc ID	Concept	Extraction Label	Extracted Match
1	replacedPart		engine, transmission, and suspension
1	replacedPart	part	suspension
1	replacedPart	part	transmission
1	replacedPart	part	engine
2	replacedPart		windshield, wipers, and mirrors
2	replacedPart	part	mirrors
2	replacedPart	part	wipers
2	replacedPart	part	windshield

Note that for each input document, the extracted matches include those for the "part" label as well as the entire span of text from the first to the last matched automotive part. This context is helpful in this scenario for determining which parts are often replaced together.

Now imagine that you might need to extract names only of malfunctioning parts that a particular company manufactures, rather than all the possible parts that were replaced. In this case, you would put a concept name between the curly braces in the extraction label. This concept could be named, for example, madeByMalCo, where MalCo is an abbreviation for a fictitious company. The madeByMalCo concept could contain only names of manufactured parts that were produced by MalCo.

```
CLASSIFIER:engine
CLASSIFIER:transmission
CLASSIFIER:suspension
CLASSIFIER:wipers
```

Then, the SEQUENCE rule in the replacedPart concept could refer to the matches that would potentially be extracted from the madeByMalCo concept.

```
SEQUENCE:(part):The _part{madeByMalCo}, _part{madeByMalCo}, and
_part{madeByMalCo} have been replaced
```

In this example, with the same input text sentences as above, the SEQUENCE rule would extract matches only if the potential matches were listed in the madeByMalCo concept. Consider the following input documents:

1. The windshield, wipers, and mirrors have been replaced.
2. The engine, transmission, and suspension have been replaced.

Pause and think: Can you predict the matches for the concept replacedPart with the input documents above?

The matches for the replacedPart concept and the input documents above are in Figure 8.4.

Figure 8.4. Extracted Matches for the replacedPart Concept

Doc ID	Concept	Extraction Label	Extracted Match
2	replacedPart		engine, transmission, and suspension
2	replacedPart	part	suspension
2	replacedPart	part	transmission
2	replacedPart	part	engine

Notice that no matches are extracted from the first document, although one of the potential matches, "wipers," is listed in the madeByMalCo concept. The rule, as written, requires that all three arguments produce matches for the concept madeByMalCo. Remember that in SEQUENCE rule types, all the elements are required to appear in the order specified before a match is returned for the concept. The second document produces three matches with the label "part" and a fourth match that extends from the first to the last of those three matches in the text.

Although the ordering of the elements in the rule definition must parallel the input text for extraction to occur, the ordering of extraction labels in the rule definition does not. Thus, the extraction label "_mal{}" could be referenced after the extraction label "_part{}" in the rule definition even if they are declared in the opposite order in the label declaration as "part" and "mal." The flexible order between two or more extraction labels in the declaration and definition is illustrated with this rule in a concept named, for example, reportedDefect.

```
SEQUENCE:(part, mal):_mal{overheating} of the _part{engine} is the
problem
```

Consider the following input documents:

1. The overheating of the engine is the problem.
2. The engine overheating is the problem.

Pause and think: Can you predict the matches for the reportedDefect concept and the input documents above?

The matches for the reportedDefect concept and the input documents above are in Figure 8.5.

Figure 8.5. Extracted Matches for the reportedDefect Concept

Doc ID	Concept	Extraction Label	Extracted Match
1	reportedDefect		overheating of the engine
1	reportedDefect	part	engine
1	reportedDefect	mal	overheating

As you can see in this output, the "_part{}" extraction label matches the term "engine," and the "_mal{}" extraction label matches the term "overheating" for the first input document. The order of the elements in the rule definition corresponds to the text of this sentence, even though the label order does not match the label declaration. There is no match for the second document because the criteria for the found text are not met: The word "overheating" is not followed by the sequence of other words defined in the rule. Simply put, the order of the extraction labels in the declaration section is irrelevant.

8.2.3. Troubleshooting

If you discover that a rule is not matching as you expected, potential causes for this could be one of the pitfalls outlined in section 5.4: namely, general syntax errors, comments, misspelling/mistyping, tokenization mismatch, or filtered matches. In addition, there are also errors that you can check for that are specific to the SEQUENCE rule type, such as the following:

- White space
- Syntax errors
- Missing extraction label
- Extra extraction label
- Tagging mismatch
- Expansion mismatch
- Concept references
- Predefined concept references
- Cyclic dependencies

In the SEQUENCE rule type, white space is reduced to a separator for a list of elements and not counted as an element itself. You cannot specify how many white space characters or what type can appear between elements. For that type of matching, where you specify white space characters, you will need to use a REGEX rule type.

The SEQUENCE rule type requires use of the output declaration, which is located between the rule type declaration and the rule definition. Make sure that you put the extraction label declaration between the two colons that delimit the section and that you format the labels as a comma-separated list between parentheses.

Another error with SEQUENCE rules includes forgetting the extraction labels and their curly braces or putting them on the wrong element, or elements. You must use all the labels you define in the declaration section of the rule at least once, and they must be spelled just as you declared them, or you will get an error. However, if you use a label in a rule that you did not declare, then you will simply get no matches. Remember the underscore and both curly braces for every label in use in the rule definition.

Every element defined in the rule must be present in the text that you are trying to match exactly as you have defined it. Mismatches in order or spelling can eliminate expected matches. If your concept is case-sensitive, then check for alignment of case, as well.

It is possible that the POS tag that you think a particular word might have is not the tag assigned to that word by the software in that particular context. The best way to prevent this error is to test your expectations with targeted examples in context before you apply the rule to a sample of documents that is like the data that you will process with the model.

In addition, it is possible that the POS tag is misspelled or does not exist. Different languages, versions, and products might use different POS tags. Consult your product documentation for lists of acceptable tags for rule-building. The spelling and case of the tags in the rules must be exactly as documented. Because writing a rule with a nonexistent tag like ":abc" is not a syntax error but a logical error, the syntax checking protocols will not catch it as an error, but there will not be any of the expected matches.

Another potential error when you are writing rules that contain a POS tag is forgetting to include the colon before specifying the tag. Without the colon, the system considers the rule to refer to a concept by that name or a string match, which might produce unexpected or no results. Syntax checking protocols will not return an error in this case.

When using the expansion symbols (e.g., @, @N, @V, @A), note that the expansion includes only related dictionary forms, not any misspellings that might have been identified by the misspelling algorithm or other variants associated with that lemma through use of a syRenonym list. To review what a lemma is, consult chapter 1. Also, remember that the forms of the words are looked up before processing, and when matching happens, the associated POS assignment of the word in the text is not considered. You can work around this issue, if you want to, by using a CONCEPT_RULE; see section 7.2 for more information. Examining the output from rules that contain an expansion symbol is recommended.

Referencing concepts by name without ensuring that you have used the correct name, including both case and spelling accuracy, can also reduce the number of expected matches. If you reference predefined concepts, be sure they are loaded into your project and always check the names because they might be different across different products.

Any rule that can reference a concept and returns matches (e.g., not REMOVE_ITEM or NO_BREAK) has the capacity to participate in a cyclic dependency error. A *cyclic dependency* is when two or more concepts refer to each other in a circle of concept references. For example, if the concept myConceptA has rules that reference myConceptB, and myConceptB has rules that reference myConceptA, then there is a cycle of references between them. This type of error will prevent your whole project from compiling successfully. This reason motivates the best practice to test your project often as you are adding concepts and rules. In this way, you will know that the latest concepts added to the model created the cyclic dependency. Another strategy to use to avoid this error is careful design for your taxonomy and model. Refer to chapter 13 to learn more about taxonomy design best practices.

Finally, if you can use a simpler rule type to do the work that you are trying to do with SEQUENCE rules, then always use the simpler rule type instead. In this case, the most likely alternative rule type is the C_CONCEPT rule. Although fact rule types are very powerful, they can be more difficult to maintain and troubleshoot in larger models because the outputs are more complex. If you use them, make sure you use them correctly.

8.2.4. Best Practices

Use the SEQUENCE rule type when fact matching is required and the order of elements is known, but only when you cannot extract enough information using a CONCEPT or C_CONCEPT rule.

When naming the extraction labels, keep in mind that they should start with a letter, followed by any series of letters, underscores, or digits. Note that in some older products, using an uppercase letter in an extraction label name could cause compilation errors. Do not use the extraction label _c{} in a fact rule, and avoid the labels _ref{}, _F{}, _P{}, and _Q{}.

To check whether your labeled elements are what you meant to extract, you will do well to complete some preliminary scoring before spending a lot of time building rules. This guideline aligns with the practice of creating a set of *method stubs* in programming to check that the end-to-end design is sound. You can put a few rules in each of your concepts to test how the input documents are transformed into new columns of structured data and plan any post-processing that might be required.

Finally, effective label names are descriptive and show why you are extracting each item. Keeping the names short is good for readability and to help avoid typographical errors, but descriptive and informative names are important for maintainability and making the rules understandable. Also, be sure to use comments to document your rules and the labels that you are using, for future troubleshooting and maintainability.

8.2.5. Summary

Requirements for SEQUENCE include the following:

- A rule type declaration in all caps and followed by a colon
- One or more comma-separated user-defined extraction labels enclosed in parentheses and followed by a colon
- Repetition of the user-defined extraction label preceded by an underscore and followed by curly braces that enclose an element or elements to be extracted somewhere within the rule definition
- Any combination of two or more elements

Types of elements allowed include the following:

- A token or sequence of tokens to match literally ("#" character must still be escaped for a literal match to occur)
- A reference to another concept name, including predefined concepts
- A POS or special tag preceded by a colon
- A word symbol (_w), representing any single token

- A cap symbol (_cap), representing any capitalized word

Allowed options for the rule type include the following:

- Comments using "#" modifier
- Morphological expansion symbols, including @, @N, @A, and @V

8.3. PREDICATE_RULE Rule Type

When you need to extract facts but cannot use a SEQUENCE rule, a PREDICATE_RULE might be effective. The SEQUENCE rule type defines a series of ordered elements, whereas the PREDICATE_RULE rule type defines a pattern of elements using Boolean and proximity operators. As in CONCEPT_RULE rules, Boolean and proximity operators allow for conjunctions, disjunctions, negations, distance, and order-free (left or right direction) constraints that specify conditions for matching. However, this flexibility of the order of elements in text in relation to one another can increase rule complexity, as well as the time required for matching, maintenance, and troubleshooting.

8.3.1. Basic Use

The basic syntax of a PREDICATE_RULE is similar to the CONCEPT_RULE type, and the set of allowed operators is the same. The primary differences are as follows:

- The addition of an extraction label declaration in the output declaration section between the rule type declaration and the rule definition
- The application of those labels in the rule to mark extracted matches, instead of using the _c{} extraction label

Here are two examples of the basic syntax:

```
PREDICATE_RULE:(label1, label2):(operator, "_label1{element1}",
"_label2{element2}")
PREDICATE_RULE:(label1, label2):(operator, "_label1{element1}",
"element2", "_label2{element3}")
```

As in the SEQUENCE rule type, the output declaration section holds the extraction label declaration, which consists of a comma-separated list of one or more extraction labels between parentheses. Remember that extraction labels must start with a letter, followed by any series of letters, underscores, or digits. Note that in some older SAS Text Analytics products, using an uppercase letter in an extraction label name could cause compilation errors.

As in the CONCEPT_RULE type, an operator and its arguments are placed in a comma-delimited list between parentheses, and every argument is fully enclosed within double quotation marks. Elements to be extracted as matches have a corresponding extraction label that is also within the double quotation marks that delimit an argument, and the curly braces enclose the element or elements to be extracted.

For example, if you want to extract two pieces of text that correspond to a vehicle part ("engine") and malfunction ("overheating") within the scope of a sentence, ignoring any other tokens in the sentence, you can use the following rule:

```
PREDICATE_RULE:(part, mal):(SENT, "_part{engine}", "_mal{overheating}")
```

This rule can be read as follows: If the strings "engine" and "overheating" are found in a sentence, then extract the match "engine" to the "part" label and extract the match "overheating" to the "mal" (malfunction) label. Note that the order of the extracted matches does not matter, as long as they are in the same sentence, because they are governed by the SENT operator, which is unordered. Moreover, the entire span starting with the first element extracted from the sentence and ending with the last element extracted from the sentence is also returned to provide insight into the context of the matches. Some SAS Text Analytics products also enable you to concatenate additional tokens onto the beginning and end of that matched string to provide even more context via a bigger window of content. The process of concatenating context to both ends of a match creates a concordance view of the match.

Consider the following input documents:

1. The report indicated overheating, which means we need to focus on the engine.
2. The customer said that the engine was frequently overheating.

Pause and think: Assuming that the rule above is in a concept named reportedDefect and the input documents above, can you predict the matches for each extraction label and the entire matched string?

Assuming that the rule above is in a concept named reportedDefect, the matches for the input documents above are included in Figure 8.6.

Figure 8.6. Extracted Matches for the reportedDefect Concept

Doc ID	Concept	Extraction Label	Extracted Match
1	reportedDefect		overheating, which means we need to focus on the engine
1	reportedDefect	mal	Overheating
1	reportedDefect	part	engine
2	reportedDefect		engine was frequently overheating
2	reportedDefect	mal	overheating
2	reportedDefect	part	engine

Both input documents produced matches despite the varied order of the extracted matches in the input text. This output shows that the order of the arguments in the definition of a PREDICATE_RULE with the SENT operator is irrelevant. Finally, if there are elements found by the rule (and not extracted) that are before the first or after the last extracted match, then they will not be included in the matched string.

Operators might have other operators as their arguments; this is called *nesting of operators*. The operator that is higher in the nesting hierarchy is the *governing* operator. If you want to restrict the order of the arguments, then you can insert an ORD operator into the rule above, governed by SENT. For more information about operators and their behavior, as well as how to select the right one, please consult both your product documentation and chapter 11. Advanced use examples in the following sections also illustrate specific applications, including nesting.

8.3.2. Advanced Use: Capture of a Sentence

Remember that, in addition to the extracted elements and associated labels, the results of a match to a PREDICATE_RULE also include a matched string that spans from the first extracted element to the final extracted element, including all the tokens between them. Potentially useful information might be contained within this span of tokens, information that can be analyzed to inform further rules.

For example, you might want to split each document into sentences. Then you can apply another model to each sentence or examine sentences with particular characteristics, such as those with mention of a vehicle part, as a smaller data set. Here is the rule to identify the first word and last word of a sentence; it assumes that your data is well formed and grammatical:

```
PREDICATE_RULE:(first, last):(SENT, (SENTSTART_1, "_first{_w}"),
(SENTEND_2, "_last{_w} :sep"))
```

This rule looks within the scope of a sentence, as defined by the SENT operator, to find its two arguments, each of which is an operator governing its own arguments. The first word of the sentence is defined as such by using the SENTSTART_n operator with n defined as 1. The other operator used is SENTEND_n with n defined as 2, which enables you to identify the last word without extracting just the sentence-ending punctuation. Keep in mind, though, that the span extracted by this rule will not include the final punctuation, because that element is not inside an extraction label's curly braces. To change the output to extract the final punctuation instead, use SENTEND_1 instead of SENTEND_2, and remove the final ":sep" element from the rule.

Consider the following input document:

The provider stopped sending me bills and therefore, I am delinquent. They sent me to a collection agency. Then they closed my account and I've been paying them all this time!

> **Pause and think**: Assuming that the previous rule is in a concept named singleSentence and the input document above, can you predict the matches for each extraction label and the entire matched string?

Assuming that the PREDICATE_RULE is in the singleSentence concept and the input document is above, the matches are in Figure 8.7.

Figure 8.7. Extracted Matches for the singleSentence Concept

Doc ID	Concept	Extraction Label	Extracted Match
1	singleSentence		Then they closed my account and I've been paying them all this time
1	singleSentence	Last	Time
1	singleSentence	First	Then
1	singleSentence		They sent me to a collection agency
1	singleSentence	last	Agency
1	singleSentence	first	They
1	singleSentence		The provider stopped sending me bills and therefore, I am delinquent
1	singleSentence	last	Delinquent
1	singleSentence	first	The

In the results above, when the extraction label column is blank, the extracted match is each sentence from the original document but without sentence-ending punctuation. This data could be the text field that you analyze in another project.

To put this type of rule into a practical situation, suppose you are running a hotel and have reviews from customers that talk about what they liked and did not like about their stay. These reviews are written for others that might be considering staying in your hotel. They include advice about what to do or see while visiting, as well as what to avoid. You want to identify such advice to use for honing your services and experiences, as well as to encourage your visitors to take advantage of great activities to engage in nearby. Your goal is for your guests to have the best time possible. You have a separate model or concept that talks about likes, dislikes, and complaints.

You can modify the rule in the previous example to get to the two types of advice when given in command form like the following:

```
PREDICATE_RULE:(pos, end):(SENT, (SENTSTART_1, "_pos{:V}"), (SENTEND_1,
"_end{_w}"))
PREDICATE_RULE:(neg, end):(SENT, (SENTSTART_3, "_neg{ Do not :V}"),
(SENTEND_1, "_end{_w}"))
```

You can see the similarity to the previous rule. This time, though, the item defined in the first position, or positions, of the sentence is meant to capture commands that start with verbs. Also, the ending punctuation is included in the match, instead of returning the final word in the sentence as the end of the matched string. If you use these two rules together—for example, in two concepts named posAdvice and negAdvice—then you might need to also use a REMOVE_ITEM rule to remove the negative comments ("do not") from the positive advice ("do") concept to disambiguate the two. Here is an example of such a REMOVE_ITEM rule:

```
REMOVE_ITEM:(ALIGNED, "_c{posAdvice}", "negAdvice")
```

See section 9.2 for more information about the REMOVE_ITEM rule type.

Consider the following input documents:

1. Visit the hotel restaurant and you will be amazed!!!
2. Do not attend the show as it is a waste of time.

Pause and think: Can you predict the matches for each extraction label and the entire matched strings for the posAdvice and negAdvice concepts with the input documents above, assuming that the REMOVE_ITEM rule removed false positives?

The matches are included in Figure 8.8.

Figure 8.8. Extracted Matches for the posAdvice Concept

Doc ID	Concept	Extraction Label	Extracted Match
1	posAdvice		Visit the hotel restaurant and you will be amazed!!!
1	posAdvice	end	!
1	posAdvice	pos	Visit
2	negAdvice		Do not attend the show as it is a waste of time.
2	negAdvice	end	.
2	negAdvice	neg	Do not attend

In the first document, the posAdvice concept matches on a verb that starts the sentence ("Visit") and spans to match the punctuation ending the sentence (the right-most exclamation point of the three). In the second document, the negAdvice concept matches on the string "Do not attend" as the first three tokens that start a sentence and spans to include the sentence-ending punctuation (a period). For each of these cases, the extracted match is the entire document. The REMOVE_ITEM rule removed the matches from the posAdvice concept that also match the negAdvice concept, so the matches in Figure 8.9 were removed from the final output.

Figure 8.9. Removed Matches for the posAdvice Concept

Doc ID	Concept	Extraction Label	Extracted Match
2	posAdvice		Do not attend the show as it is a waste of time.
2	posAdvice	end	.
2	posAdvice	pos	Do

Both rules are defined in two separate concepts, named posAdvice and negAdvice respectively, to semantically associate each positive and negative set of rules with its respective dedicated concept.

You can later restrict the first rule to limit the verbs to the ones you expect reviewers to use, because POS tagging can be error-prone. This type of exploratory approach can be used to learn many things in your data, when you already know some things or can use the structure of the text to focus in on what you are interested in. You can also explore your data with

SEQUENCE rules, but they are less flexible and you can fill only gaps that are modeled with elements like _w, POS tags or _cap.

For more information about sentence boundary detection with CAS, consult Gao (2018).

8.3.3. Advanced Use: More Complex Rules

Multiple Boolean and proximity-based operators can be used within a PREDICATE_RULE. As mentioned in section 8.3.1, a feature that makes this rule type as powerful as the CONCEPT_RULE type is *nesting*, the ability to embed an operator and its arguments as an argument of another operator. This allows for interactions between the operators to help you specify the exact conditions under which the pattern in the text will be a match for the desired information. The number of nesting levels are not constrained, although you should keep your rules logical and readable to the extent possible.

As an example, you may find several variations of an argument are needed as part of your rule. You can achieve this result by listing each of the variations as arguments to a single OR operator, separated from another via a comma-delimited list:

```
PREDICATE_RULE:(part, malfunction):(SENT, (OR, "_part{fender}",
"_part{wing}", "_part{mudguard}"), (OR, "_malfunction{shaking}",
"_malfunction{vibrating}")
```

In this example, any one of the three variants of the idea of a vehicle part ("fender," "wing," or "mudguard") can match and will evaluate to a value of true for the OR operator. Similarly, when either of the ways that something can move back and forth ("shaking" or "vibrating") match, the second OR operator will evaluate to true, as well. If both OR operators are true within a sentence, then the SENT operator is also made true, and the match is returned for the entire rule.

> **Tip**: When the list of arguments under an OR operator is bigger than 4–5 arguments, consider adding them as a list of CLASSIFIER or CONCEPT rules in a new concept and referencing that concept for better readability.

Another aspect of PREDICATE_RULE rules to be aware of is that not all elements require a corresponding extraction label. Elements used in the rule definition can serve as additional conditions that must hold true for the rule to match. Such elements specify the context of the rule match, much as with the elements without the _c{} extraction label in a CONCEPT_RULE rule type.

For example, in medical records, drug names are often followed by text that explains the means for delivery or administration of drugs and then by a date of application. Extracting matches for the drug name and date of application in the context of the string that represents the drug delivery method can be done with a PREDICATE_RULE that leverages two other concepts: nlpDate, which is an enabled predefined concept, and drugName, which includes the following rules:

```
CLASSIFIER:prednisone
CLASSIFIER:methylprednisolone
CLASSIFIER:fluticasone
```

The PREDICATE_RULE given here is in the drugDelivery concept:

```
PREDICATE_RULE:(drug, date):(SENT, (ORDDIST_10, "_drug{drugName}",
"administer@", "_date{nlpDate}"))
```

This rule can be read as follows: Within a sentence, within a span of 10 tokens or less, first find a drug as defined in the drugName concept, then find a delivery string that contains variants of the token "administer," and, finally, find a date of application as defined in the predefined concept nlpDate. The rule returns a match of the drugName concept with the "drug" label, a match for the nlpDate concept for the "date" label, and the entire span of text between the drugName match and the nlpDate match.

In this case, each argument found in the text must be in the same order as specified in the rule because of the use of the ORDDIST_n operator. If specifying the ordering is not required for your data, you could use DIST_n instead. One additional benefit of this specific rule is that the drug names have been collected in a separate concept called drugName to avoid writing a separate rule for each drug. Also, leveraging the predefined concept nlpDate gives you the flexibility to match on many types of date variants without writing explicit rules. By using the @ modifier with the "administer" element, you extend the rule beyond the usefulness of a simple string to cover forms such as "administered."

Consider the following input documents:

1. Due to inflammation, we are prescribing Prednisone to be administered starting today.
2. I took half a dose of fluticasone nasal spray yesterday.
3. Resulted because IV fluid and methylprednisolone was administered on 30.11.04 and swelling was observed in forearm on 4.12.04—that is, 4 days after fluid administration.

Pause and think: Can you predict the matches for each extraction label and the entire matched string for the drugDelivery concept and the input documents above?

The matches for the drugDelivery concept and input documents above are in Figure 8.10.

Figure 8.10. Extracted Matches for the drugDelivery Concept

Doc ID	Concept	Extraction Label	Extracted Match
1	drugDelivery		Prednisone to be administered starting today
1	drugDelivery	date	today
1	drugDelivery	drug	Prednisone
3	drugDelivery		methylprednisolone was administered on 30.11.04
3	drugDelivery	date	30.11.04
3	drugDelivery	drug	methylprednisolone

The output shows matches for the first and third document and not for the second one because it did not contain a morphological variation of the token "administer," as the rule definition required. In addition, the extracted matches for the two labels include only the drug name ("Prednisone" and "methylprednisolone") and the date of application ("today" and "30.11.04"), and not the strings related to the token "administer." Because morphological variations of that token were defined in the rule, they must be present and reside between the other two arguments in order for matches to be returned at all. But because the rule did not specify that the token should be extracted with a label, the variations of "administer" are not part of the labeled matches. The entire string from the match for the drug to the match for the date is also included in the output.

8.3.4. Advanced Use: Single Label, Multiple Extracted Matches

As with the SEQUENCE rule type, you can also match against the same extraction label more than once in a PREDICATE_RULE. For example, there might be several vehicle parts mentioned within the space of a couple of sentences, and you want to know when multiple parts are mentioned in close proximity to see whether those parts are interacting poorly. For this purpose, you can use a single PREDICATE_RULE extraction label, named "part," and use it more than once in the same rule definition:

```
PREDICATE_RULE:(part):(SENT, "_part{partListA}", "_part{partListB}")
```

You can read this rule this way: Within the span of a sentence, extract any match to the rules in the concept partListA and the concept partListB as matches for the label "part." Each of the two referenced concepts contains a list of parts which are of a certain type. In other words, this rule will find situations where one type of part is mentioned by a customer in the same sentence as another type of part. This approach enables you to explore the relationships between two types of parts (from partListA and partListB) and to produce both sets of matches as outputs to a third concept, named, for example, partInteraction.

The concept partListA includes rules such as the following:

```
CLASSIFIER:rear defrost
```

The concept partListB includes rules such as the following:

```
CLASSIFIER:back windshield
```

Consider the following input document:

Immediately after turning on my rear defrost I heard that oh too familiar cracking noise coming from the passenger side of my back windshield—the same sound I heard the first time I came outside to find my windshield shattering on its own.

Pause and think: Can you predict the fact matches and matched string for the partInteraction concept with the input document above?

The matches for the partInteraction concept with the input document above are in Figure 8.11.

Figure 8.11. Extracted Matches for the partInteraction Concept

Doc ID	Concept	Extraction Label	Extracted Match
1	partInteraction		rear defrost I heard that oh too familiar cracking noise coming from the passenger side of my back windshield
1	partInteraction	part	back windshield
1	partInteraction	part	rear defrost

The PREDICATE_RULE in this example would also work if the parts were all together in a single list; however, in that case, you would get more false positive matches of items you already knew were related or variant ways of referring to the same thing. For example, you would get extracted matches for both "back windshield" and "windshield," which is much less useful.

At this point, you might ask why you would use a PREDICATE_RULE over a CONCEPT_RULE when attempting to match multiple items using a single argument. Although a CONCEPT_RULE type does accept Boolean and proximity operators, it does not allow for capturing multiple matches at the same time because the _c{} extraction label is used to yield a single result each time text is found. Therefore, you could not show the relationship in the example above between different parts in a CONCEPT_RULE.

You might remember that the _c{} extraction label can be used more than once in a CONCEPT_RULE but only when used with an OR operator to mark multiple sister arguments. Even then, only one match will be returned. The PREDICATE_RULE will enable you to capture multiple values for the same argument and should be used when you want to associate the same items in some relationship. If instead you do want to extract only one of the items, a CONCEPT_RULE should be used because it is the less computationally expensive rule type.

8.3.5. Advanced Use: More Than Two Returned Arguments

Remember that fact rule types (SEQUENCE and PREDICATE_RULE) are intended to capture relationships between elements. As you have already seen, elements do not all have to be extracted. You can extract more than two elements with one PREDICATE_RULE rule;

the number of labels should correspond to the elements that you are attempting to extract. For example, consider the following rule in a concept named checkInfo:

```
PREDICATE_RULE:(checkNo, amount, date):(SENT_2, "_checkNo{checkNumber}",
"_amount{nlpMoney}", "_date{nlpDate}")
```

You can read the rule this way: Within a span of 2 sentences, find a match for the rules in the custom concept checkNumber and return it as a match for the label "checkNo," a match for the rules in the predefined concept nlpMoney, and return it as a match for the label "amount," as well as returning a match for the rules in the predefined concept nlpDate for the label "date." Note that the rule declaration consists of three extraction labels, corresponding to the information that you want to extract: the check number, amount, and date. The concept checkNumber is a supporting concept that contains the definition for how a check is expected to appear, which starts with a single hash symbol, followed by one or more digits (that is, the check number itself). The concept contains the following rule:

```
REGEX:\#\d+
```

As in SEQUENCE rules, the order of the extraction labels in the declaration does not matter, and you can change it if you want to. The order in the rule definition depends on whether you are using operators that require a particular order to match, like ORD or ORDDIST.

Consider the following input documents:

1. I have written a personal check in the amount of $125.00 and it is dated from Monday. The check number is #2501. Why is this check not shown on my current statement?
2. My accountant noticed that our check #3889, in the amount of $889.23 from 3/24/2016 bounced.

Pause and think: Can you predict the matches for the checkInfo concept and the input text above?

The fact matches for the checkInfo concept and the input documents above are shown in Figure 8.12.

Figure 8.12. Extracted Matches for the checkInfo Concept

Doc ID	Concept	Extraction Label	Extracted Match
1	checkInfo		$125.00 and it is dated from Monday. The check number is #2501
1	checkInfo	date	Monday
1	checkInfo	amount	$125.00
1	checkInfo	checkNo	#2501
2	checkInfo		#3889, in the amount of $889.23 from 3/24/2016
2	checkInfo	date	3/24/2016
2	checkInfo	amount	$889.23
2	checkInfo	checkNo	#3889

Note that there are matches for both documents, even though the order of the three elements in the two documents is different.

8.3.6. Advanced Use: Discovery of Terms to Add to a Model

Imagine that you are building a list of adjectives used to describe your product in reviews. There are several approaches you could take. One way to find adjectives in your data is to use the POS tag :A in a CONCEPT rule. You will, however, get a lot of adjectives that are not used to describe your product. A better approach would be to use a PREDICATE_RULE with a SENT operator like the following:

```
PREDICATE_RULE:(prod, adj):(SENT, "_prod{productList}", "_adj{:A}")
```

But, using this rule, you are still likely to get some matches that are not references to your product, and you will miss some that are correct. If you want to adjust your results further, one option is to use context to target words that are likely to be adjectives.

```
SEQUENCE:(prod, adj)::DET _adj{:A} _prod{productList}
PREDICATE_RULE:(prod, adj):(SENT, (ORDDIST_5, ":DET", "_adj{:A}",
"_prod{productList}"))
```

Comparing the output of the two rules above, the second rule is broader in that it allows for other words to come between the adjective and the product mention. It is also more constrained in scope: It is limited to within a sentence. Both rules look for a determiner like "the" or "a," followed by an adjective, and then followed by a mention of the product. Taking into consideration your specific data, you can use the rule that returns better results. You can also model additional contexts where adjectives are likely to occur grammatically:

```
SEQUENCE:(prod, adj): _prod{productList} be@ _adj{:A to :V}
PREDICATE_RULE:(prod, adj):(SENT, (ORDDIST_5, "_prod{productList}",
"be@", "_adj{:A to :V"))
```

These rules look for mention of your products, followed by some form of the word "be," and then an adjective followed by an infinitive verb construction. Again, try both to see which one is most suitable for your data. Then you can expand or add similar rules to continue your investigation. As you find examples of useful adjectives in your data, you can add those adjectives to a list and put them in their own concept to be referenced by other rules.

8.3.7. Troubleshooting

If you discover that a rule is not matching as you expected, potential causes for this could be one of the pitfalls outlined in section 5.4: namely, general syntax errors, comments, misspelling/mistyping, tokenization mismatch, or filtered matches. In addition, there are also errors that you can check for that are specific to the PREDICATE_RULE type of rule, such as the following:

- White space
- Syntax errors
- Missing extraction label
- Extra extraction label
- Logical error with operators
- Tagging mismatch
- Expansion mismatch
- Concept references
- Predefined concept references
- Cyclic dependencies

White space in a PREDICATE_RULE is not very important because of the use of the parentheses, commas, and double quotation marks to set off pieces of the rule. However, within an argument (double quotation marks), white space is a separator for a list of elements and not counted as an element itself.

Every PREDICATE_RULE includes an output declaration section between the rule type declaration and the rule definition. Make sure that there is a colon on either side of this section and that the declaration of the names of labels is a comma-separated list between parentheses.

One of the common syntax errors that are specific to PREDICATE_RULE is forgetting or misplacing the extraction label (or labels), underscore (or underscores), or curly braces of the extraction label: The braces must always be inside the double quotation marks defining an argument. Remember also that the elements inside a set of parentheses are a comma-separated list. Do not forget the commas. Finally, parentheses and quotation marks must come in pairs.

You must use all the labels you define in the declaration section of the rule at least once, and they must be spelled just as you declared them, or you will get an error. If you use a label in a rule that you did not declare, you will simply get no matches.

Do not forget that if you have marked all or part of an argument of an OR operator with a user-defined label, then you will also have to place the label somewhere on all of the sister arguments, as well. Otherwise, you will not see the matching behavior that you expect. Avoid using _ref{}, _F{}, _P{}, or _Q{} as an extraction label, as well, because there might be unexpected behavior if you do use them.

It is possible that the POS tag that you think a particular word might have is not the tag assigned to that word by the software in that particular context. The best way to prevent this error is to test your expectations with targeted examples in context before applying the rule to a sample of documents that is like the data that you will process with the model.

In addition, it is possible that the POS tag is misspelled or does not exist. Different languages, versions, and products might use different POS tags. Consult your product documentation for lists of acceptable tags for rule-building. The spelling and case of the tags in the rules must be exactly as documented. Because writing a rule with a nonexistent tag like ":abc" is not a syntax error but a logical error, the syntax checking protocols will not catch it as an error, but there will not be any of the expected matches.

Another potential error when you are writing rules that contain a POS tag is forgetting to include the colon before specifying the tag. Without the colon, the system considers the rule to refer to a concept by that name or a string match, which might produce unexpected or no results. Syntax checking protocols will not return an error in this case.

When using the expansion symbols (e.g., @, @N, @V, @A), note that the expansion includes only related dictionary forms, not any misspellings that might have been identified by the misspelling algorithm or other variants associated with that lemma through use of a synonym list. To review what a lemma is, consult chapter 1. Also, remember that the forms of the words are looked up before processing, and when matching happens, the associated POS assignment of the word in the text is not considered. You can work around this issue using a CONCEPT_RULE; see section 7.2 for more information. Examining your output from rules that contain expansion symbols is recommended.

Referencing concepts by name without ensuring that you have used the correct name, including both case and spelling accuracy, can also reduce the number of expected matches. If you reference predefined concepts, be sure they are loaded into your project, and always check the names because they might be different across different products. Concept names are always case-sensitive.

Any rule that can reference a concept and returns matches (e.g., not REMOVE_ITEM or NO_BREAK) has the capacity to participate in a cyclic dependency error. A *cyclic dependency* is when two or more concepts refer to each other in a circle of concept references. For example, if the concept myConceptA has rules that reference myConceptB, and myConceptB has rules that reference myConceptA, then there is a cycle of references between them. This type of error will prevent your whole project from compiling. This is why you should test your project often as you are adding concepts and rules. In this way, you will know that the latest concepts added to the model created the cyclic dependency. Another strategy to use to avoid this error is careful design for your taxonomy and model. Refer to chapter 13 to learn more about taxonomy design best practices.

One common error reported by users who write rules programmatically is to add an additional colon between the name of the concept and the names of the labels. Although this unnecessary colon will not produce a syntax checking error, the rule will produce no matches. To avoid this situation, ensure that there only two colons in the fact rule written programmatically: one between the rule type declaration and the concept name, and the other between the extraction labels and the rule definition. See the programmatically formatted example rule that follows, which defines the "part" and "mal" labels in the replacedPart concept:

```
PREDICATE_RULE:replacedPart(part, mal):(SENT, "_part{engine}",
"_mal{overheating}")
```

Be careful: This rule is correct when you are using the programmatic ways of building a model, but it will not work as expected in the GUI environment. In the GUI, you should not use the concept name as a part of the rule, because the GUI interprets the name from your taxonomy structure and location of your rule in the editor associated with a specific concept.

If you have checked all the above and are still having problems with your rules, then you should look at the logic defined by your combination of operators. A full understanding of operators is recommended if you are combining them together in a single rule. Consult chapter 11 to learn more about operators and how they interact. Review the project design and match algorithm sections in chapter 13 if you need more help with troubleshooting these rule types.

Finally, if you can use a simpler rule type to do the work that you are trying to do with these rules, always use the simpler rule type instead. Although these rule types are very powerful, they can be more difficult to maintain and troubleshoot in larger models. If you use them, make sure you use them correctly.

8.3.8. Best Practices

As rule complexity grows, the potential exists for increasing compilation and run-time costs. Because of the flexible nature of elements and operators that can be used in a PREDICATE_RULE, it is advised to keep each rule as lightweight as possible. You can write less computationally intensive rules by opting for the following:

- Minimizing the number of rule arguments
- Limiting the number of nested Boolean and proximity operators
- Referencing less computationally expensive concepts

Remember, PREDICATE_RULE arguments are used to match against specific parts of a text. If you are extracting elements from many arguments in a PREDICATE_RULE type of rule, then you should evaluate whether all extracted elements require extraction as a set. Can the rule be split into smaller, less expensive rule types with fewer restrictions? If so, select those rule types over the more computationally expensive PREDICATE_RULE.

PREDICATE_RULE arguments contain two types of elements: the ones with an extraction label specify what part of the match to return, and the ones without a label specify context. You can think of the latter in the same way you do the unmarked contextual elements in a CONCEPT_RULE rule type. Minimize the number of these elements needed in each rule in order to reduce processing time, but leverage them where useful. Remember that extraction labels must start with a letter, followed by any series of letters, underscores, or digits. Note that in some older products, using an uppercase letter in an extraction label name could cause compilation errors. Do not use the extraction label _c{} in a fact rule, and avoid the labels _ref{}, _F{}, _P{}, and _Q{}.

When PREDICATE_RULE rules refer to concepts that are themselves potentially computationally expensive, the costs associated with compilation and run-time processes are compounded. It is recommended to have PREDICATE_RULE rules depend on concepts with only more simplistic matching or comprising less computationally expensive rule types, like CLASSIFIER, CONCEPT, or C_CONCEPT rules.

Having PREDICATE_RULE definitions depend on concepts which themselves contain PREDICATE_RULE definitions, also known as *scaffolding*, is not recommended. A referring PREDICATE_RULE rule might be dependent on whether another concept contains PREDICATE_RULE matches, but does not use the results of the matches themselves (e.g., the matching fact arguments). It is recommended to have the rule in the referent concept use a less computationally expensive rule type. If operators are required, use a CONCEPT_RULE type to feed one level of PREDICATE_RULE at the very top.

To check whether your labeled elements are what you meant to extract, you will find it a good idea to do some preliminary scoring before spending a lot of time building rules. This guideline aligns with the practice of creating a set of *method stubs* in programming to check that the end-to-end design is sound. You can put a few rules in each of your concepts to test how the input documents are transformed into new columns of structured data and plan any post-processing that might be required.

Finally, the best way to use label names effectively is to use descriptive labels that help show why you are extracting each item. Keeping the names short is good for readability and to help avoid typographical errors, but descriptive and informative names are important for maintainability and making the rules understandable. For ease of troubleshooting and maintainability, be sure to use comments to document your rules and labels.

8.3.9. Summary

Requirements for a PREDICATE_RULE include the following:

- A rule type declaration in all caps and followed by a colon
- One or more comma-separated user-defined extraction labels enclosed in parentheses and followed by a colon
- Repetition of the user-defined extraction label preceded by an underscore and followed by curly braces that enclose an element or elements to be extracted somewhere within the rule definition
- One or more Boolean or proximity operators, in a comma-separated list with its arguments enclosed in parentheses
- One or more elements enclosed in double quotation marks in each argument

Types of elements allowed include the following:

- A token or sequence of tokens to match literally (# character must still be escaped for a literal match to occur)
- A reference to other concept names, including predefined concepts
- A POS or special tag preceded by a colon
- A word symbol (_w), representing any single token
- A cap symbol (_cap), representing any capitalized word

Allowed options for the rule type include the following:

- Comments using # modifier
- Morphological expansion symbols, including @, @N, @A, and @V

Chapter 9: Filter Rule Types

9.1. Introduction to Filter Rule Types

In chapter 5, you learned about four groupings of LITI rule types:

- Concept rule types (including CLASSIFIER, CONCEPT, C_CONCEPT, and CONCEPT_RULE)
- Fact rule types (including SEQUENCE and PREDICATE_RULE)
- Filter rule types (including REMOVE_ITEM and NO_BREAK)
- REGEX rule type

The REMOVE_ITEM and NO_BREAK types of rules are grouped together because they can be leveraged to filter out unwanted matches. For example, there may be cases when you want to extract a particular match in most cases but with some exceptions. You can write a rule or set of rules to cover most of the cases where you want a match and then specify the conditions for the exceptions in a filter rule. You will see concrete examples throughout this chapter.

The most important point to understand about filter rules is that they remove matches from the result set when triggered. The "best match" and "longest match" algorithms can also remove matches from the result set. If you want to see your result set without any matches removed, then you should avoid both of these rule types and set your match algorithm to "all matches." Troubleshooting rule matches will be much easier under these conditions, especially for novices.

Each of these two rule types is described briefly in the SAS Text Analytics product documentation, and you have already encountered examples of REMOVE_ITEM rules in sections 7.5 and 8.3.2. This chapter will extend your understanding by including examples that show both the basic and advanced uses of each of the rule types.

To aid with troubleshooting unexpected behavior, each rule type section in this chapter includes a checklist of possible errors specific to that rule type. To help you make the most out of each rule type in your models, this chapter also contains best practices. Finally, the requirements and optional elements for each rule type are summarized at the end of each section so you can keep coming back to that section as a quick reference when you are building your models.

After reading this chapter, you will be able to do the following tasks:

- Use the LITI syntax to write efficient and effective REMOVE_ITEM and NO_BREAK rules
- Avoid common pitfalls and use best practices to create better rule sets
- Troubleshoot common rule-writing errors

9.2. REMOVE_ITEM Rule Type

The REMOVE_ITEM rule type prevents a match for a specific concept from passing through to the final result set under specified conditions; in other words, it filters matches. A prerequisite for this rule type to do anything is that a referenced concept exist and contain rules that match text in documents. This referenced concept is the taxonomy node from which matches will be removed with the REMOVE_ITEM rule. Note that this rule type is global, which means that you can put the rule itself in any part of the hierarchy, in any concept, and its behavior will be exactly the same.

9.2.1. Basic Use of the REMOVE_ITEM Rule Type

The basic syntax is the following:

```
REMOVE_ITEM:(ALIGNED, "_c{toRemove}", "equivalent extracted text")
```

This rule specifies the removal of the extracted match from the concept in the first argument (toRemove) if it is matching the same span of text as the string specified in the second argument. Remember, because this rule type filters results, you must specify a concept name in the _c{} extraction label somewhere in the first argument, or else the rule will do nothing. In other words, you cannot put a literal string or any other type of element inside the brackets for the _c{} extraction label.

The operator used in REMOVE_ITEM rules is always ALIGNED, and only two arguments are allowed with no nesting. The concept name you specify in the first argument within the _c{} label must contain rules that extract matches from your data. Those matches, along with any other elements specified in the first argument, must span the same text in the document text as is matched by the elements in the second argument, or else the rule will do nothing. Just as in CONCEPT_RULE and PREDICATE_RULE, the arguments are inside double quotation marks.

For example, suppose that a company has two lists of employees maintained in two concepts: a list of current employees in the concept currEmp and a subset of retired employees in concept retiredEmp. The currEmp concept contains rules such as the following:

```
CLASSIFIER:John Solder
CLASSIFIER:Mary Pensky
CLASSIFIER:Lou Messer
CLASSIFIER:Barry LaMountain
```

The retiredEmp concept contains rules such as the following:

```
CLASSIFIER:Lou Messer
CLASSIFIER:Barry LaMountain
```

To ease the maintenance of these two concepts, the company has added a REMOVE_ITEM rule to the taxonomy in a third concept, globalConcept:

```
REMOVE_ITEM:(ALIGNED, "_c{currEmp}", "retiredEmp")
```

You can read this rule this way: When the same match is extracted for both the currEmp concept and the retiredEmp concept, remove the match from the currEmp concept. This approach allows the company to maintain the list of current employees by updating only the retiredEmp concept with the name of an employee when that employee retires. The rule will automatically remove a match of that name from the currEmp concept when that name is encountered in the input text.

Consider the following input documents:

1. Mary Pensky got married last month, so updates to her benefits are allowed.
2. I sent the healthcare forms to Lou Messer and Barry LaMountain yesterday.
3. On Friday, John Solder contacted me in regards to his employment status.

Pause and think: Can you predict the extracted matches with these input documents?

The output for the currEmp concept based on the input documents is as represented in Figure 9.1.

Figure 9.1. Extracted Matches for the currEmp and retiredEmp Concepts

Doc ID	Concept	Matched Text
1	currEmp	Mary Pensky
2	retiredEmp	Lou Messer
2	retiredEmp	Barry LaMountain
3	currEmp	John Solder

The results correctly depict that Mary and John are both current employees, whereas Lou and Barry are retired. Even though Lou and Barry also matched the currEmp concept, because of the REMOVE_ITEM rule, they are correctly logged only as retired employees.

9.2.2. Advanced Use of REMOVE_ITEM: Additional Elements

You may place elements into the first argument in addition to your concept name enclosed in the _c{} extraction label. You can also place multiple types of elements into the second argument position, including a concept name, multiple concepts, and a combination of strings, concepts, and elements such as "_w." Essentially, anything that is allowed in a CONCEPT rule can go in that slot, except coreference rule modifiers. So the following is a valid rule as well:

```
REMOVE_ITEM:(ALIGNED, "_c{toRemove} concept2 so", "concept1 concept2
_w")
```

Only the match to the concept named toRemove will be removed by this rule, because it is bracketed with _c{}. None of the matches to the other participating concepts (concept1 and concept2) will be affected. They are used only to specify the circumstances for the removal. The ALIGNED operator defines that the matched text in the first argument must be identical to the matched text in the second argument for the rule to be applied. If that condition is met, then the match specified in the _c{} extraction label is removed.

For example, suppose you have a federal government data source where the string "the States" is used either as an alias for the United States as a country, or as references to the individual states themselves. To extract only the references to the "states" as an alias for the country, you may want to write a series of concepts. One concept, usAlias, may contain the following rule:

```
CLASSIFIER:the States
```

But you would not want matches returned to that concept if the match was part of the strings "one of the States," "each of the States," "all of the States," or "none of the States." Notice that in each of these strings, the preposition "of" precedes the match to the usAlias concept. In this simple example, a REMOVE_ITEM rule like the following one is appropriate:

```
REMOVE_ITEM:(ALIGNED, "of _c{usAlias}", "of the States")
```

You can read this rule this way: When the string "of the States" is encountered, remove the match "the States" from the usAlias concept. Consider the following input documents:

1. Each of the States ratified the amendment.
2. None of the States were concerned about their borders.
3. Immigrants built the States and have always supported the economy.

Pause and think: Assuming that the rule above is in a concept named globalConcepts, can you predict the matches for the usAlias concept for the input documents?

The output for the usAlias concept based on the input documents in this example is in Figure 9.2.

Figure 9.2. Extracted Matches for the usAlias Concept

Doc ID	Concept	Matched Text
3	usAlias	the States

The REMOVE_ITEM rule has removed the matches in the first two documents because "the States" was preceded by "of." So the output consists of only one extracted match to the usAlias concept, coming from the third input document.

Remember that to test that the match is removed, you must find the concept that you are removing matches from (in this case, the usAlias concept) and test from that concept. If running your test only on that concept versus the whole project, be aware that you will not see the behavior of the REMOVE_ITEM rule unless it is also in the tested concept. See chapter 11 for more information about how to set up your hierarchy and use this rule type properly.

9.2.3. Advanced Use of REMOVE_ITEM: Negation

In many projects, keywords are a useful approach to either early model-building or exploration of the data. A common challenge that arises is addressing negation. Using a REMOVE_ITEM rule to address negation may be necessary. This section will show you how to do this in a simple example and provide some guidance to extend this to more complex examples.

The data used in this example comes from 2007 reports of adverse events associated with vaccinations, as reported to the U.S. Centers for Disease Control and the U.S. Food and Drug Administration via the Vaccine Adverse Event Reporting System (https://vaers.hhs.gov/). This site enables reporting of adverse events from individual patients, health care professionals, and vaccine manufacturers. The data set includes a column headed SYMPTOM_TEXT, which is a text that describes the situation and symptoms of the patient. It is often in a narrative (story) format.

Imagine that you want to look for systemic patterns of symptoms across patients, timeframes, or geographies. You build a model to find the symptoms, starting with a list of symptoms you expect to see in the generalSymptom concept. The rules include the following:

```
CLASSIFIER:fever
CLASSIFIER:difficulty breathing
CLASSIFIER:diarrhea
```

After running the model, you notice results for symptoms found in a context that indicates that they were not present in the patients' experience. These symptoms are false positives and should be removed from the output.

Consider the following input documents, representing a subset of those false positives with shaded extracted matches for the generalSymptom concept:

1. No fever.
2. Fever 101 but no difficulty breathing.
3. The patient did not have a fever.
4. The patient had since been administered her second dose, at 4 months of age, of Rotateq and did not develop any diarrhea.

These examples illustrate two primary patterns in the data. First, the word "no" may appear within a few words before the symptom, negating it. Second, the word "not" may appear in patterns before the symptom, negating it. A REMOVE_ITEM approach can remove these false positives, but it must be as specific as possible to avoid removing legitimate symptoms. The two rules shown below account for the observed patterns.

```
REMOVE_ITEM:(ALIGNED, "no _c{generalSymptom}", "no generalSymptom")
REMOVE_ITEM:(ALIGNED, "did not _w _w _c{generalSymptom}", "did not _w
_w generalSymptom")
```

The matches to be removed are the ones in the generalSymptom concept, so that is the concept name with the _c{} extraction label in the REMOVE_ITEM rules. The other elements in the first argument specify the context, including "no" and "not" as observed in the two negating patterns that need to be removed. The elements in the second argument are just meant to exactly represent the same string of text as the first argument represents. One way to do this is to repeat the first argument, but without the _c{} extraction label, as shown in this example. These rules remove all the false positive matches. The only extracted match that remains is the first word of the second document.

This simple example illustrates the process of eliminating false positives with REMOVE_ITEM rules. Realistically speaking, the process of finding patterns in the data, creating rules, observing outputs, and then creating REMOVE_ITEM rules to eliminate false positives is a cyclical development process. With complex data, this process often needs to be repeated, and matches frequently need to be tested as the model grows. The most important point to remember when you are attempting this type of model building is to build slowly, testing each piece to ensure that the results are what you expect. When the rules are working as planned, document what you did to build them, anything you learned to avoid through your testing, and the results you expect from the rules.

For more exploration of and extraction from this data, see the scenarios in the supplemental online materials.

9.2.3. REMOVE_ITEM Troubleshooting

If you discover that a REMOVE_ITEM rule is not filtering the matches as you expected, potential causes could be one of the pitfalls outlined in section 5.4; namely, general syntax errors, comments, misspelling/mistyping, tokenization mismatch, or unfiltered matches. In addition, there are also errors that you can check for that are specific to the REMOVE_ITEM rule type, such as the following:

- Extraction label
- Syntax errors
- ALIGNED operator
- Concept references
- Predefined concept references
- Tagging mismatch
- Expansion mismatch
- Concept placement

In a REMOVE_ITEM rule type, you must use the extraction label _c{}. The label marks what part of the matched content should be acted on. The name of the concept from which you want to remove matches goes in between the curly braces. Nothing else should be placed between the curly braces.

The elements defined along with the extracted concept must be enclosed in one of the two arguments delimited by double quotation marks. The ALIGNED operator is required, and only two arguments are allowed under a single ALIGNED operator. The elements within each of the two arguments are ordered and generally delimited by white space.

Additionally, for the REMOVE_ITEM rule type, it is very important for the first part of the rule to be an exact match for the same text as the second part of the rule. The ALIGNED operator requires that the offsets for the two parts be identical. The argument for each part includes everything inside the double quotation marks. Check this carefully, because it is easy to miss this type of error, when building this rule with more than two elements in each argument, or when using concepts that can generate results of different token lengths.

One way to examine the elements is to count the elements on each side, then to line them up, and then to check each pair to see that it matches the same text in your test data one-by-one. When counting what a concept contributes to the span of text matched by one of the arguments, you must consider the returned match from that concept, so keep this guideline in mind when pointing to concepts containing advanced rule types. Do not nest operators inside either of the two arguments; nesting is not supported in this rule type. Referencing concepts by name without ensuring that you have used the correct name, including both case and spelling accuracy, can also reduce the number of filtered matches. If you reference predefined concepts, be sure that they are loaded into your project, and always check the names, because they may be different across different products.

It is possible that the part-of-speech (POS) tag you think a particular word may have is not the tag assigned to that word by the software in that particular context. The best way to prevent this error is to test your expectations with targeted examples in context, before applying the rule to a sample of documents that is like the data you will process with the model.

In addition, it is possible that the POS tag is misspelled or does not exist. Different languages, versions, and products may use different POS tags. Consult your product documentation for lists of acceptable tags for rule-building. The spelling and case of the tags in the rules must be exactly as documented. Because writing a rule with a nonexistent tag like ":abc" is not a syntax error, but a logical error, the syntax-checking protocols will not catch it as an error, but there will not be any of the expected matches.

Another potential error when you are writing rules that contain a POS tag is forgetting to include the colon before specifying the tag. Without the colon, the system considers the rule to refer to a concept by that name or a string match, which may produce unexpected or no results. Syntax-checking protocols will not return an error in this case.

When using the expansion symbols (e.g., @, @N, @V, and @A), note that the expansion includes only related dictionary forms, not any misspellings that may have been identified by the misspelling algorithm or other variants associated with that lemma through use of a synonym list. To review what a lemma is, consult chapter 1. Also, remember that the forms of the words are looked up before processing, and when matching happens, the associated POS assignment of the word in the text is not considered. You can work around this issue, if you want to, by using a CONCEPT_RULE; see section 7.2 for more information. Examining your output from rules that contain expansion symbols is recommended.

9.2.4. REMOVE_ITEM Best Practices

Use REMOVE_ITEM rules when you are seeing matches that you do not want, but otherwise believe your model to be a successful approach. If you realize that you are using many REMOVE_ITEM rules, then you should revisit your design or taxonomy, or collect additional data to analyze.

As mentioned in the troubleshooting section, do not put anything other than a single concept name inside the _c{} extraction label in the first section. You are removing a match to that concept by using the rule. Putting something like a string or multiple elements inside the braces would make no sense, because that would not represent a single match to a specified concept. The _c{} extraction label marks the match that you are targeting for removal from the result set with your rule.

The elements outside the _c{} braces can be any element allowed in CONCEPT rules. This is also true of elements in the second argument. Remember that, if you want to match the "#" character, then you must escape it like this: "\#" in the rule. Also, you cannot use coreference symbols in this rule type.

> **Tip**: Use the REMOVE_ITEM rule type carefully in your model. Do not put anything other than a single concept name inside the extraction label _c{}.

The best place to put your REMOVE_ITEM rules is in a concept you have selected to hold all global rules. This concept can be anywhere in your taxonomy, but keeping it in a prominent position, such as at the top, is a good practice so that it is easy to find when you are troubleshooting matches (Figure 9.3).

Figure 9.3. SAS Visual Text Analytics Concepts Node List of Custom Concepts

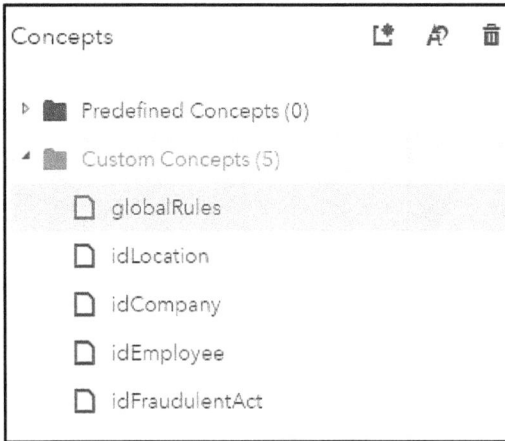

With all REMOVE_ITEM rules in one place, you can quickly scan your rules to troubleshoot unexpected behavior in rule matches to determine whether your global rules are affecting your model in ways you did not predict. Another reason to keep REMOVE_ITEM and other global rules in a single node of your hierarchy is that doing so helps you to prevent creating rules that offset each other. For example, if you have these two rules in a single location, then you are more likely to realize that they are mirror images of each other, and you can then adjust them accordingly:

```
REMOVE_ITEM:(ALIGNED, "_c{concept1}", "concept2")
REMOVE_ITEM:(ALIGNED, "_c{concept2}", "concept1")
```

Note that the result of these rules will be to remove both matches to concept1 and matches to concept2. If each of these rules appears in separate nodes, you may not notice how similar but opposite they are. It is possible that you would have a valid reason for having both rules: for example, if you want no matches if both concepts match a span of identical text. However, that scenario is less likely than that you meant for one concept to "win."

Another option is to place all your REMOVE_ITEM rules into a set of concept definitions designated to hold all global rules (Figure 9.4). Keeping them all in the same small number of concepts helps to gain some of the benefits of putting them into a single node, but also provides the possibility that you can label and group such rules according to their purpose.

Figure 9.4. SAS Visual Text Analytics Concepts Node List of Custom Concepts and Subconcepts

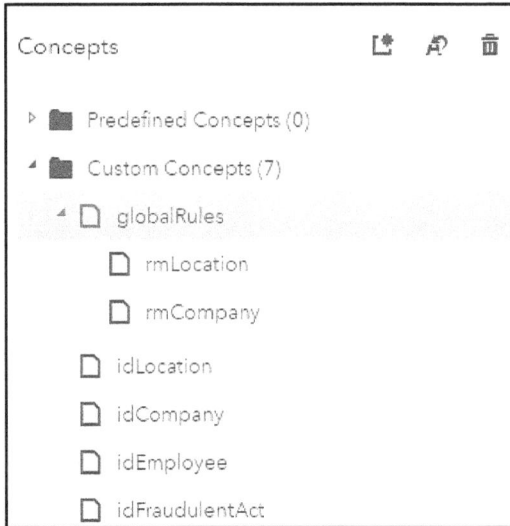

```
Concepts                        �  �  🗑

  ▷ ▮ Predefined Concepts (0)

  ▲ ▮ Custom Concepts (7)

      ▲ ☐ globalRules

          ☐ rmLocation

          ☐ rmCompany

      ☐ idLocation

      ☐ idCompany

      ☐ idEmployee

      ☐ idFraudulentAct
```

A less preferred option is to put your global rules into the concept definition that you are removing matches from, as shown in Figure 9.5. Typically, if you take this approach, then you should put all the REMOVE_ITEM rules into a designated section of the rule set—for example, at the top. Otherwise, you will quickly forget that you have the rule buried somewhere in your model, other users will be flummoxed by the odd behavior they are seeing with certain parts of the model, and they will have no easy way to track down the cause.

Figure 9.5. SAS Visual Text Analytics Concepts Node and Rule Definitions

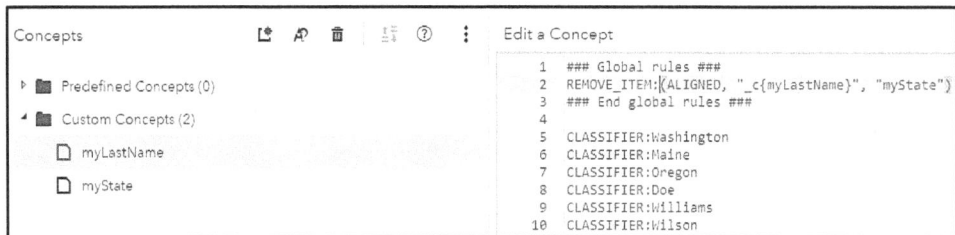

```
Concepts              �  �  🗑  �  ⑦  ⋮    Edit a Concept

                                              1   ### Global rules ###
  ▷ ▮ Predefined Concepts (0)                 2   REMOVE_ITEM:(ALIGNED, "_c{myLastName}", "myState")
                                              3   ### End global rules ###
  ▲ ▮ Custom Concepts (2)                     4
                                              5   CLASSIFIER:Washington
      ☐ myLastName                            6   CLASSIFIER:Maine
                                              7   CLASSIFIER:Oregon
      ☐ myState                               8   CLASSIFIER:Doe
                                              9   CLASSIFIER:Williams
                                             10   CLASSIFIER:Wilson
```

This third option shown in Figure 9.5 is much less preferred than the other two options described above, because you can easily lose track of what these rules are doing and make false assumptions when you place them in the concept definition where you expect them to operate. However, because of the way testing in some products works, you may need to put them into the node temporarily while the building and fine-tuning of that node is in progress. Remember that, once the testing of other nodes is again in focus, collecting them in a single concept in your model is advised for maintenance and troubleshooting purposes.

Do not put these rules in any other location in your model. You will eventually regret doing so and have more trouble understanding the behavior of matches, when you have such rules operating on your model results and do not realize it. *You have been warned.*

> **Tip**: After designing and testing the model, put REMOVE_ITEM rules in a concept you
> have selected to hold all global rules in the taxonomy. This approach will save you time
> when you are troubleshooting.

The benefit of using the REMOVE_ITEM rule is that you can take out of your models the
matches that you did not want to match without changing other aspects of your model. This is
called *filtering* matches. Unlike the NO_BREAK rule type, which is discussed next, the
REMOVE_ITEM rule type can target removal of matches from only one concept. The
NO_BREAK rule type removes matches from any node that meets the definition. Therefore,
REMOVE_ITEM rules are safer and easier to troubleshoot.

9.2.5. REMOVE_ITEM Summary

Requirements for REMOVE_ITEM include the following:

- A rule type declaration in all caps followed by a colon
- ALIGNED operator in parentheses with two arguments enclosed in quotes and
  separated by a comma
- A concept reference as part of the first argument, enclosed in the curly braces of the
  _c{} extraction label
- At least one other element in the second argument

The syntax is similar to the CONCEPT_RULE type (with only ALIGNED operator allowed).
Types of elements allowed in either argument outside the c{} label include the following:

- A token or sequence of tokens to match literally ("#" character must still be escaped
  for a literal match to occur)
- A reference to other concept names, including predefined concepts
- A POS or special tag preceded by a colon
- A word symbol (_w), representing any single token
- A cap symbol (_cap), representing any capitalized word

Allowed options for the rule type include the following:

- Comments using "#" modifier
- Morphological expansion symbols, including @, @N, @A, and @V

9.3. NO_BREAK Rule Type

The NO_BREAK type of rule prevents a match from passing through to the final result set, if
it has the potential to break up a specified set of elements. In other words, the matches from
other rules are removed or filtered from the result set. NO_BREAK is a global rule type,
which means that it can be placed in any node in the taxonomy and operate the same way,
with one exception, which will be described in section 9.3.2.

9.3.1. Basic Use of the NO_BREAK Rule Type

The basic use of NO_BREAK is with a set of literal strings, as will be illustrated in this section. The advanced use section 9.3.2 delves further into referencing a concept match or a more complex set of elements. In both cases, the targeted set of elements can optionally be limited by context, using the same method as in a C_CONCEPT rule. The NO_BREAK rule type is not recommended for frequent use, because of the side effects discussed later in this section. If a filtering rule is needed, then you should first try to use REMOVE_ITEM instead.

The basic syntax is the following:

```
NO_BREAK:_c{element1 element2}
```

You can read this rule this way: Two or more specific elements in curly braces should not be split or interrupted by a match in any concept. In other words, one of the elements cannot be part of a match, while the other one is in the text but is not part of that same match. For example, here is a rule in the globalRules concept that specifies the disallowance of any match to break or interrupt the series of literal strings in the curly braces ("life insurance").

```
NO_BREAK:_c{life insurance}
```

If you had two concepts, one called insuranceType and the other called lossType, with the rules shown below, the CLASSIFIER rules in both concepts could extract matches with the input text. The insuranceType concept includes the following rule:

```
CLASSIFIER:life insurance
```

The lossType concept includes the following rule:

```
CLASSIFIER:loss of life
```

Consider the following input document:

> Failure to properly identify the beneficiary of a life insurance policy can result, as it did in the Morey case, in the loss of life insurance proceeds to creditors of the deceased person's estate.

> **Pause and think**: Assuming the taxonomy above, can you predict the matches for the insuranceType concept with the input document in this example?

The matches for the insuranceType concept with the input document above are shown in Figure 9.6.

Figure 9.6. Extracted Matches for the insuranceType Concept

Doc ID	Concept	Matched Text
1	insuranceType	life insurance
1	insuranceType	life insurance

The match to "loss of life" before the last instance of "insurance" is a match to lossType, but it is filtered out of the results because of the NO_BREAK rule in the globalRules concept.

Note that the NO_BREAK rule does not have to be in the globalRules concept. It could be in any concept in the model because this rule works across all nodes in the hierarchy when the full project is run.

To limit the restricted string by context, you can specify the context outside of the curly braces.

```
NO_BREAK:_c{life insurance} policy
```

This rule means that, when the match "life insurance" is followed by the word "policy" and there could potentially be another match extracted that would partially overlap with "life insurance" or be a subset of the strings in this match, only "life insurance" should be extracted as a match. Using the same rules for the insuranceType and lossType concepts but changing the NO_BREAK rule to this latter form, you get a slightly different output with the same input text document:

> Failure to properly identify the beneficiary of a life insurance policy can result, as it did in the Morey case, in the loss of life insurance proceeds to creditors of the deceased person's estate.

Pause and think: Assuming the modified NO_BREAK concept and the previous taxonomy and input document, can you predict the matches for the insuranceType and lossType concepts?

This time, the matches for the insuranceType and lossType concepts are in Figure 9.7.

Figure 9.7. Extracted Matches for the insuranceType and lossType Concepts

Doc ID	Concept	Matched Text
1	insuranceType	life insurance
1	lossType	loss of life
1	insuranceType	life insurance

As you can see, there are still two matches to the CLASSIFIER rule in insuranceType. However, the NO_BREAK rule will filter matches only if the term "life insurance" is followed by "policy." So the CLASSIFIER rule in lossType is matching as before, but the match is no longer filtered out of the results.

It is very likely that you see this change as less useful, because in this sentence the phrase "loss of life" is not referring to death, but to the loss of money (the life insurance proceeds). But consider this additional input document:

Life insurance does not simply apply a monetary value to someone's life. Instead, it helps compensate for the inevitable financial consequences that accompany the loss of life.

Pause and think: Assuming the same taxonomy as before, can you predict the matches for the insuranceType and lossType concepts with the new input document above?

The matches for the insuranceType and lossType concepts with the input document in this example are shown in Figure 9.8.

Figure 9.8. Extracted Matches for the insuranceType and lossType Concepts

Doc ID	Concept	Matched Text
1	insuranceType	Life insurance
1	lossType	loss of life

In this example, "loss of life" is truly a type of loss that "insurance" is meant to be triggered by. The first question is why must "life insurance" always be analyzed as if it were a single unit? In other words, is there a valid reason to treat it as if it were added to the dictionary? In essence, this is what the NO_BREAK rule does. However, when a word is added to the dictionary as a multiword, a word with internal spaces, that combination of strings can never be analyzed as two separate words again. So one question to ask yourself is this: When you see this pair of words in sequence, will there ever be a time that you just want to match one of them? Or is either of the parts meaningful to you on its own?

If the answer to these questions is ever "yes," then do not make a NO_BREAK rule to keep them together, or do so with as much specific context around it as possible. In fact, this section wraps up with a warning to avoid using the NO_BREAK rule type whenever possible. You can usually reach the same types of goals with more control if you use a REMOVE_ITEM rule, which is preferable to using the NO_BREAK rule type. Here are some options for solving the example just presented:

- Option 1: Remove NO_BREAK rule and allow situations of overlap to match both concepts.
- Option 2: Use REMOVE_ITEM rule instead, like this rule that removes the "loss of life" match if it overlaps with a "life insurance" match:

```
REMOVE_ITEM:(ALIGNED, "_c{lossType} _w", "loss of life
insurance")
```

- Option 3: Use the NO_BREAK rule type with more context to restrict the times when you are treating the item as a multiword, as in this rule that only filters out matches that conflict with the phrase "loss of life:"

```
NO_BREAK: loss of _c{life insurance}
```

9.3.2. Advanced Use of NO_BREAK: Specifying a Concept Name

You can also place a concept reference or other elements in the curly braces. This is considered advanced use because it can have unintended consequences, or side effects. These examples show some of the possibilities:

```
NO_BREAK: _c{myConcept}
NO_BREAK: _c{myConcept in _w} place@
```

You can read the first rule above this way: If a potential match from any concept partially overlaps with or is a partial match with a match from the myConcept concept, then that potential match will be discarded in favor of the match in myConcept.

The second rule adds more elements: If a potential match from any concept partially overlaps with or is a partial match with a match from the myConcept concept, followed by the word "in" and any token, and is found preceding any dictionary form of the word "place," then that potential match will be discarded in favor of the match in myConcept.

For example, a life insurance company may have the following concepts. The first one, lifeInsurance, is for the types of life insurance it provides, such as term life and whole life insurance:

```
CLASSIFIER:term life insurance
CLASSIFIER:whole life insurance
```

The second one, permanentLife, lists types of whole life insurance:

```
CLASSIFIER:traditional whole life
CLASSIFIER:universal life
CLASSIFIER:variable life
CLASSIFIER:variable universal life
```

To make sure that a match for "whole life insurance" in the lifeInsurance concept does not break the match for "traditional whole life" in the permanentLife concept when "insurance" follows "life," the taxonomy also contains the following NO_BREAK rule in a globalRules concept:

```
NO_BREAK: _c{permanentLife}
```

Consider the following input documents:

1. The process for applying for our whole life insurance policy was long.
2. The representative explained the differences between variable universal life and traditional whole life insurance.

Exercise: Assuming the concepts just introduced, can you predict the matches for the input documents in this example?

The matches for the model and input documents are in Figure 9.9.

Figure 9.9. Extracted Matches for the lifeInsurance and permanentLife Concepts

Doc ID	Concept	Matched Text
1	lifeInsurance	whole life insurance
2	permanentLife	variable universal life
2	permanentLife	traditional whole life

Note that there is no match for the string "whole life insurance" and the lifeInsurance concept in the second document, because that match would break the string "traditional whole life" in the permanentLife concept.

Although this example is simple and limited to just a few rules, concepts containing many rules can, in general, go awry if you try this approach. The best practice is to use this rule type only with simple taxonomies like this one.

Tip: If you reference a concept name within the _c{} label, make sure you test the effects on all your concepts in the entire document collection rigorously, because you cannot ever know without testing which of your other concepts a NO_BREAK rule will filter results from.

9.3.3. NO_BREAK Troubleshooting

If you discover that a particular NO_BREAK rule is not filtering the matches as you expected, potential causes could be one of the pitfalls outlined in section 5.4; namely, general syntax errors, comments, misspelling/mistyping, tokenization mismatch or missing matches. In addition, there are also errors that you can check for that are specific to the NO_BREAK rule type, such as the following:

- Extraction label
- Syntax errors
- Concept placement

In NO_BREAK rules, you must use the extraction label _c{}. The label marks what part of the matched content should be acted upon. You can put one concept name into the curly braces (although this is not recommended) or put two or more other elements in the braces.

The syntax of the NO_BREAK rule is much like that of the C_CONCEPT rule type. The elements are ordered and generally delimited by white space. There are no arguments or operators in this rule type.

If you notice that the NO_BREAK rule is not working as expected, make sure that it is not in the same concept you referenced in the extraction label. This placement can have undefined behavior and prevent your model from operating properly. In other words, if you write the following rule, do not put it into the concept named riskType, because the riskType concept is referenced inside the _c{} extraction label.

```
NO_BREAK:_c{riskType} occurs
```

To prevent unexpected missing matches, remember to assess the effect of the rule on the entire project. Move your rules to a globalRules concept, where you keep track of these rules for maintenance and troubleshooting purposes. Imagine having a taxonomy with hundreds of nodes and in one of them you have a NO_BREAK rule that filters out matches from somewhere in your hierarchy. You might not even know it is there and wonder why your rules just fail to match sometimes. Placing all your global rules in a single node will help to alleviate this problem because you can look at them to determine whether a match is being filtered from your results.

See the example below where using NO_BREAK is troublesome because it impacts matches that you did not intend it to remove.

Rules in the concept named mentionsArt include the following:

```
CLASSIFIER:art
NO_BREAK:_c{art museum}
```

There are two rules in the mentionsArt concept. One rule says to match anytime the word "art" appears in the text. The other rule says not to match "art" when next to "museum." So the rule says not to break "art museum" with any match, and your intention is to apply this filter to matches of mentionsArt.

Consider the following input documents:

1. I'm an art major.
2. I love to go to the art museum.
3. I don't like the science museum.

Pause and think: Assuming the rules in the mentionsArt concept just presented, can you predict the matches for these input documents?

The model and input documents produce the match shown in Figure 9.10.

Figure 9.10. Extracted Matches for the replacedPart Concept

Doc ID	Concept	Matched Text
1	mentionsArt	art

Imagine that, after getting the result you expected above, you move the NO_BREAK rule into the globalRules node, as recommended, and move on to other parts of your model. At some point, you decide to target locations in your model, too, intending to extract any type of museum. So you make this rule in the concept named museumType:

```
CLASSIFIER:museum
```

You run the model with the same input data as above to see the matches, as illustrated in Figure 9.11.

Figure 9.11. Extracted Matches for the museumType Concept

Doc ID	Concept	Matched Text
3	museumType	museum

You do not see a match to the second sentence, and you wonder why your simple CLASSIFIER rule is not matching. You might try other rule types, which also do not extract matches for "museum." You might try matching other terms, which would produce matches as expected, leaving you in a conundrum. Then you might remember the best practice of troubleshooting missing matches by looking at your globalRules node. You notice that the NO_BREAK rule contains the word "museum" and realize that you have blocked the match to "museum" yourself.

Remember that you cannot apply your NO_BREAK rule to matches from one concept only. But you can often use REMOVE_ITEM instead. In this scenario, you could substitute the following rule instead:

```
REMOVE_ITEM:(ALIGNED, "_c{mentionsArt} _w", "art museum")
```

You check to make sure that your rule matches the same text on both sides of the comma. Then you test and see that the matches you wanted are now as expected and shown in Figure 9.12.

Figure 9.12. Extracted Matches for the mentionsArt and museumType Concepts

Doc ID	Concept	Matched Text
1	mentionsArt	art
2	museumType	museum
3	museumType	museum

This approach works more accurately because you can target removal of only matches from the mentionArt concept.

9.3.4. NO_BREAK Best Practices

As mentioned already, if you use NO_BREAK rules, then you should put them into a single node in a prominent place in your taxonomy, such as the globalRules concept. In addition, when testing for global rule behavior, you must run the entire project.

> **Tip**: Filtering rules are global and remove matches. Therefore, matches for filtering rules are not displayed. To see their effect, test your project with and without them, and compare the results to see which matches have been removed.

In general, the recommendation is not to use NO_BREAK, because it can cause many problems and is difficult to control. Instead, use REMOVE_ITEM because it is easier to control. The NO_BREAK rule type cannot be limited to one concept only, whereas the REMOVE_ITEM rule type filters matches from only one specified concept and will not operate on matches from other places in the taxonomy.

9.3.5. NO_BREAK Summary

Requirements for NO_BREAK include the following:

- A rule type declaration in all caps followed by a colon
- _c{} extraction label in the rule definition with elements enclosed in the curly braces; must be more than one to show what to keep together or a concept name where some matches cross two or more tokens

Types of elements allowed include the following:

- A token or sequence of tokens to match literally ("#" character must still be escaped for a literal match to occur)
- A reference to other concept names, including predefined concepts
- A POS or special tag preceded by a colon
- A word symbol (_w), representing any single token
- A cap symbol (_cap), representing any capitalized word

Allowed options for the rule type include the following:

- Additional elements outside braces to specify context; same list allowed as above
- Comments using "#" modifier
- Morphological expansion symbols, including @, @N, @A, and @V

Chapter 10: REGEX Rule Type

10.1. Introduction to the REGEX Rule Type

In chapter 5, you learned about four groupings of LITI rule types:

- Concept rule types (including CLASSIFIER, CONCEPT, C_CONCEPT and CONCEPT_RULE)
- Fact rule types (including SEQUENCE and PREDICATE_RULE)
- Filter rule types (including REMOVE_ITEM and NO_BREAK)
- REGEX rule type

This chapter describes the use and best practices associated with the REGEX rule type. It is treated separately because it has some key differences from the other rule types, and it has the potential to be the most computationally expensive type. The REGEX rule type has some similarities to the common PERL-based regular expressions that are used in many programming languages. You may be tempted to overuse this rule type if you are familiar with the regular expression syntax.

After reading this chapter, you will be able to do the following tasks:

- Use the LITI syntax to write effective REGEX rules
- Avoid common pitfalls of overuse and complexity
- Understand and be able to avoid errors relating to differences between REGEX rules and regular expressions

10.2. Basic Use

The REGEX rule type is similar to the CLASSIFIER and CONCEPT rule types in that the entire found text (i.e., everything that matches the rule is extracted). The REGEX rule defines a character pattern that is used for searching for particular characteristics in text data. It uses the basic PERL-style regular expression syntax after the rule name and colon. However, the syntax allowed is a limited subset of the capabilities of PERL regular expressions: There is no capacity for look-ahead, look-behind, capture groups, or back-references. The only parentheses used in LITI REGEX rules are used for grouping and alternation, as in "(?:match this|or this)." These limitations serve to optimize LITI regular expressions for better performance.

If you have no experience with PERL-style regular expressions, then you should take a quick break and find a tutorial that introduces the syntax with good examples. A good book for this purpose is *Introduction to Regular Expressions in SAS*, by K. Matthew Windham. Alternatively, you can consult your product documentation for an introduction. Only the basics will be demonstrated in this section.

One unique feature of LITI REGEX rules is that rules must match at token boundaries. There is no match to a partial token, although you can match one or multiple tokens with a single rule. The reason for this limitation is that the results of a REGEX rule match can be passed to other concepts and therefore referenced by other rules. Other rule types function over tokens, so if a REGEX rule passed a partial token as a match, the receiving rule would not be able to handle it properly. For more information on tokenization in SAS products, see section 1.2.1.

The basic syntax for a LITI REGEX rule is as follows:

```
REGEX:PERL-style regular expression
```

The PERL-style regular expression comprises a combination of literal characters and special characters. Literal characters stand for exactly that same character: What you see is what you get. Special characters serve some function in the regular expression. For example, square brackets around a set of literal characters serves as a command to treat those characters as a set of possible characters in that position of the expression.

```
REGEX:[Big]
```

This rule will match one character, "B," "i," or "g." Because writers seldom use these letters as independent tokens, the rule is unlikely to match. However, a situation where it could match is found in the following example.

Assume that the rule above is in a concept named myRegex. Consider the following input documents:

1. The pizza delivery girl knocked on apartment 402 B, and quietly listened for any sounds.
2. The pizza delivery girl knocked on apartment 402B, and quietly listened for any sounds.

Pause and think: Assuming the rule above, can you predict the matches with the input text above?

With the rule and input documents above, the output includes only one match for the myRegex concept:

Doc ID	Concept	Matched Text
1	myRegex	B

As you can see, only the token "B" that appears after "402" in the first input document is returned as a match. To illustrate why this is the only match, the tokens of the first sentence are shown below between each double slash.

The // pizza // delivery // girl // knocked // on // apartment // 402 // B // , // and // quietly // listened // for // any // sounds // .

Only three tokens are one character long, so the rule considers only these as a possible match: B, comma, period. The first one, "B," does satisfy the rule's requirements of being one of three possible letters, so this token matches the REGEX rule. Consider the tokenization for the second example.

The // pizza // delivery // girl // knocked // on // apartment // 402B // , // and // quietly // listened // for // any // sounds // .

The rule did not produce any matches for the second sentence because the token is "402B," which is longer than the single character specified in the rule.

Below is a new version of the rule that would match this additional token: It leverages a hyphen as a special character to include any digit from 0 to 9 in the character class, and the plus sign after the second square brackets is a multiplier that allows 1 or more characters to match anything inside the brackets. This rule is in a concept named myRegex2.

```
REGEX:[Big0-9]+
```

This rule says to match one or more of the following characters in a sequence, starting and ending at token boundaries: "B," "i," "g," "0," "1," "2," "3," "4," "5," "6," "7," "8," "9." It can now match multiple characters because of the plus sign, so it can match the token "402B."

Consider the following input document:

Kunal Nayyar, from the hit-show "The Big Bang Theory," has purchased a brand-new BMW i8. Now he can just hit g00000000!

Pause and think: Can you predict the matches for the myRegex2 concept with the input text above?

The matches for the myRegex2 concept and the input document above are as illustrated in Figure 10.1.

Figure 10.1. Extracted Matches for the myRegex2 Concept

Doc ID	Concept	Matched Text
1	myRegex2	Big
1	myRegex2	i8
1	myRegex2	g00000000

To reiterate, in LITI rule matching, the token is the focus of the match algorithm. One or more tokens may be matched by a REGEX rule; however, white space is never treated as a token. You cannot write a rule to capture only white space or to capture white space on one or both ends of a token. The only way to capture white space with a REGEX rule, is to define the white space between two defined tokens. You can define white space in REGEX by inserting into a rule one of the following:

- A literal space
- \n
- \r\n
- \r
- \t
- \s

> **Remember**: You cannot write a rule to capture only white space or to capture white space on one or both ends of a token. The only way to capture white space with a REGEX rule, is to define the white space between two defined tokens.

While regular expressions are powerful tools to find certain patterns in text data, in the context of LITI there are two key things to remember. One is that, although LITI regular expressions are optimized for performance, they still are the slowest of all the rule types generally. Therefore, if you can write a rule using another type that gets the same matching behavior, you should select the alternative rule type. Second, REGEX rules can never use any of the special modifiers or other elements, including referencing another concept. In that way, they are similar to CLASSIFIER rules. They are limited to matching either strings or patterns depicted by the regular expression syntax.

> **Remember**: REGEX rule syntax includes a limited subset of the capabilities of PERL regular expressions. You cannot reference other concepts, use special modifiers, or other elements in REGEX rule definitions.

10.3. Advanced Use: Discovery of Patterns

You see patterns of characters every day. Right now, you can probably imagine a common format for a phone number, a social security number, an age, a birth date, an address, and the name of a tax form.

Words are also a pattern you recognize. You know that words usually use the characters in the alphabet. Sometimes they have numbers or hyphens in them, like "59-year-old." Rarely, other punctuation characters play a role, like the comma in "39,000-square-foot auditorium" and the period in an abbreviation like "U.S.A.," and you recognize these strings of characters as carrying specific meaning in the language.

REGEX rules in LITI are a good way to extract the types of data that follow patterns. For example, if you wanted to find the Social Security numbers in your documents that represented people from Ohio issued a social security number in 1975, you could start by using this REGEX rule.

```
REGEX:268-68-[0-9]{4}
```

The rule definition starts after the colon and says to find tokens that start with the series 268-68- and end with any 4 digits; the curly braces are special characters. But be aware that this rule will find any number in your data that matches this pattern, even if it is not a Social Security number or that number was never issued to a cardholder.

Another situation where looking for a pattern instead of specific lexical items might be useful is with part numbers, product numbers, ticket numbers, and the like. For example, if you want to make sure that your technicians are ordering the right parts for repair work, you might extract the part numbers out of their tech notes and compare them with the list of ordered parts for that account. If there is a discrepancy, then the account can be flagged for review or logged as a potential error.

Suppose that this list is representative of part numbers to find in the notes:

- EE28624
- EE54981
- EE700469
- EE8202
- EE8762
- EE9088
- EE9256
- EEM214

A REGEX rule to find these types of strings could look like the following:

```
REGEX:EE[0-9M][0-9]{3,5}
```

This rule says to find a token that starts with two E characters, then any digit or M character, followed by between three and five more digits. You will need to write some SAS code once you have done the extraction to compare the ordered parts and the parts from the notes.

> **Pause and think**: Assuming the rule above is in the concept partNumber, can you predict the matches with the list of part numbers text above?

The matches are in Figure 10.2.

Figure 10.2. Extracted Matches for the partNumber Concept

Doc ID	Concept	Matched Text
1	partNumber	EE28624
2	partNumber	EE54981
3	partNumber	EE700469
4	partNumber	EE8202
5	partNumber	EE8762
6	partNumber	EE9088
7	partNumber	EE9256
8	partNumber	EEM214

All the part numbers in the sample are extracted.

10.4. Advanced Use: Exploration

Data exploration is a good use for REGEX rules. Maybe you want to explore particular aspects of your data or patterns that you believe should exist. Sometimes, using a quick REGEX rule can stand in for multiple simpler rules and can give you a quick view into your data while you are developing your rules.

Perhaps you are looking at customer reviews and you want to get a sense of when your customers are getting confused or upset. One way to explore this is to look for sentences that are questions or exclamations. Here is a simple rule to help you do so:

```
REGEX:  [\?\!]
```

This rule, in the questionExclaim concept, looks for any question mark or exclamation mark in the text. The backslashes indicate that these special characters should be treated as literal characters in this rule. As you apply the rule above to reviews of various airlines, you are surprised to find that customers had put in more than one exclamation point or question mark in some cases. Now you can use the number of fact matches per document as a column to sort on so you can determine which reviews were full of these signs of confusion or anger. In order to see this directly in SAS Text Analytics products, you can reference the questionExclaim concept in a SEQUENCE rule to sort by the number of fact matches in the interface. Here is the rule in the tempFact concept:

```
SEQUENCE:(ques):_ques{questionExclaim}
```

The results are represented in Table 10.1.

Table 10.1. Visual Text Analytics Concepts Node Matches from a SEQUENCE Rule

Text Excerpt	Fact Matches
I would like to bring to your attention a problem I encountered with your airline's experience. We were held on the tarmac for over 6 hours the first 4 hours were without food or drink!!! We were only ever updated with more promise to be updated at a later time. What were we to think??? After Sept 11th most of us were thinking were we being hijacked? What was wrong. No one would tell us anything!!! We were not allowed to leave the aircraft hours would pass and we would not see or hear anything from a flight attendant. At one point one of the flight attendants yelled at me and a few others stating that she was about to lose it! That she couldn't take anymore. That is her job to comfort us when we are in a panic...This now 5 hours of sitting aboard the aircraft with only having been fed a small portion of food. Most of us had been at the airport since 11:00 am. We did not get any food until 6:30 PM. (…)	93 (11 in the excerpt)
(…) THESE TICKETS I THOUGHT???—!!!!!!!!!!) WERE RETURNED/FOR REFUND/CREDIT BY MY SISTER. (…)	59 (13 in the excerpt)
I lost it!!!!!! I totally lost it!!!! I had been told (…)	59 (10 in the excerpt)
I know yours is a frequently criticized industry, so it gives me great pleasure to send this compliment about your airline's on-time performance. I hope you'll let everyone involved in this great experience know that their work is greatly appreciated. I just wanted to say of the excellent service XYZ Airlines has performed in my last trip. They left on time and handle me like if I was in first class. It has been a while since I have travel on any plan because of the service experience I have had. XYZ has changed my mind about traveling. I would take XYZ anytime I have to fly again. Thank you XYZ for changing my way of thinking on flying Perhaps it would help you to know a little bit about me. I've flown five times or less in the past 12 months, mostly for pleasure. I usually buy a discount coach ticket. I am a true fan of your company, and this reinforces my feelings about it. You can certainly count on my business in the future, and I have every intention of urging others to fly with you. Thanks again for everything. Keep up the good work!	1

The first document has the most markers in the document collection: a total of 93 matches in about 9 paragraphs. The final document has the fewest matches (only one exclamation point at the end) and shows that the theory of using these markers as cues to strong sentiment is accurate for these reviews.

Of the 7,589-document collection, 4,370 of the reviews matched the rule. Twenty-seven had between 30 and 93 matches. Twenty-four had between 20 and 29 matches. One hundred eighty-one documents had at least ten matches, and the rest had fewer than 10 matches. One lesson here is that punctuation alone may be enough to identify customers who need more urgent attention or may be a good marker when combined with other characteristics, depending on the types of documents you are processing.

Now that you know this information, you can build it into the model. Instead of using the REGEX rule, which was used for exploration above, you can use two CLASSIFIER rules to do the work of identifying the punctuation:

```
CLASSIFIER:?
CLASSIFIER:!
```

These rules are preferred from a maintenance and a performance efficiency perspective. Replace the REGEX rule in the questionExclaim concept with these two rules for best performance.

10.5. Advanced Use: Identification of Tokens for Splitting in Post-processing

You cannot directly split tokens in LITI. However, you can use a REGEX rule to identify the tokens you are interested in splitting, and then post-process your data column of matches to get the subpart you are interested in. This process is demonstrated below.

Suppose you need the age of patients that have been in a particular clinical study, but some ages are missing in the original data. You have doctors' notes that sometimes mention the patient's age, and you want to fill in missing ages. Sometimes the approach is easy and entails writing a C_CONCEPT rule:

```
C_CONCEPT: born on _c{nlpDate}
```

You simply extract the data from a sentence that indicates a birth date. However, other times the data contains references to age in a form like the following:

> The patient is a 34-year-old male . . .

Now the digits are buried inside the hyphenated token "34-year-old" and you need a way to extract them for further analysis. Here is the REGEX rule to start with:

```
REGEX:\d{1,3}-(?:day|week|month|year)-old
```

This rule will find ages from 1 to 3 digits on the front of a hyphenated string that includes a reference to the days/months/years of the age inside a grouping set of parentheses. The parentheses, the question mark, the colon, and the hyphen are all special characters, along with the single bar that separates all the options. So it matches and extracts all the following tokens:

- 55-year-old
- 15-week-old
- 1-year-old
- 5-day-old
- 11-month-old
- 101-year-old

It does not match the following, although you could extend your rule to do so:

- 5-yr-old
- 10wk-old
- 17d old

The extracted matches include the full tokens, so if you want to just use the numbers, then you will need to use post-processing code like the following SAS code to identify them:

```
/*This code puts data in the work directory; use a libname statement if
you want to use a different location*/
data mydata;
 input age $ 1-12;

datalines;
55-year-old
15-week-old
1-year-old
5-day-old
11-month-old
101-year-old
;
run;

proc contents data=mydata; run;
proc print data=mydata; run;

/*This code analyzes the data you put into the age variable above and
moves it to previous_age*/
/*The new data you create is just the number and is placed into the age
variable*/
data newdata(drop=text);
  length text $ 12 nage 8.;
  set mydata;
  text = PRXCHANGE("s/(\d{1,3})-(day|week|month|year)-old/$1/o",1,age);
  nage = put(text, 12.);
  previous_age = age;
  drop age;
  rename nage=age;
run;

proc contents data=newdata; run;
proc print data=newdata; run;
```

This code works on the column in your data where you have put the matches listed above and will convert them to keep just the number portion of the match. In this way, your data will be transformed from the items in the right column of Figure 10.3 below (previous_age) to that of the middle column (age).

Figure 10.3. Post-processing for Splitting Tokens and Extracting Numbers

Obs	Age	Previous_age
1	55	55-year-old
2	15	15-week-old
3	1	1-year-old
4	5	5-day-old
5	11	11-month-old
6	101	101-year-old

But wait! You have lost important information about the unit of measurement: years, months, days, or weeks. So patient 2 will be recorded as being "15 years old" rather than "15 weeks old." You could modify the SAS code above to pull out two pieces of information to accomplish the following result shown in Figure 10.4.

Figure 10.4. Post-processing for Splitting Tokens and Extracting Numbers and Unit of Measure of Time

Number	Unit	Match
55	year	55-year-old
15	week	15-week-old
1	year	1-year-old
5	day	5-day-old
11	month	11-month-old
101	year	101-year-old

However, in the next section, an alternative, more useful approach will be examined: application of the information field in REGEX rules.

10.6. Advanced Use: Information Field

Another way that REGEX rules are similar to CLASSIFIER rules is that both can have an information field, which can store special information associated with the match. The information field can be used by SAS Text Analytics products such as SAS Enterprise Content Categorization as a means for specifying the lemma (parent or canonical form) of the match. The lemma acts as an umbrella term under which various forms of the same matched term are aggregated in the Terms list after parsing. You can read more about lemmas in chapter 1.

However, in some SAS Text Analytics products, the information field is not displayed or used and in others, this information is lost if the concept containing the REGEX rule is referenced by another concept. Therefore, you should use this option with caution and always consult the documentation for your specific product and version before using this feature.

The way to signal use of the information field in a REGEX rule is through the use of "INFO" between commas, like so:

```
REGEX:rule-definition,INFO,information field
```

The information works just like a text field, and any characters may be entered there, including spaces. So, returning to the example in the previous section, you have a rule like this to find mentions of ages within a single token:

```
REGEX:\d{1,3}-(?:day|week|month|year)-old
```

This rule finds the mentions of various types of ages in the doctors' notes for a patient and can help to fill in missing ages for the patient's record. Once the information is extracted, SAS code can pull out the relevant information, including the digits representing the value and the measurement units like "day" or "year." Another way to handle the latter is to break the rule into four rules and use the information field to hold the unit of measurement, like so:

```
REGEX:\d{1,3}-year-old,INFO,year
REGEX:\d{1,3}-month-old,INFO,month
REGEX:\d{1,3}-week-old,INFO,week
REGEX:\d{1,3}-day-old,INFO,day
```

These rules will extract the match in Figure 10.5 when data like "11-month-old" is found in the text.

Figure 10.5. SAS Enterprise Content Categorization Displays an INFO Value

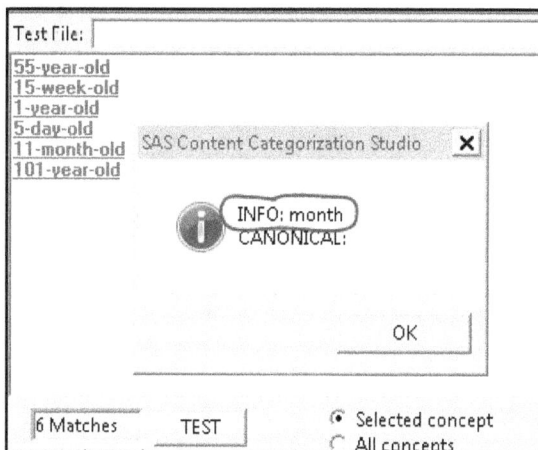

Users can request the addition of this feature in products that do not yet support it.

10.7. Troubleshooting REGEX

If you discover that a particular REGEX rule is not matching as you expected or your model is running very slowly, potential causes for these effects could be the following:

- Comments
- Tokens
- Limited syntax
- Efficiency
- Precision
- Case variation
- Syntax errors

You cannot use comments inside this rule type, so if you want to comment a line that contains a REGEX rule, you must place it before the rule type declaration. This example shows a REGEX rule that has been turned off by the placement of a comment mark in this fashion:

```
#REGEX:[My][Rr][Uu][Ll][Ee]
```

When you are writing the rules themselves, there are a few errors that are common and should be avoided. One is trying to match less than a full token. If you are knowledgeable about PERL regular expression syntax, then you should envision "\b" on each end of your rules, because that is how each of your rules is interpreted by the system—but you do not need to add them explicitly.

Keep in mind that it is possible for a token to contain punctuation like hyphens or apostrophes or spaces. If you have a word you are trying to match and cannot seem to make your rule work, try looking it up in the terms list to see if there are variants that might account for this problem. For example, trying to match the word "once" even when it appears in URLs, multiwords, hashtags, or hyphenated words, you may find that a regular CLASSIFIER rule is not working as you expect it to. It may not be obvious at first, but if you look up "once" in the terms list, you may see tokens like those in Figure 10.6.

Figure 10.6. Tokens that Include the Term "Once"

Terms
once
once again
once more
once-over
onceuponatime
all-at-once
all at once

Consider the following sentence:

> Thousands of commuters once again decided to stay at home rather than try to beat the rail strike.

With a CLASSIFIER rule for the string "once" and a term identified as "once again," the rule will not produce a match because "once again" is processed as a single token.

You have two choices: You can add another CLASSIFIER rule that finds "once again," or you can write a REGEX rule to capture every token containing "once." The former strategy is preferred from an efficiency perspective, but you may need the alternative strategy in certain cases, so you would create the REGEX rule here:

```
REGEX:[ \w]*once[ \w]*
```

Because this rule is not very efficient, it will try to match every token and only fail when the string "once" is not found inside. It will also match words like "sconce." You may decide to use this rule while building and then add all the correct terms you find as other rule types like the following example. Remember to remove the REGEX rule from your model at the end of your exploration so you regain efficiency.

```
CLASSIFIER:once
CLASSIFIER:once-over
CLASSIFIER:once again
CLASSIFIER:once more
CLASSIFIER:all-at-once
CLASSIFIER:all at once
CLASSIFIER:onceuponatime
```

A second error that is common when one is writing REGEX rules is trying to use PERL regular expression features that do not exist in the subset of options supported by the rule. Check to see that the only parentheses you have in rules are either escaped literals or the alternation/grouping kind as used in the following rule that finds abbreviations for 3 months followed by one or two digits with no intervening characters:

```
REGEX:(?:apr|may|jan)\d\d?
```

A third error is to write inefficient rules that will slow the application of your model. If possible, put the most specific things at the front of your rule. Also, avoid using "*" and "+" operators whenever possible. Avoid using a period to stand for any character, when you could use "\d" or "\w" instead.

A fourth error type is to use syntax in your rules that is less precise than needed so your rule is "simpler." For example, using "\s" when you intend to match only one or two spaces is not advised, because "\s" will match across tabs and newlines, as well. Effective testing practices should help to show these types of errors. It is recommended that you collect test data that has some of the characteristics of your target matches but is data you do not expect to match with your rule. Test this data, as well as data you do expect to match, to check that your rule is well behaved.

A fifth error type is to forget case variations in your rules. Uppercase and lowercase letters may need to be represented in your rules explicitly. Some SAS products and versions will leverage the project-level setting for case sensitivity and apply it to REGEX rules, and some will ignore that setting for the REGEX rule type only. Notice the rule above, where the first letter of each word is allowed in both uppercase and lowercase forms. If you have all-caps text in your data sources, then you will need to add more variants to your rules. One example in the three key forms in many text types are "year," "Year," and "YEAR."

Keep in mind when working with REGEX rules that they are very precise instruments that can easily go awry. Test often and thoroughly. Also, remember that you cannot ever reference a concept within a REGEX rule; in this sense they are just like CLASSIFIER rules. The validation code will not catch this type of error.

Additionally, the REGEX rule is like the CLASSIFIER rule in that it allows use of an information field inside the rule. You must signal your use of this field by placing these characters in a row: comma, INFO, comma. Then you can replace INFO with any text you want to record in the information field. This convention is different from a CLASSIFIER rule, where you signal the use of an information field by only using one comma.

10.8. Best Practices for Using REGEX

When using REGEX rules, the first tip is to make sure that there is no other rule type that will meet the need. REGEX rules are generally more expensive in terms of processing load and will therefore make your model run more slowly if overused. If it is possible to write CLASSIFIER rules or some other rule type, even if you need to write several such rules to replace one REGEX, it will lead to a more efficient model. Use special tags like ":sep," ":digit," ":time," and ":date" whenever possible to avoid writing a REGEX for such items. Refer to chapter 1 for explanations of these special tags. Use REGEX rules only for those patterns that are impossible to encode in other rule types. For example, during corpus exploration, rather than writing a REGEX rule to return every token in your corpus, use a CONCEPT rule with the _w modifier.

> **Tip**: Because REGEX rules are very computationally expensive, use them only when there is no other rule type or combination of rule types that can meet your needs.

Remember to put a comment above every REGEX rule you write, while you are working on it. You may think you will remember what you were trying to do, but chances are good that you will forget or that someone else may need to look at your rules at some point in the future. Putting in a good comment will save you time in the long run. Also, make sure that, as you update rules, you update the associated comments as well.

> **Alert**! Some products allow the case sensitivity setting for the project to impact the matches in REGEX rules. Not being able to adjust this project setting will impede your ability to write effective REGEX rules. Test to be sure before writing a lot of REGEX rules.

Finally, when testing your REGEX rules, you can verify that you have not written the rules too broadly or too narrowly. First, check that they are not too narrow by collecting as many types of variants that you want to match as possible. It is also useful if you can collect examples that look similar to those you want to match but are not targeted by your rule. Run your rule over your collected examples to ensure that the matches that are found are the ones you thought your rule would return. Next, to check for rules that are too broad, run the rule over a data set that is at least as varied as the real data set you plan to apply your model to. Review the matches in that sample data to ensure that all the matches are valid. If some are not valid, then look for patterns or contexts that you could add to your rule to constrain it further.

10.9. Summary of REGEX

Requirements for a REGEX include the following:

- A rule type declaration in all caps followed by a colon
- Literal and special characters for the rule definition
- Use of "\" to transform any special character to a literal character, where needed

Allowed options for the rule type include the following:

- Comments using # modifier (at the beginning of the line only; before the rule type)
- Grouping parentheses only, signaled by the characters "?:" right inside the left parenthesis
- Use of the information field, signaled by "comma + INFO + comma"

Chapter 11: Best Practices for Custom Concepts

11.1. Introduction to Boolean and Proximity Operators

In chapters 7 and 8, it was mentioned that the CONCEPT_RULE and PREDICATE_RULE rule types can contain Boolean operators, such as AND, OR, and NOT, and distance operators, such as SENT_n, DIST_n and ORDDIST_n. Many operators are available in LITI, and because they can be used in isolation as well as together, it can be difficult to know which operator or operators to choose for a particular purpose. Likewise, it can be challenging to know which rule type is best for a particular situation. After reading this chapter, you will be able to do the following tasks:

- Rely on best practices when choosing operators in isolation and in combination
- Choose the most appropriate rule type for your project on the basis of computational cost and performance factors

11.2. Best Practices for Using Operators

Each *operator* is a logical command over a set of arguments. The command controls the requirements for a match to be found in text data. In other words, the operator over a set of arguments defines how many and in what relationships the arguments may occur to make the rule "true" in the data. The operators include both the standard Boolean operators AND, OR, and NOT, as well as additional proximity operators that add constraints about the context the arguments must appear in.

Operators are used in CONCEPT_RULE, PREDICATE_RULE, and REMOVE_ITEM rule types. In the first two rule types, they may be used in almost infinite combinations to control the conditions for a match, because all the operators except ALIGNED allow other operators to be arguments in addition to any other elements that may appear in the rule type. In other words, an operator may govern another operator in those two rule types.

> **Remember**: Arguments are always one or more elements between double quotation marks. Elements may also have modifiers such as @ or an extraction label like _c{}.

11.2.1. Behavior of Groupings of Single Operators

The operators have a basic behavior that spans sets of operators, and this behavior is useful to know for choosing the right operator for your purposes. This common behavior of operators is summarized in Table 11.1 and described in more detail in the next sections.

Table 11.1. Operator Groupings

Description	Operators
Any argument found in the text triggers a match; if one has _c{} modifier or a fact label, then all must.	OR
All arguments are required to be found in the text to trigger a match; arguments' order and distance constraints apply as well. When used, the *n* is replaced by a digit.	AND DIST_n ORD ORDDIST_n
All arguments are required to be found in the text to trigger a match; distance from the start or end of a sentence constrains the match. When used, the *n* is replaced by a digit.	SENTEND_n SENTSTART_n
All arguments are required to be found in the text to trigger a match; document structure criteria constrain the match as well. When used, the *n* is replaced by a digit.	SENT SENT_n PARA
These special operators require a specific context to work.	ALIGNED ▶ allowed only in REMOVE_ITEM rule type UNLESS ▶ second argument should be headed by one of the following operators: AND, SENT, DIST_n, ORD, ORDDIST_n NOT ▶ must be an argument of AND; cannot stand alone

The OR Operator

First, the OR operator requires only one argument, but is generally used to govern a list of items. At least one of the arguments in the list must match to satisfy the requirements of the OR. If there is only one argument under an OR, then there is probably a simpler way to write the rule, such as using a CLASSIFIER or CONCEPT rule type. Usually an OR is applied in combination with other operators in the same rule. Here is a simple rule with only an OR operator as an example:

```
CONCEPT_RULE:(OR, "_c{love}", "_c{joy}", "_c{peace}")
```

The OR governs three arguments, each in double quotation marks. If at least one of the three words is present in data, then the requirements of the OR operator are satisfied, and because it is the only operator in the rule, the rule matches. In other words, OR is "true," and the rule is therefore also "true." This same result could also be achieved with three CLASSIFIER rules, and would be easier to read and maintain:

```
CLASSIFIER:love
CLASSIFIER:joy
CLASSIFIER:peace
```

The reason that the _c{} extraction label is required in each argument of an OR operator in a CONCEPT_RULE, if it appears in any of them, is that only one of the arguments has to match to satisfy the conditions, and the others are not required. For example, if the _c{} extraction label was not present on the argument "joy," then if the text matched that argument, there would be no return command in the part of the rule that matches, and no match would be returned—it would be as if the rule did not match. This type of error is difficult to catch during syntax validation because of potentially embedded operators, so the logic in the rule must be manually verified.

Operators Related to AND

The second group of operators in Table 11.1 governs two or more arguments and requires all to match in order to satisfy the operator requirements. The AND operator works this way: All arguments are required to match to make AND "true." The scope of AND is the entire document, so arguments may appear anywhere in the document and in any order. The other arguments in this group work like the AND operator but have a second test that makes each of them different from the others.

First, the DIST_n operator works like AND, except it specifies a restricted scope. All the arguments of DIST_n must match within a distance of *n* tokens, where *n* is a digit. Next, the ORD operator works just like AND, except it requires that the arguments appear in the document in the same order that they appear in the rule; the scope is still the entire document. Finally, the ORDDIST_n operator both limits the scope to *n* tokens, and requires that the arguments appear in the same order in both the rule and the document text.

The next example uses data from a city government's records of 311 service requests that include a text field describing the resolution of each citizen request (available online at https://data.cityofnewyork.us/dataset/311-Service-Requests-From-2015/57g5-etyj). Imagine that you are doing an audit of the resolution of the complaints for a period of time, and you want to specifically look at any complaint that would have been resolved without a specific action being taken to fix or address the issue. You can then compare the results of your search with the department responsible for each request. Two rules using the operators discussed above are provided below in a concept named, for example, noAction, showing the resolution of government action to 311 service requests:

```
CONCEPT_RULE:(ORDDIST_2, "no", (OR, "_c{_w action}", "_c{_w evidence}"))
CONCEPT_RULE:(ORDDIST_2, "not", (OR, "_c{_w violate@}", "_c{_w
necessary}", "_c{_w found}"))
```

Consider the following input documents:

1. The Police Department responded to the complaint and determined that police action was not necessary.
2. The Police Department responded and upon arrival those responsible for the condition were gone.
3. Unfortunately, the behavior that you complained about does not violate any law or rule. As a result, no city agency has the jurisdiction to act on the matter.
4. The Police Department responded to the complaint and with the information available observed no evidence of the violation at that time.

Pause and think: Assuming the rules above, can you predict the matches for the input documents above?

The matches for the noAction concept with the input documents above are in Figure 11.1.

Figure 11.1. Extracted Matches for the noAction Concept

Doc ID	Concept	Matched Text
1	noAction	not necessary
3	noAction	not violate
4	noAction	no evidence

The two rules look for indications that a complaint was resolved without any direct action being taken to correct a given condition or situation. Each requires a relationship that is narrowly defined between a negation word and another marker, which closely follows the negation word, of intention to act. Each of the input documents is a situation in which the government found that it could or should take no action, but the second document does not match either rule. Another rule is needed to capture the finding that "those responsible" were "gone." Note that in order to extract extra context as a part of the extracted match, an extra _w was placed before each of the extracted terms in this rule. Variations on this trick are useful ways to work around optional components in a match when you need a particular one to be there. As you collect examples and analyze patterns, you can continue adding rules to your model until you are satisfied by your testing that you have found a good sample of reports to review more closely.

Note that in the group of operators described in this section, there should be two or more arguments under each operator type. Be cautious: The software will validate and run if the operators are used with only one argument, but that is a logical error. Avoid such errors, because they make your rules more difficult to read and to maintain, as well as troubleshoot. For example, you should avoid rules like the following:

```
ERROR! -> CONCEPT_RULE:(ORD, (AND, "_c{go@}"), (AND, "stay@"))
```

In this rule, the ORD operator has two arguments, which is correct. However, each of the AND operators has only one argument, which contributes nothing to the rule, as if it were not there. The correct way to write this rule is as follows:

```
CONCEPT_RULE:(ORD, "_c{go@}", "stay@")
```

This version looks cleaner and is much easier to understand; there is a match if the terms "go" and "stay" appear in the document in that order, and it returns the match for "go."

Operators Related to Sentence Start and End

The third group of operators in Table 11.1 governs one or more arguments. SENTEND_n and SENTSTART_n each rely on the structure of sentences to bound the distance between arguments. They work much like the DIST_n in that they consider token count and add the criterion of a sentence boundary. SENTEND_n will match one or more arguments that occur within n tokens of the end (last token) of a sentence. Counting backwards from the end of a sentence to the number of tokens specified defines the scope of a possible match; all arguments must then be found within that distance. SENTSTART_n works the same way but starts the count at the beginning (first token) of each sentence.

Here is an example of using the SENTSTART_n operator in a rule. The data consists of reports on restaurant inspection results in a large city (available at https://data.cityofnewyork.us/Health/DOHMH-New-York-City-Restaurant-Inspection-Results/43nn-pn8j). Each record is usually short, but some are a few sentences long. The goal of this rule in the mainTopic concept is to find the best summary in the form of a noun phrase that will be used to categorize each report:

```
CONCEPT_RULE:(SENTSTART_5, "_c{nounPhrase}")
```

This rule looks for a noun phrase within 5 tokens of the beginning of the sentence, because you observed that the first noun phrase in your data usually indicates the main topic of the report. The nounPhrase concept is a custom concept that has rules that handle singular nouns, plural nouns, proper nouns, pronouns, possessive nouns, and adjectival modifiers. Some of these rules are provided for you in the supplementary code that accompanies this book and is available online.

Here are a few records from the data set and the results of running the rule set described above on each input document. The matches are shaded gray:

1. Hot food item not held at or above 140° F.
2. Food contact surface not properly washed, rinsed and sanitized after each use and following any activity when contamination may have occurred.
3. Proper sanitization not provided for utensil ware washing operation.

4. Bulb not shielded or shatterproof, in areas where there is extreme heat, temperature changes, or where accidental contact may occur.

5. Facility not vermin proof. Harborage or conditions conducive to attracting vermin to the premises and/or allowing vermin to exist.

After reviewing the results, you decide that the first noun phrase found will be used as your summary unless it is a single word in length; then it will be used with the second one, if another one is found. You derive your final summaries by postprocessing the matches shown above. Figure 11.2 is the final summary_report, based on running your own postprocessing code with the algorithm to select the first noun phrase or first pair of nouns.

Figure 11.2. Postprocessed Matches for the mainTopic Concept

Doc ID	Concept	Matched Text
1	mainTopic	Hot food item
2	mainTopic	Food contact surface
3	mainTopic	Proper sanitization
4	mainTopic	Bulb
5	mainTopic	Facility vermin

You have successfully extracted the most important noun phrases from the restaurant inspections data set, creating a new, structured data set that can be used for counts and reporting.

Operators Related to Sentence or Paragraph Structure

The fourth group of operators uses the structure of the document to manage scope constraints, overriding the default document-level scope. If governing one argument, that argument is usually another operator. The SENT and PARA operators define the scope of the match as within one sentence or one paragraph respectively. For SENT_n, you can specify the number of sentences that will scope the match—all arguments must appear within the bounds of *n* sentences, where *n* is some digit. These three operators are useful for matching items that are in grammatical, topical, or discourse relationships. They are also useful for helping to constrain matches in longer documents instead of using AND. They frequently govern the operators discussed in the first three groups above in combination.

The goal in the example below is to find mention of health issues near the discussion of senior citizen needs in political speeches. The concept seniorHealth contains the rule below, which uses the PARA operator to look in each paragraph to find sentences that mention health-related topics, such as "healthcare," "healthy," "drug," "drugs," or "medicine," within three sentences of the discussion of senior citizen issues, as defined in the seniorCitizen concept. The PARA operator governs the SENT_n operator, which in turn governs an OR operator.

```
PREDICATE_RULE:(health, senior):(PARA, (SENT_3, (OR,
"_health{healthcare}", "_health{healthy}", "_health{drug@}",
"_health{medicine}"), "_senior{seniorCitizen}"))
```

The concept seniorCitizen includes the following rules relevant to the example:

```
CLASSIFIER:elderly
CONCEPT:senior@
```

Consider the following input documents:

1. 450,000 of our citizens will lose access to healthcare because of the lack of funding for our Medicaid programs and 800,000 meals for the elderly will be eliminated.
2. We increased funding to help Alabama seniors get free prescription drugs. More citizens than ever can get help buying the medicine they need. Now they won't have to choose between eating and taking their prescriptions.
3. Congressional leaders promised help, but they failed to deliver on a prescription drug benefit program. I'm not waiting any longer. During this session, we will create a prescription drug program that will lower the cost of drugs for Alabama seniors.

> **Pause and think**: Assuming the model above, can you predict the matches for the seniorHealth concept and the input documents above?

The matches for the seniorHealth concept and the input documents above are in Figure 11.3.

Figure 11.3. Extracted Matches for the seniorHealth Concept

Doc ID	Concept	Extraction Label	Extracted Match
1	seniorHealth		healthcare because of the lack of funding for our Medicaid programs and 800,000 meals for the elderly
1	seniorHealth	Senior	elderly
1	seniorHealth	Health	healthcare
2	seniorHealth		seniors get free prescription drugs. More citizens than ever can get help buying the medicine
2	seniorHealth	Senior	seniors
2	seniorHealth	Health	medicine
2	seniorHealth		seniors get free prescription drugs
2	seniorHealth	Senior	seniors
2	seniorHealth	Health	drugs
3	seniorHealth		drug benefit program. I'm not waiting any longer. During this session, we will create a prescription drug program that will lower the cost of drugs for Alabama seniors
3	seniorHealth	Senior	seniors
3	seniorHealth	Health	drug
3	seniorHealth		drug program that will lower the cost of drugs for Alabama seniors
3	seniorHealth	Senior	seniors
3	seniorHealth	Health	drug

Doc ID	Concept	Extraction Label	Extracted Match
3	seniorHealth		drugs for Alabama seniors
3	seniorHealth	Senior	seniors
3	seniorHealth	Health	drugs

Note that the unlabeled matched strings for the second and third input documents overlap. If you change the "all matches" algorithm to "longest match," the duplicate matches without a label and the corresponding extracted matches with labels will be removed automatically, resulting in the output in Figure 11.4.

Figure 11.4. Extracted Matches for the seniorHealth Concept

Doc ID	Concept	Extraction Label	Extracted Match
1	seniorHealth		healthcare because of the lack of funding for our Medicaid programs and 800,000 meals for the elderly
1	seniorHealth	senior	elderly
1	seniorHealth	health	healthcare
2	seniorHealth		seniors get free prescription drugs. More citizens than ever can get help buying the medicine
2	seniorHealth	senior	seniors
2	seniorHealth	health	medicine
3	seniorHealth		drug benefit program. I'm not waiting any longer. During this session, we will create a prescription drug program that will lower the cost of drugs for Alabama seniors
3	seniorHealth	senior	seniors
3	seniorHealth	health	drug

For each input document in these results, there is only one set of extracted matches, comprising one match for the "senior" label, one for the "health" label, and the text span between them.

Special Operators

The final set of operators is special, because they are less universal than the ones described above. To work properly, each of these operators requires a special context or structure of a rule.

First, the ALIGNED operator matches two arguments when both arguments match the same text in the document. In other words, you define the two arguments to extract the same exact span of text. For example, suppose that you want to match the string "love," when it is also a noun—the two arguments could be "love" and ":N." Theoretically, these two arguments would satisfy the requirements of the ALIGNED operator if used in a rule.

The second restriction on ALIGNED is that it must be used only in a REMOVE_ITEM rule. If you want this behavior to apply to a single token in CONCEPT_RULE or PREDICATE_RULE rules, then you can use DIST_0 to get two criteria applied to the same token. See the example in section 7.2. The REMOVE_ITEM rule allows two arguments governed by ALIGNED: The first argument must contain a _c{} extraction label on a concept name, specifying what match to remove. For more information and examples of this rule type, see section 9.2.

The next special operator is UNLESS, which governs two arguments, the second of which can be AND, DIST_n, ORD, ORDDIST_n, or SENT. Except for SENT, the remaining operators were all described in the second set in Table 11.1. The UNLESS operator requires that the first argument not be present within the match scope of the second. It is a way of filtering matches and restricting a rule that is capturing false positive matches. For example, you can use the UNLESS operator to eliminate sentences containing negation, as illustrated in section 7.5.

The final operator is NOT, which takes only one argument. It is a basic operator that seems simple at first, but there are some special restrictions that make this operator tricky. First, this operator must be under the AND operator in the hierarchy and, in this case, the AND operator must be at the top of the hierarchy.

> **Alert!** The only operator that can govern a NOT operator is AND. Do not put any other operator above NOT in the hierarchy. The part of the rule containing the NOT operator is applied to the entire document.

If you do not follow this best practice, then the rule may validate, but not work the way you would expect. For example, in the rule below, it is erroneous to put NOT under a SENT operator (two levels up):

```
ERROR! -> CONCEPT_RULE:(SENT, (AND, "drive@", (NOT, "crazy")),
"_c{nlpMeasure")
```

The intention of this rule is to find mentions of driving and some measure amount, like "200 miles," in the same sentence as long as the word "crazy" is not also in the sentence. This approach avoids idioms, such as "drives me crazy," when matching literal driving events and extracting the distance driven. However, because the NOT operator cannot be governed by the SENT operator, what really happens is that the word "crazy" found anywhere in the document will cause the rule to fail to match. This formulation of the rule better matches its behavior:

```
CONCEPT_RULE:(AND, (SENT, "drive@", "_c{nlpMeasure}"), (NOT, "crazy"))
```

This formulation of the rule better illustrates that NOT acts independently of the SENT operator restriction; the preceding rule works the same way, but its form obscures the expected results.

You may ask why this restriction exists on the NOT operator, because operators like SENT and DIST_n are really a type of AND plus scope restrictions, as are all the operators that one may use with UNLESS above. The answer is that additional capability within the LITI syntax would be possible, and if SAS customers request this addition, then it will likely be provided.

11.2.2. SAS Categorization Operators

If you are familiar with SAS categorization models, then you recognize the use and syntax of the CONCEPT_RULE as similar to those rules. The main differences are that there is no rule type declaration—the rule just starts with an open parenthesis. The other difference is that there are no extraction labels because, in categorization, no information is truly extracted. However, this boundary is blurred due to the match string information that may be used as output in categorization.

The syntax of LITI is different from categorization in some unexpected ways, and you might be tempted to use shortcuts from categorization that are not supported by LITI. For example, there is no support for using the following symbols in a rule in LITI:

- * as a wildcard match on beginning or end of a word
- ^ to tie match to beginning of a document
- $ to tie a match the end of the document
- _L to match a literal string
- _C to specify case-sensitivity

The set of operators that you can use in categorization rules includes several that are currently <u>not available in LITI</u> including: NOTIN, NOTINSENT, NOTINPAR, NOTINDIST, START_n, PARPOS_n, PAR, MAXSENT_n, MAXPAR_n, MAXOC_n, MINOC_n, MIN_n, and END_n. Do not attempt to use these operators, because they will only give you a compilation error. If you need any of these operators, consider whether you could combine a concept model and a categorization model together. Concepts can be referenced in categorization models in the same way concepts are referenced in LITI rules, but with a slightly different syntax. If users request implementation of any of these categorization-only operators for LITI rules, then these operators could be added in the future.

> **Alert!** There are differences between the syntax of rules for information extraction and those for categorization. In addition, the set of operators available for information extraction is narrower than the set available for categorization.

11.2.3. Combinations of Operators and Restrictions

Earlier, it was mentioned that the operators may be combined in almost infinite ways to control the characteristics of matches to CONCEPT_RULE and PREDICATE_RULE types of rules. Some exceptions have been described in the previous sections, and next you can learn about some of the most and least useful types of combinations. Note that these are general tips and guidelines, but there are situations in which it may be fine to ignore them. Some combinations will compile, but not work the way that you might expect. This section will clarify those situations.

Rules with multiple layers of embedded operators are evaluated in the system via a bottom-up approach. At each layer, the governed operator passes on true or false information to the governing operator, and that one passes it to its governing operator and so forth through the layers until the entire rule is evaluated. As you are writing custom rules with multiple layers of embedded operators, consider this approach and test to make sure that the results meet your needs.

Tips for Use of OR, NOT, and UNLESS

The first tips are about the use of OR. Do not generally use an OR operator to govern the top level of your rules. If OR is at the top of your rule structure, then you could likely write two rules that would be easier to read and maintain. Remember that if OR is the only operator in your rule, then you should be using a different rule type. The perfectly correct example below could be rewritten to four CLASSIFIER rules instead, with much less complicated syntax:

```
Avoid this! -> CONCEPT_RULE:(OR, (OR, "_c{love}", "_c{kindness}"), (OR,
"_c{joy}", "_c{happiness}"))
```

The approach with CLASSIFIER rules follows:

```
CLASSIFIER:love
CLASSIFIER:kindness
CLASSIFIER:joy
CLASSIFIER:happiness
```

Keep in mind the restrictions on use of NOT and UNLESS. When using NOT, be sure to connect it to a top-level AND operator, and do not artificially embed it under other scope-restricting operators. Keep the NOT sections of your rule where you can use the rule itself to remind you that NOT cannot be limited to less than document scope.

Use UNLESS carefully and be mindful of its restrictions; see section 7.5 for details. At the time of this writing, it is the newest and potentially the most brittle of all the operators, so test such rules carefully at every stage of your project if you use them.

Basic Combinations and Pitfalls

One good basic guideline is that the items in the second and third groups of Table 11.1 usefully govern each other and OR. The operators in these groups include AND, DIST_n, ORD, ORDDIST_n, SENTEND_n, and SENTSTART_n. However, there is a caveat to this guideline, which is discussed next.

A useful situation where this guideline works well is when an AND operator governs an ORD and a DIST_n, each of which has arguments of its own. Here is an example:

```
CONCEPT_RULE:(AND, (ORD, "arg1", "arg2"), (DIST_n, "arg3", "_c{arg4}"))
```

This rule reads that, if arg1 and arg2 are in that order in the document AND arg3 and arg4 are within *n* tokens of each other in the document, then the rule will match and extract arg4. It does not matter whether the matches for the ORD and the DIST_n operators overlap, because the AND operator has no restrictions other than both pairs of arguments appearing in the document scope.

However, there are some combinations that may not work the way you would expect. One example involves ORD and ORDDIST_n. It is redundant for ORD to govern ORDDIST, because the ordering command exists for the arguments of ORD and applies to the arguments of any operators that it governs. Consider each of the following two rules. The first one can be interpreted this way: Find "good" within five tokens preceding "job," both of which should precede "not" within seven tokens preceding "quit." The second one could be interpreted this way: Find "good" within five tokens of "job," both of which should precede "not" within seven tokens of "quit."

```
CONCEPT_RULE:(ORD, (ORDDIST_5, "good", "_c{job}"), (ORDDIST_7, "not",
"quit"))
CONCEPT_RULE:(ORD, (DIST_5, "good", "_c{job}"), (DIST_7, "not", "quit"))
```

For distinguishing between matches, the first rule is in a concept named jobEval1, and the second is in jobEval2. Consider the following input documents:

1. I have a good job, so I will not quit.
2. I have a good job, and if I quit, I will not be happy.

> **Pause and think**: Can you predict the matches for jobEval1 and jobEval2 with the input documents above?

Both jobEval1 and jobEval2 extract the same match, as seen in Figure 11.5.

Figure 11.5. Comparison of Extracted Matches for the jobEval1 and jobEval2 Concepts

Doc ID	Concept	Match Text
1	jobEval1	job
1	jobEval2	job

Although the ordering is not explicit in the "("DIST_7, "not", "quit")" part of the rule in the jobEval2 concept, there is no match for the second document because ORD applies to the arguments of the DIST_7 operator that it governs.

Just as the ORD operator's governing ORDDIST is redundant, so is ORDDIST's governing ORD. Therefore, the following two rules in the jobEval concept produce the same matches with the two input documents above as the previous two rules:

```
CONCEPT_RULE:(ORDDIST_10, (ORD, "good", "_c{job}"), (ORD, "not",
"quit"))
CONCEPT_RULE:(ORDDIST_10, (AND, "good", "_c{job}"), (AND, "not",
"quit"))
```

In fact, the first rule is an error, because its formulation gives the impression that, if you find the pairs of words under the ORD operators in the right order, then the pairs could even overlap and still the rule would match. However, that is not the case. If you run the first rule above on the following two documents, the shaded match is the only one extracted:

1. Good, you did not quit your job.

2. Good job, you did not quit.

To go even further, the second rule above also contains redundant operators, which is an additional error. The rule will behave the same way if you write it without the AND operators, so the right way to write this rule is to remove the redundant operators completely, as in the following rule:

```
CONCEPT_RULE:(ORDDIST_10, "good", "_c{job}", "not", "quit")
```

This rule is also much easier to read and to maintain.

Semantic Hierarchy of Operators

All the information presented so far points to a semantic hierarchy between these operators. When you understand the operators and their hierarchy, you can write better rules.

Remember that ORD is like AND, but with an added ordering constraint. You can interpret that to mean that ORD means [and] + [order], where each of the items in the square brackets is a part of the meaning of the ORD operator. The square brackets are used in the rest of this section to denote a component of meaning or characteristic of each operator. This approach means that the most useful rule of operator combination will be a heuristic one, as described in this tip:

Tip: Use operators that are governed by other operators where the governing operator does not already imply the same characteristics as the governed one. In other words, the lower-level operator should add elements of meaning or constraints in order to be useful.

The exception to this rule is where the two related operators share the [distance] constraint. In that case, the higher operator should have the same or larger digit on the distance operator.

Putting this tip into practice implies certain recommendations for the first three groups of operators from Table 11.1. Each operator has specific meaning components. Table 11.2 shows the list of operators each can effectively govern.

Table 11.2. Operator Governance for OR, AND, ORD, DIST_n, and SENTEND_n, SENTSTART_n, and ORDDIST_n

Operators	What the Operators Can Govern
[or]	OR ▶ any but OR (unless using groupings for enhanced readability or maintenance)
[and]	AND ▶ any but AND
[and] + [order]	ORD ▶ any but AND, ORD, ORDDIST_n
[and] + [distance]	DIST_n ▶ any but AND
[and] + [distance]	SENTEND_n ▶ any but AND
[and] + [distance]	SENTSTART_n ▶ any but AND
[and] + [order] + [distance]	ORDDIST_n ▶ any but ORD, AND

Table 11.2 shows that OR can govern any of the other operators, but keep in mind the caveat about using it at the top of your rule structure. If you put multiple OR operators in a hierarchical relationship with each other, then it will work to organize arguments into sets,

but will not make the rule behave differently. For example, suppose you want to capture specific drink types and mention of sugar content with the following rule:

```
PREDICATE_RULE:(drink, sugar):(DIST_8, "_sugar{nlpMeasure}", (OR, (OR,
"_drink{grape juice}", "_drink{apple juice}", "_drink{orange juice}"),
(OR, "_drink{vodka}", "_drink{beer}", "_drink{wine}")))
```

You can see two OR lists under OR that is the second argument of DIST_8. This OR does all the work of creating a list of drink types; The lower-level OR operators do nothing other than allow the rule builder to group types of drinks together. A better place to do this type of organization is in a separate concept for drinks, but this approach may be useful during the exploration phase of rule-building.

The meaning of AND, which is by default the same as [document scope], is included in all the other operators' constraint set, and all the other operators add their own constraints. Therefore, putting an AND operator under any of the others is redundant, as is putting an [order] operator under another [order] operator.

As the caveat implies, the [distance] operators work differently, because distance is always defined by a number. It is possible and logical to put a [distance] operator under another [distance] operator, assuming that the lower-level operators are more constrained by their number than the governing operator. This rule illustrates that approach:

```
CONCEPT_RULE:(DIST_18, (DIST_5, "good", "_c{job}"), (DIST_5, "not",
"quit"))
```

Each of the items that are most closely related are constrained to within 5 tokens of each other; however, the entire rule can match across a total of 18 tokens. Assuming the four elements do not overlap (for example, "not" appearing between "good" and "job"), then the top-level operator adds 8 more tokens that can appear between the two subordinate matches. If that number were 10, then one would understand that it is not intended that there be intervening tokens between the matches or that the matches should overlap one another. An even smaller number like 8 would constrain the matches even further, never allowing both DIST_5 operators to reach their full distance at the same time in a given match scenario. If the upper-level operator goes as low as 5, then the lower operators become redundant and should be removed.

DIST_n and ORDDIST_n operators can also be used together, with the same caveat in mind, plus the basic rule that says [order] will constrain all the arguments if ORDDIST_n is used as a top operator, but only its own arguments if it is used under a DIST_n operator. So, the following rules produce different matches:

```
CONCEPT_RULE:(DIST_18, (ORDDIST_5, "good", "_c{job}"), (DIST_5, "not",
"quit"))
CONCEPT_RULE:(ORDDIST_18, (DIST_5, "good", "_c{job}"), (DIST_5, "not",
"quit"))
```

For the purpose of distinguishing between matches, the first rule is in a concept named jobEval1, and the second is in jobEval2. Consider the following input documents:

1. She does not have a good job, so she will quit.
2. He has a good job, but he will still quit, though not right away.

Pause and think: Can you tell which of the above rules match the input documents?

The extracted match is represented in Figure 11.6.

Figure 11.6. Extracted Match for the jobEval1 Concept

Doc ID	Concept	Match Text
2	jobEval1	job

The first rule above matches the second input document, because there is no operator that requires that "not" and "quit" be in that order. In the first input document, "not" and "quit" are just too far apart to match, because both rules require that they be no more than 5 tokens apart.

The second rule does not match either of the documents. It cannot match the first document because DIST_5 is too small of a distance to capture "not" and "quit" in this sentence. It also cannot match the second document because "quit" comes before "not" and the rule requires the reverse ordering due to ORDDIST_18, which governs all operators.

Sentence Start and End Combinations

The two operators, SENTEND and SENTSTART, are a little more complicated when used together. If you want the match to be on the same token, then you can construct rules like the following, encapsulating one of the operators within the other:

```
CONCEPT_RULE:(SENTSTART_10, (SENTEND_10, "_c{job}"))
CONCEPT_RULE:(SENTEND_10, (SENTSTART_10, "_c{job}"))
```

Either operator can be first and you will see the same match pattern, so both rules above will match the second sentence below, but not the first. Even though in the second sentence, the word "job" appears within 10 tokens of the start of the sentence and again within 10 tokens of the end of the sentence, the rule specifies that the token match be on one item in the sentence, not on two separate identical items, because one operator governs the other in each rule. The input documents are as follows:

1. He has a good job, but he will still quit, though not until he finds another job.
2. I have a good job, so I will not quit.

If you want to match the first document, then use the AND operator in your rule to put each of the other operators on the same level, as in this example:

```
CONCEPT_RULE:(AND, (SENTSTART_10, "job"), (SENTEND_10, "_c{job}"))
```

Assuming the rule above is in a concept named jobEval, the matches are shown in Figure 11.6.

Figure 11.6. Extracted Matches for the jobEval Concept

Doc ID	Concept	Match Text
1	jobEval	job
2	jobEval	job

Note that only the second occurrence of the string "job" in the first sentence is returned as a match.

Scope Override Operators

Turning to the fourth set of operators, SENT, SENT_n, and PARA as shown in Table 11.3, you see that they all have in common that they override the default scope constraint of AND and limit the scope of the match. Because of this, they are not usually used to govern the AND operator. They are often used to constrain the other groups of operators discussed earlier in this chapter. Also, they have another constraint of interacting with each other that is similar to the [distance] operators above. In general, the [scope] operator at the higher level should specify a larger scope. SENT is always smaller than SENT_n and PARA and should not govern them. PARA and SENT_n may each have larger scope than the other, depending on the value of *n* and type of documents, so you must decide which should govern the other. Usually, PARA is considered to have greater scope than SENT_n unless *n* is larger than 6.

Table 11.3. Operator Governance for AND

Operators	What the Operators Can Govern
[and] + [scope]	SENT -> any but AND, SENT_n, or PARA
[and] + [scope] + [distance]	SENT_n -> any but AND or if n < 6 also PARA
[and] + [scope]	PARA -> any but AND or SENT_n where n > 6

Some examples of using the [scope] operators with the other operators include the grammatical and topical strategies described in this section and the advanced use sections for CONCEPT_RULE and PREDICATE_RULE.

Use SENT to constrain matches to within a sentence, while using ORD or ORDIST to specify the order of items. This approach can be used to explore the grammatical relationships, like the one between subjects and verbs, once you have defined some basic concepts for the head noun of a phrase and an active verb using part-of-speech tags:

```
PREDICATE_RULE:(subj, verb):(SENT, (ORDDIST_3, (OR, "_subj{headNoun}",
"_subj{:Pro}"),  "_verb{activeVerb}"))
```

This rule requires that, within the scope of a sentence, a subject head noun or pronoun appear in the text within three tokens and be ordered before an active verb. You can move elements around and focus on passive verbs as well:

```
PREDICATE_RULE:(subj, verb):(SENT, (ORDDIST_5, "_verb{passiveVerb}",
(DIST_2, "by",  (OR, "_subj{headNoun}", "_subj{:Pro}"))))
```

You can read this rule as follows: Within the scope of a sentence, match a passive verb that precedes (within the span of five tokens) the word "by" which itself is within two tokens of either a head noun or a pronoun. The passive verb is returned as a match for the label "verb," and the head noun or pronoun match is returned for the label "subj." This type of rule will become much more effective when a new operator called CLAUS_n is released. This operator is on the product roadmap for SAS Visual Text Analytics. The use of CLAUS_0 restricts the scope of a match to within any single main clause in a sentence. The use of CLAUS_1 restricts the scope of a match to within any single clause, either main or subordinate, in a sentence. This type of grammatical scope will make rules like the one above or rules for negation much easier to write and test.

SENT_n is useful for when you are looking for a relationship, but suspect that there is a high potential for use of anaphora (pronouns and general nouns used in place of more specific nouns) that could obscure the relationships you are looking for. In this rule, you are looking beyond single-sentence matches to find a birth location for an individual:

```
PREDICATE_RULE:(per, loc):(SENT_4, (ORD, "_per{nlpPerson}", (OR, "she",
"he"), "born", "in _loc{nlpPlace}"))
```

This rule says that you will look in a scope of four sentences for a Person predefined concept match first, then either "she" or "he," then the word "born," and then a combination of the word "in" with a Location predefined concept match. The matches to the labels "per" and "loc" represent the fact that the extracted match for person was born in the extracted match for location. PARA may be used in some products to identify the first head noun in a paragraph, which may be a good indicator of the topic of that paragraph, depending on how your data is structured.

```
CONCEPT_RULE:(PARA, (SENTSTART_5, "_c{headNoun}"))
```

This rule will find the first head noun from each of the sentences in the paragraph, but you can filter the results in postprocessing by selecting the matches with the lowest offset values to carry forward into your analysis. What about governing [scope] operators with the other operators described above? You can combine them in some cases. For example, if you want to match two items within a sentence and you want one of the matches to come before the other, then the following rule will work to some extent:

```
CONCEPT_RULE:(ORD, (SENT, "bank", "_c{fee@}"), (SENT, "close@",
"account@"))
```

This rule will find the two items governed by the first SENT operator within the same sentence and then will find the other two items governed by the second SENT operator. The matches for the first pair must come before the matches of the second pair, because of the ORD operator; however, the matches could appear in the same sentence or different sentences at the beginning and end of the document, because ORD has document-level scope.

If you want to constrain the distance of the two matches, then you might try to use ORDDIST or DIST operators instead of ORD. The rule might look like the following with a large value of *n* to try to allow for some sentence variation:

```
CONCEPT_RULE:(DIST_50, (SENT, "bank", "_c{fee@}"), (SENT, "close@",
"account@"))
```

The discussion of bank fees and closing the account can appear within a scope of 50 tokens in either order. Even though the individual arguments produce matches (shaded gray below), the input document would not match this rule, because the shaded relevant element pairs are just too far apart.

Consider the following input document, modeled after public data from the U.S. Consumer Financial Protection Bureau (https://www.consumerfinance.gov/data-research/consumer-complaints):

> A month ago I commented that closing my account at Bank Y was really easy. A week or two later, I found all this mail from Bank Y—overdraft notices for my checking account, which was supposedly closed. The notices are for two debit card transactions and two auto-pay electronic checks. Instead of the payments being rejected by my bank, like you would expect, all four were paid by Bank Y, which then added an overdraft fee of $34 to each one, meaning $136 in overdraft fees.

A better approach might be to use PARA or SENT_6 instead of the DIST operator. You can also provide a higher value of *n* for the SENT_n operator. These operators give you more control over the number of sentences used to relate the issue of closed accounts to bank fees. This rule would match the text above, providing more control over matches than either ORD or DIST:

```
CONCEPT_RULE:(SENT_6, (SENT, "bank", "_c{fee@}"), (SENT, "close@",
"account@"))
```

Keep in mind, however, that this rule will also allow the matches to all be in the same sentence. To try to specify that they must be at least in two separate sentences, you will need to add ORD and some marker of the sentence division like the following. Note that in this version of the rule, the ordering constraint also applies to each of the arguments of the SENT operators, so you may need more variations of the rule in your model:

```
CONCEPT_RULE:(SENT_6, (ORD, (SENT, "bank", "_c{fee@}"), "sentBreak",
(SENT, "close@", "account@")))
```

The concept sentBreak used in the rule above could contain a REGEX rule that looks for sentence-ending punctuation, or an even better option would be a concept containing a rule using the SENTSTART_n operator like this:

```
CONCEPT_RULE:(SENTSTART_1, "_c{_w}")
```

Best Practices for Operator Combinations

In summary, the combinations that work best across the operators are the following:

- OR can govern any other operator but should not be the top-level or only operator in the rule.
- NOT and UNLESS may appear only in very constrained contexts.
- The variants of AND with document-level scope can usefully govern each other so long as the lower-level operators in the rule add meaning or have smaller distance constraints than the higher-level operators in the rule.
- The variants of AND that change scope can usefully govern the other operators.
- The variants of AND that change scope usefully govern each other, if the scope is greater for the higher-level operators in the rule and is smaller for the lower-level ones.
- The variants of AND with document-level scope can be used to govern the variants of AND that change scope but may not be as effective as you want; be careful and aware of how the operators will interact.

11.3. Best Practices for Selecting Rule Types

Each rule type has its own processing requirements, which means that, by selecting different rule types, you have control over how efficiently your model processes data. This section will help you make such decisions.

11.3.1. Rule Types and Associated Computational Costs

To better inform the selection of rule types for your models, the following list ranks the rule types from least to most computationally expensive:

- CLASSIFIER is the least costly rule type because it includes only tokens, and because the found text is the extracted match.
- CONCEPT is the second least expensive rule type because it works with token literals, refers to a set of sequential elements and rule modifiers, and the found text is the extracted match.
- C_CONCEPT works like the CONCEPT rule type at first by matching all the defined elements and modifiers. Additional processing then returns a part of the rule match using the _c{} extraction label, making the rule type slightly more expensive.
- CONCEPT_RULE is the most expensive of the concept rule types because it allows for Boolean and proximity operators. The number of operators in a rule can increase its overall cost. It is possible to create a CONCEPT_RULE that is more expensive than even some of the other rule types below.
- SEQUENCE is the less expensive of the two fact-matching types of rules because elements and modifiers are sequential, which parallels the C_CONCEPT rule type. Additional processing then extracts all matches for each label. More labels in the rule can further increase the cost of the rule.
- PREDICATE_RULE is more flexible, but more expensive, than the SEQUENCE rule type because of the use of Boolean and proximity operators. It is similar in cost

to the CONCEPT_RULE type plus extra processing for extracting matches for multiple labels. More operators or more labels can contribute to increases in the overall cost of this type of rule.

- REMOVE_ITEM is generally the less costly filtering rule type of the two; it operates over only matches of a specified concept. It depends on the number of matches for that concept to determine the cost, so keep that factor in mind as you apply the rule.

- NO_BREAK is the costlier of the two filtering rule types because it operates over all matches in the model across all concepts.

- REGEX rule cost can vary widely because of seemingly endless combinations and because it depends on the makeup of the regular expression rule. It must be used with caution. Although this rule can have minimal cost for certain definitions, it can potentially be the most expensive. See chapter 10 for additional advice on special characters and strategies to avoid.

Each of the available rule types have been designed for specific purposes, and it is advised that you use these rule types for those purposes. Although some rule types can be used in place of others, this approach can lead to inefficiencies that may not surface until a later time when you are scoring documents at scale. It is thus best that you use the appropriate rule type from the start of authoring rules.

If you are relatively new at writing rules, you may fall into the trap of always using a given rule type that has worked for you in the past. This approach can lead to a misunderstanding of when to use certain rule types, and potentially develops a habit of using the wrong rule type when authoring larger sets of rules. Instead, select the rule type by always keeping in mind the goals of the model, the type of data you are working with, and the tips about each rule type in this book.

11.3.2. Use of the Least Costly Rule Type for Best Performance

Take for example the CLASSIFIER and CONCEPT rule types. Both produce a match on the same input token or tokens, so the result appears to be the same. The CONCEPT rule type is used to match against everything to the right of the colon in its definition (in order), just as the CLASSIFIER rule type. However, the CONCEPT rule type can do more than the CLASSIFIER rule type can, including referring to rule modifiers and other element types. With these additional capabilities and because of the various ways in which it can be expanded, the CONCEPT rule type is more expensive in terms of complexity and run-time cost. In contrast, the CLASSIFIER rule type allows only literal strings in the rule definition. Repeated use of the CONCEPT rule type for literal strings should be converted only to using the CLASSIFIER rule type.

For the example below, a series of CONCEPT rule types each have a single named symptom:

```
CONCEPT:burning
CONCEPT:itching
CONCEPT:redness
```

Given that the rules above define only literal strings, they should be rewritten as
CLASSIFIER rules:

```
CLASSIFIER:burning
CLASSIFIER:itching
CLASSIFIER:redness
```

Alternatively, two of them can be kept as CONCEPT rules that match in a broader fashion by
converting the rule definition to include a lemma form and @ expansion symbol. There is no
need for the expansion symbol in the third rule, so it could be converted to a CLASSIFIER
rule:

```
CONCEPT:burn@
CONCEPT:itch@
CLASSIFIER:redness
```

Remember that you cannot put an @ modifier on an adjective like "red" to get matches for
the noun "redness," because the @ modifier expands only to nominal, adjectival, or verbal
forms that are inflectionally derived. In other words, the adjective "red" is not the parent of
the nominal form "redness."

The same conservative approach just described for CLASSIFIER and CONCEPT rule types
is also recommended for the CONCEPT and C_CONCEPT rule types in comparison to one
another. Matches extracted because of CONCEPT rules correspond to the full found text
based on the rule definition. In other words, when a CONCEPT rule matches input text, the
extracted match will be the entire rule definition body. The C_CONCEPT rule will likewise
match input text in accordance with its full rule definition, but the extracted match is only the
part of the found text specified in the _c{} extraction label. When this extraction label
includes the entire definition of the rule, it is better to use the CONCEPT rule type instead of
the C_CONCEPT rule type, because the latter is designed for extracting only a portion of the
found text. Even though technically it is allowed, _c{} should never be used to match against
an entire rule definition, because it is a misuse of the C_CONCEPT rule type. Instead,
consider whether the CONCEPT rule type can be used in its place.

For the example below, assume a concept with the name skinSymptom has been defined as
containing a list of known symptoms that can impact the skin. The first rule set is incorrect,
and should be replaced by the second set or the third set:

```
Avoid this! -> C_CONCEPT:_c{skinSymptom sensation}
Avoid this! -> C_CONCEPT:_c{skinSymptom feeling}
Avoid this! -> C_CONCEPT:_c{skinSymptom}
```

In the case where both the match from the concept skinSymptom and the token after it should
be returned, use the following set of rules:

```
CONCEPT:skinSymptom sensation
CONCEPT:skinSymptom feeling
CONCEPT:skinSymptom
```

In the case where only the match from the skinSymptom concept should be extracted, use the following set of rules:

```
C_CONCEPT:_c{skinSymptom} sensation
C_CONCEPT:_c{skinSymptom} feeling
CONCEPT:skinSymptom
```

11.3.3. When Not to Use Certain Rule Types

Although using one rule type in place a of a less costly rule type is one type of misuse, another is improperly using the results of one rule in another rule. For instance, using the SEQUENCE or PREDICATE_RULE rule types to define a concept that is referenced in the rules of another concept is generally not a proper use of the rule type, because the fact aspect of the matches will be lost. In other words, the labels and associated extracted matches will be lost. Only the matched string will be passed along.

If you have a reason to extract the full match string from the first to the last match element, and if your elements are in a known pattern, then you can use a CONCEPT rule instead of a SEQUENCE rule. On the other hand, if you need to use operators to find all the elements that are required for your match, then PREDICATE_RULE is the only rule type that enables both operators and the extraction of the full matched string. This use case may have a use in your model but must be applied with caution.

If you have no purpose for either of the output results of the rule match, and you are throwing away both types of extracted data, then you are using the existence of the match as a binary decision. This is a misuse of the SEQUENCE and PREDICATE_RULE rule types because they are meant to produce the information about relationships between labeled items or between them and the extracted match string. In such a situation, you should use the C_CONCEPT or SEQUENCE or CONCEPT rule types instead, because your model will run faster. For example, the CONCEPT_RULE type is used in place of the PREDICATE_RULE type when fact matches are not needed but operators are required to define the rule and the result of finding a relationship among the elements is still desired.

The example below shows two concepts, each with a PREDICATE_RULE definition. The first concept, named reportedIssue, contains a PREDICATE_RULE definition containing two labels, a part, defined as a match to the partList concept, and mal, a malfunction often connected to vehicle air bags. The partList concept contains the following rule:

```
CLASSIFIER:air bags
```

The concept named reportedIssue contains the following rule:

```
PREDICATE_RULE:(part, mal):(SENT, "_part{partList}", "_mal{deploy@ on
:DET own}")
```

The second concept, named legalClaim, contains a CONCEPT_RULE containing two keywords, *insurance* and *claim*, and a reference to the reportedIssue concept:

```
CONCEPT_RULE:(SENT_2, "insurance", "_c{reportedIssue}", "claim")
```

The rule defined in the legalClaim concept is attempting to match the token "insurance," a match on the reportedIssue concept, and the token "claim," and to return the reportedIssue as the match for the CONCEPT_RULE rule definition. The extracted matches from the PREDICATE_RULE are being used only to define the bounds of the matched string, which is being passed forward to the CONCEPT_RULE. That matched string then leads to output via the result of the CONCEPT_RULE, which is a legitimate way to use the rules. One other legitimate reason for choosing this combination of rules is that you need both legalClaim and reportedIssue output from scoring your data in production.

Consider the following input document:

It was foggy. We were going about 30 mph when the air bags deployed on their own, broke the windshield and caught on fire. The damage to the car was $5100.00 and when the insurance put a claim into the manufacturer, they replied that they would have to examine the "alleged faulty parts" before honoring the claim or taking responsibility. How frustrating!

Pause and think: Assuming the model with reportedIssue and legalClaim concepts, can you predict the matches for the reportedIssue concept with the input document above? What if you also output the legalClaim concept?

With the input document above, the legalClaim concept produces the match in Figure 11.7.

Figure 11.7. Extracted Match for the legalClaim Concept

Doc ID	Concept	Match Text
1	legalClaim	air bags deployed on their own

With the input document above, the reportedIssue concept produces the matches in Figure 11.8.

Figure 11.8. Extracted Matches for the reportedIssue Concept

Doc ID	Concept	Extraction Label	Extracted Match
1	reportedIssue		air bags deployed on their own
1	reportedIssue	mal	deployed on their own
1	reportedIssue	part	air bags

If you did not place the _c{} extraction label on the reportedIssue concept, but somewhere else in the rule, then the use would be incorrect unless you were generating output via both concepts above, because all the information passed from the PREDICATE_RULE would have then been lost. Be careful not to make this error, because such fact rules buried in your model with no purpose can contribute to slow run-time speeds when you are scoring data with your model.

```
Avoid this! -> CONCEPT_RULE:(SENT_2, "_c{insurance}", "reportedIssue",
"claim")
```

To solve the error of losing all the extracted information from the PREDICATE_RULE in higher levels of your model, convert the original PREDICATE_RULE type of rule to a CONCEPT_RULE type. The CONCEPT_RULE type of rule returns a match only on either of the tokens: either the malfunction, or the part. It would probably be better to return the latter. After this modification, the concept named reportedIssue contains the following rule:

```
CONCEPT_RULE:(SENT, "_c{partsList}", "deploy@ on :DET own")
```

The output for the reportedIssue concept has changed as detailed in Figure 11.9.

Figure 11.9. Extracted Match for the reportedIssue Concept

Doc ID	Concept	Matched Text
1	reportedIssue	air bags

Considering how models are constructed and how they pass information forward through the layers of concepts is covered in more detail in chapter 13. Please refer to that chapter before designing and setting up your taxonomy and before building your model.

11.3. Concept Rules in Models

Custom concepts are useful when you know what information you are trying to extract from your data and you need a way to target that information. You can use a single rule or a series of rules to accomplish your goals. The information in chapters 5–10 introduced each of the rule types and showed you how they relate to one another in terms of complexity and usage scenarios. With the addition of the important details and best practices in the current chapter, you are well equipped to start building your own custom rules successfully, using the LITI syntax.

Chapters 12–14 take advantage of what you have learned in the previous chapters and equip you to build a full information extraction model. Chapters 12 and 13 include tips on designing and setting up a model, taking into consideration data characteristics, whereas chapter 14 focuses on testing and maintenance of models.

Chapter 12: Fundamentals of Data Considerations

12.1. Introduction to Projects

In chapters 2–11, you practiced with the examples, extended your skills with respect to information extraction (IE), and learned many new ideas about how to apply LITI rules to your own data. Now you are ready to set up your own IE projects and build models to extract information from documents. Before you start building models, there are several considerations for setting up your own text analytics IE project:

- What text data will you use and what are its characteristics?
- What are your business goals and what types of questions do you want to answer?
- What is the set of entities or relationships you need to find in the data to answer the questions?
- How will you design your taxonomy and models?
- How will you measure the accuracy of your models?

These five questions that guide project setup can be grouped into three focus areas:

- Data preparation and business goals, covered in this chapter
- Project design, covered in chapter 13
- Measurement design, covered in chapter 14

Experience will teach a lot as well, so if you are new to text analytics projects, then start small and build on your understanding as you expand your goals so that you set yourself up for successful outcomes.

There is another consideration to add to the ones listed, and that is integration of your IE models into the larger context. This integration includes using resources from the larger context to accelerate your model-building, such as feeding information into models from other exploratory, machine learning, and statistical methods. When your models are completed, integration also includes feeding your results into the appropriate location or variables so that you can use the results in predictive models, reports, or databases to answer business questions. These advanced topics are not addressed in this book.

If you are working on a simple project or one with relatively low expectations of accuracy, then you may be able to skip most of this chapter and chapter 14 altogether. However, if you plan to build a complex IE model or if the quality of your models is very important, then take the time to absorb and practice the information in this chapter and chapter 14. The methods introduced here could spell the difference between a successful and unsuccessful large-scale text analytics project.

12.2. Data Considerations

The data is an important element in project planning. Unstructured text data encompasses a variety of forms and structures. This complexity of variation is important to understand when you are building models. For example, a focus on form and purpose would lead to questions like the following:

- What textual data do you have?
- What are the characteristics of this data?
- Is it homogeneous or heterogeneous? That is, were the documents in the data collection written with the same purpose in mind or for all different purposes? Is the type of document the same: all reviews, all call center notes, or all medical discharge notes? Or are there many types of document?

The word cloud in Figure 12.1 illustrates this vast variation in document type.

Figure 12.1. The Breadth of Types of Variation in Text Data

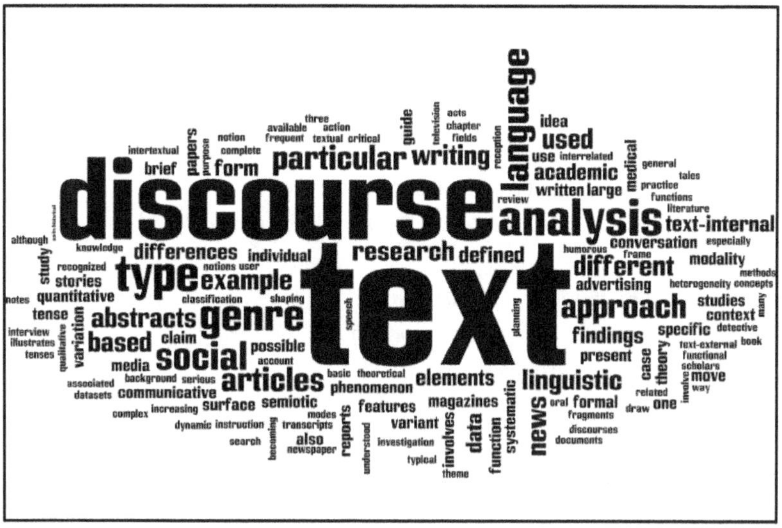

After investigating the form of the data, you can examine the language of the data. Questions you can ask include the following:

- Is the language formal and grammatically correct, or noisy and filled with errors?
- Are the documents long, short, or of varying length?
- Are there different age groups, genders, language proficiency levels, socioeconomic backgrounds, cultures represented among the authors of the documents?
- What languages or dialects may be present?

Another facet to consider is the impact of the data on your organization. Does this data have a life cycle or not; that is, does it have a short or long duration of usefulness within your organization? Is your unstructured text data tied directly to any types of structured data? What is the source of the data—is it created internally to your organization or it is found in the public domain?

As you answer the questions in this chapter, you will come to understand your data better. In particular, you will understand the sources of variation within your data. If you do not have data yet, you will know what to consider when collecting it.

12.3. Data Evaluation

When you analyze unstructured text data, it is important to understand what aspects of the data can impact your models: heterogeneity, noise, availability, and relevance, among other aspects. If you select input data with lots of linguistic variation, your models will need to either be more complex to reach higher accuracy, or remain simpler but with an expectation of lower accuracy. Understanding and managing this inherent variation is one of the skills needed to construct effective text analytics projects.

> **Tip**: Use the checklist below to get you started with evaluating sources of variation in your data.

1. Evaluate content:
   a. One or more than one document type?
   b. Purpose, or purposes, of creating documents?
   c. Grammatical proficiency and correctness of the language?
2. Evaluate authors:
   a. Internal to organization, external, or both?
   b. One or more than one author or author group?
   c. Cultures or language groups?
   d. Age, gender, and education level of authors?
3. Evaluate mode:
   a. Written or spoken language?
   b. Short or long documents?
   c. How is context understood?

The easiest IE models to build will be applied to data that has been created for one purpose or is all the same document type, has relatively good grammatical structure, and comprises documents that are roughly the same length and generally shorter than one page. Does this mean that other types of data sets cannot be targeted with good text analytics models? Absolutely not! However, other types of data sets may take more effort to build good models for, and the types of information you can get out of them may be different.

For example, news articles and product reviews are commonly used document types in text analytics models because they are each written with a single purpose: News articles tell about an event, and product reviews express an opinion or experience with a product. Both are usually edited to some extent, although the latter will be written by authors with a wider variance in education and language backgrounds, leading to more errors and less clarity. Generally, both of these document types are relatively short and stay focused on a single relevant topic. Though building models for language is never simple, the models needed to analyze documents like these will be simpler than for some other types of data.

At the other end of the spectrum, you may have a data set that was made up of all the documents produced as a part of the discovery portion of a legal case. If one company or organization takes another to court, then they may exchange huge data sets to allow each of the legal teams to prove their claims in the case. These data sets may represent all types of documents, from email, to Microsoft Word, Microsoft Excel, and Microsoft PowerPoint documents, as well as reports, notes, financial materials, work tickets, call center notes, and so on. The data may come from many groups within the organization and across an extended period of time. Because this type of data set is very noisy, it is difficult to use it to build a single IE model that will be very effective. Instead, it would be better to filter out the noise and perhaps even do some categorization on the data to divide it into more homogeneous sections before applying one or more IE models. Some creative preprocessing steps may also be useful.

> **Tip:** Preprocess noisy or long documents to increase the effectiveness of the IE model.

When you have diverse or difficult data, there are many ways to think creatively about your documents and prepare them for use in text analytics. For example, if you have very long documents, but you are interested in extracting information from only a certain section or sections, then you can first extract those sections, and then apply your model to the data without the extra noise. You can also break longer documents into sentences or sets of sentences. Breaking up longer documents or extracting sections before applying complex models is recommended, because the SAS Text Analytics products process long documents (greater than 32KB) by breaking the documents up into chunks for processing efficiencies. This type of chunking could divide the text into parts that you wanted to match across, thereby eliminating important matches. To avoid this issue, preprocess your very long documents to pre-separate sections or remove noise and extra materials that you do not intend to match. For an example of dividing your document into sentences, see section 8.3.2. You can extend the rule provided in that section by replacing SENT with SENT_n or PARA.

Another idea for preprocessing is to filter out the documents that are less relevant according to the presence or absence of specific keywords or entity types found in the data. Preprocessing may also be useful to combine multiple text fields into one. For example, perhaps you want to investigate customer relationships, but have multiple records of interactions with each customer. If you combine each customer's encounters with the company into a single record, perhaps for a given year, then you can see the "big picture" in each customer relationship. You can use a double bar (‖) or some other type of section marker to keep the combined sections distinct.

If you have data that is heterogeneous, ungrammatical, or noisy, you may need to reorganize and clean the data up front, build separate models for different subsets of the data, or simply adjust your expectations to focus on easier IE tasks in your models. Any of these approaches will be successful.

The least successful approach is to ignore the characteristics of your data and blindly create models that are too ambitious to be effective when applied to your data. If you are uncertain about the nature of your data or do not have all the information you need to make these decisions, then create a sample from your data and explore its characteristics before deciding how you want to build your models. This type of exploration is elaborated on in the next section.

12.4. Data Exploration

When you want to explore your data, make a sample that is as close as possible in its characteristics to your target data. In other words, extract your sample from data that you want to apply your models to in the future, or ensure that your sample has the same characteristics as the target data. Usually, you need to draw only a random sample.

However, sometimes the items of most interest are not sufficiently represented in the sample. There are two reasons that this could happen. The first is if the sample itself is too small. In this case, one solution is to draw a larger random sample. The second reason is if your data contains rare entities or events of interest and you do not get a sufficient number of instances of those items in a random sample. In this case, you can draw a stratified sample that will increase the proportion of your targeted entities or events in your sample and make modeling easier.

To prepare your full corpus for stratified sampling, first identify what characteristics of your data make it important to you or contribute to important types of diversity. For example, if you have a set of customers, then you may want to ensure that your sample includes data from customers in all geographical regions that your company works with or across all marketing segments. If you have medical data, you may want to ensure that your sample represents genders or ages of patients in the same proportions as your population. If you have data from customer reviews, you may want to divide them by length to ensure that you get an even number of long, medium, and short reviews in your sample. Make sure that your corpus contains a variable or variable that represent this information, and use the variables to designate strata. Then you can draw your sample in a targeted fashion. For more discussion on stratified sampling, see section 12.4.4.

Once you have your exploratory sample, you can apply a clustering analysis to the sample data to see whether the clusters align with the known characteristics in your data. If they do not align with your expectations, then explore each cluster to see if you can learn something new about the data characteristics. Alternatively, you can discover topics in the data and see whether the topics align with other attributes of your data. For example, if politeness terms like "thank you" or "greetings" always align with your email in a topic, then you can see that the structure of the data, and not just the content, is relevant enough to surface in such exploratory tests.

> **Tip**: Use random sampling to create your exploratory data set. However, if you need to control certain characteristics of your sample or you want to increase the number of instances of a targeted item in your sample, then use stratified sampling.

You can also use these same techniques to compare various random samples of your exploratory corpus with one another to determine how similar the samples are. If they vary outside the expected norm, then you probably need to "drill down" to find out what parts are very different. You can also do this with subsets that you expect to be different to determine how different they are. For example, you might have five different sources of data, and you take an exploratory sample from each one to compare the samples with one another. If you have results that show a lot of variation between the corpora, then you may need to consider building separate models for each or, at least, should test them separately as you build your models in order to see how the variation impacts your models and your strategies for testing and improving them.

After you have determined how to create your sample and done some initial exploration using topics or clusters, another type of exploration is testing for linguistic variation. You can test for diversity of word usage in your exploratory sample or compare the diversity of word usage between multiple samples or subsections of your sample by creating word frequency histograms and visual aids. You can also review statistics on your data to understand information density, information complexity, formality level, and domain specificity. When a corpus is less dense and complex, but more formal or structured, models will be easier to build in general. More detail about each of these measures will be discussed in the next section.

The data sets used for illustrations in this chapter represent various types of corpora. Some are publically available, and you can experiment with them yourself. Others are data sets that the authors have analyzed for customers or during research, and those are not accessible to readers. The characteristics of these data sets will help you to compare your data with the ones presented here and set some expectations of what types of analyses may yield the best level of information. Table 12.1 briefly describes the characteristics of each corpus, for your reference.

Table 12.1. Characteristics and Descriptions of Various Corpora

Corpus	Total Words	Description	Availability
Amazon Reviews	310,859	Product reviews relating to gaming consoles	Source: http://www.amazon.com
VAERS 2017	293,847	Patient and medical caregiver reports of vaccine side effect from 2017 as reported via the Vaccine Adverse Events Reporting System (VAERS)	Source: https://vaers.hhs.gov/data/datasets.html
Skittles Tweets	18,393	Based on search for word "Skittles"	Source: Collected via Twitter API
Park Reviews	162,829	Reviews from visitors to various public parks	Not publicly available
Sleep Abstracts	3,404,367	Abstract portion of research papers on sleep	Not publicly available
Treebank – WSJ	1,082,713	Wall Street Journal section of the Treebank data set	Source: https://catalog.ldc.upenn.edu/LDC2015T13
Brown Corpus	1,009,371	A scientifically-collected corpus of American English: https://en.wikipedia.org/wiki/Brown_Corpus	Source: https://catalog.ldc.upenn.edu/LDC99T42
Airline Reviews	138,659	Set of customer reviews of multiple airlines	Not publicly available
Casino Reviews	187,554	Set of customer reviews of casinos and related hotels	Not publicly available
Technical Notes	246,879	Set of mechanics notes created while fixing vehicles	Not publicly available
Billion Word Corpus	663,930,711	Sentences to be used as modeling benchmark for English; not documents https://ai.google/research/pubs/pub41880	Source: https://github.com/ciprian-chelba/1-billion-word-language-modeling-benchmark

Corpus	Total Words	Description	Availability
British National Corpus (BNC)	938,972	Designed to represent written and spoken British English from the latter part of the 20th century	Source: http://www.natcorp.ox.ac.uk/corpus/

12.5. Data Analysis

In general, when you investigate your text data, you are doing what linguists call *corpus analysis*, which is a way of applying statistical measures to unstructured data. You can use statistics to explore the characteristics of your data in isolation to get some insight into your data. However, even better insight will be gained from comparing two or more data sets with each other.

You can use a reference corpus as a baseline for comparison, or divide your corpus into subsets to compare the sets to one another. It is especially useful to divide your data by strata you identified earlier, or by any other characteristics that you think may cause more linguistic variation, in order to understand how much variation exists. For example, you may divide your data on the basis of the source of each record, such as documents created in marketing as opposed to human relations, or by document type, as in customer reviews as opposed to customer surveys. Another way to divide your text data is to leverage structured data associated with each record. For example, in medical care environments, you could group all patients' records from the orthopedic group as opposed to the pediatric group, or group patient records by age or gender.

12.5.1. Vocabulary Diversity

Word usage in your corpus can be very uniform or very diverse. It is more difficult to build complex models on diverse data, so you will need to plan extra time to tune and refine such models. To investigate diversity of word usage, in some SAS Text Analytics products, you can view a Zipf's chart that shows term-by-frequency from largest number of occurrences to smallest. Consult your product documentation to find out whether your product supports this visualization.

Another way to review your vocabulary diversity is to view the coverage of your vocabulary by charting the number of different word forms in descending frequency order, mapping a line from the smallest group to 100% coverage. This coverage-rank distribution plot is essentially the integral of the ranking plot and normalized to 1. The vertical axis is linear, while the horizontal one is logarithmic in order to ensure a display ratio of 1 to 10.000.000. You can read more about this approach in Németh and Zainkó (2002). A simpler version of this approach is to graph the cumulative percentage coverage from most frequent word form to the next, all the way through the list. Figure 12.2 illustrates this simpler approach with the BNC Corpus, which contains 100,098,044 words; 4,000 word forms total about 80% of the corpus.

Figure 12.2. BNC Cumulative Percentage: 4,000 Word Forms Cover 80% of the Corpus

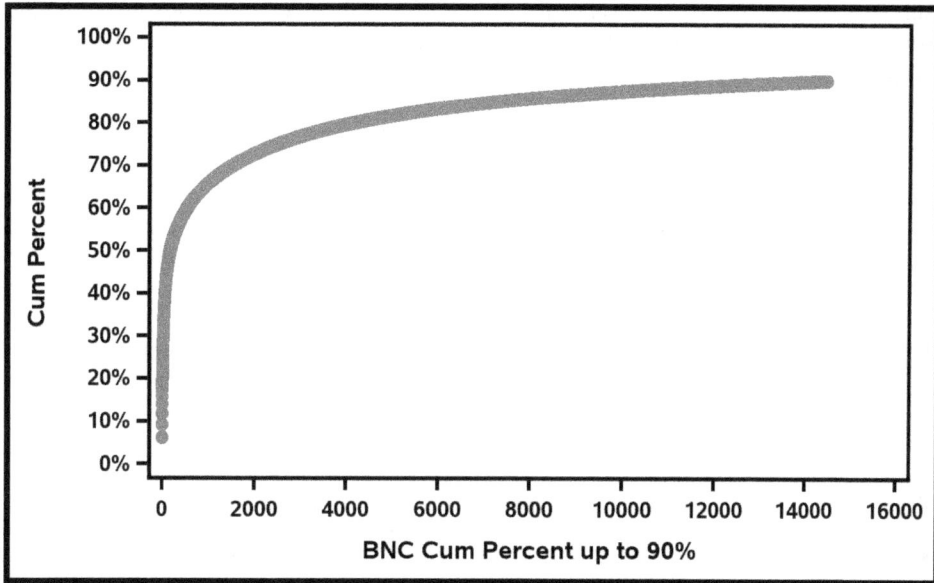

This approach provides some insight into a specific corpus, but is not easy to use to compare corpora of different sizes to each other. The Amazon reviews contain 310,859 words, for example, and Figure 12.3 shows that about 500 unique word forms covers 80% of the data.

Figure 12.3. Amazon Reviews Cumulative Percentage: 500 Word Forms Cover 80% of the Corpus

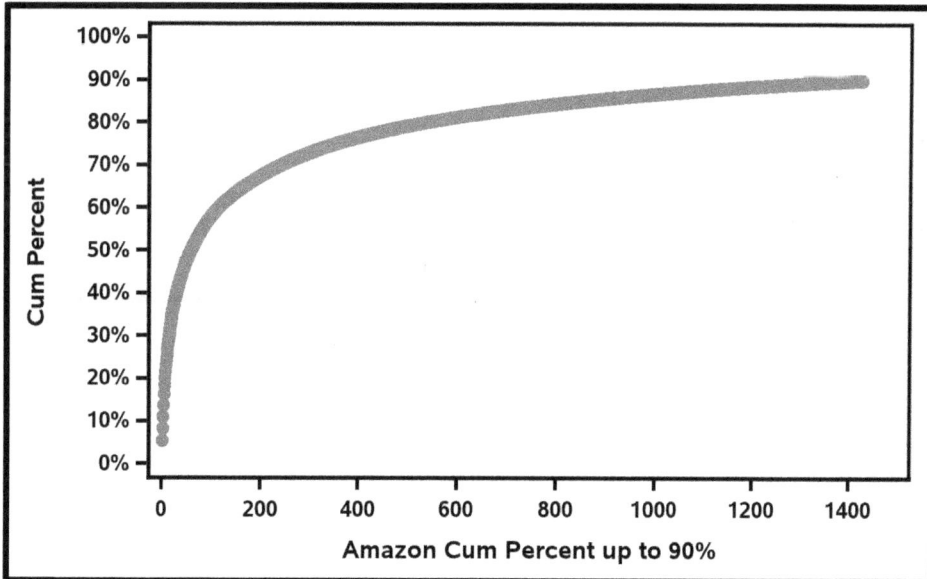

If you want to understand the vocabulary diversity in only one corpus, then you can use this simple approach. The more advanced approach is recommended for comparing corpora. Also, some of the methods in this chapter illustrate additional ways to understand and evaluate your corpus.

12.5.2. Information Density

Information density in your data can be low or high. If it is low, then you will have a higher proportion of shorter words or function (stop) words in your data. If it is high, then the proportion of content words and longer words will be greater. When you are charting the word length in characters by frequency, a weighted distribution where every instance of a word is counted gives a better view than just using a list of unique words. The width and height of the histogram can tell you how sophisticated and varied your corpus is. For example, in the Airline Reviews data written by various customers of airlines all over the world, a histogram shows that most of the words are less than 11 characters, and peak is at 7 characters (Figure 12.4).

Figure 12.4. Airline Reviews Word Length Peaks at 7 Characters

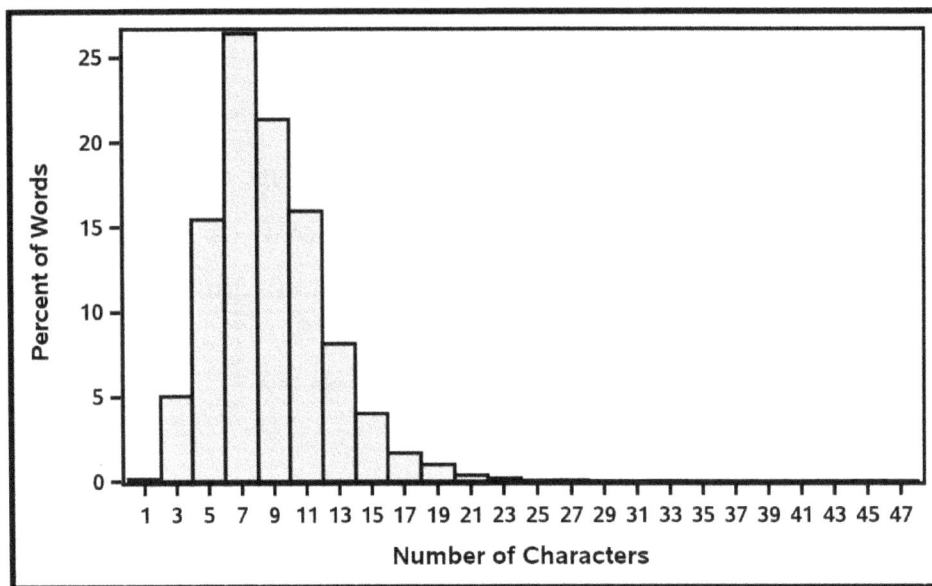

The longest word in this data is "brisbane-singapore-london-singapore-melbourne." This analysis also uncovered that various white space characters between words are missing, resulting in artificially long words like "incomparablycramped." Before you use such data, an issue like this one should be investigated to see if the words are properly separated in an earlier version of the data and the issue can be prevented at an earlier stage of data collection. This chart was created from a listing of word forms in the data, and how many times each word appeared. Then the character count was added for each word form.

Figure 12.5 is another example of a histogram showing the number of characters per word form across the data of abstracts written by researchers working the area of diagnosing sleep problems and addressing them. You can quickly see the difference between this data and the

Airline Reviews data informing Figure 12.4. For example the peak number of words is 9 characters, rather than 7, and the descrease down to the tail is much more gradual, showing that even words with 20 characters are fairly common in the data. The longest word in this data is "tetrahydro-5-hydroxy-5h-benzocyclohept-6-ylideneacetic," and words at the 25-character level include "electroneurophysiological" and "ethylcarboximidoadenosine." This data of sleep abstracts is likely to be more difficult to model in general, because of the greater density of information.

Figure 12.5. Sleep Abstracts Word Length Peaks at 9 Characters

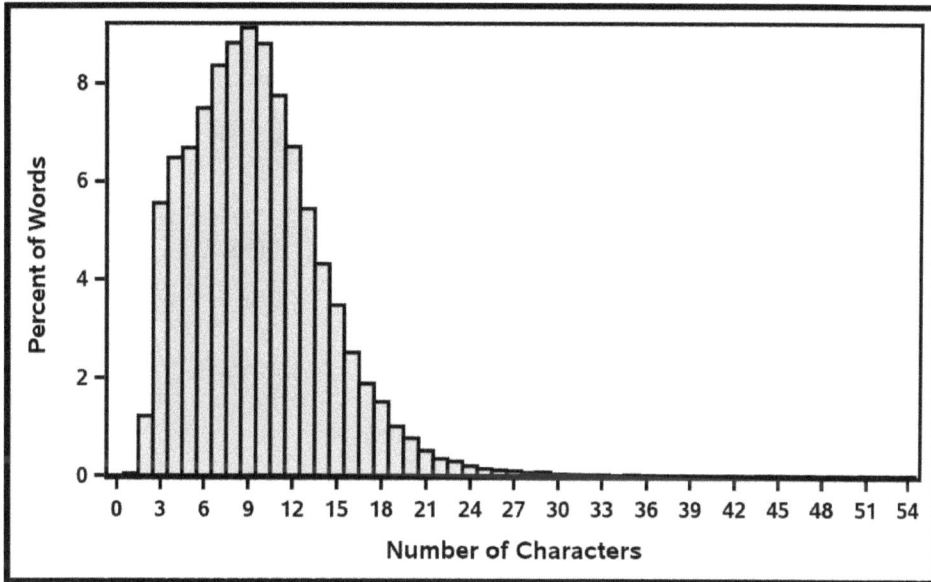

To count function versus content words, you can capture the set of function words by identifying a list of stop words or using the one provided with some SAS Text Analytics products. You may also want to designate words containing numbers as different from other types of content words. Tables 12.2 and 12.3 list the results of dividing the unique word forms from several data sets into three categories: stop words, numeric words, and other content words. Table 12.2 shows the percentage when using each unique form only once.

Table 12.2. Types of Word Forms by Corpus

	Total Forms	Stop Forms	Content Forms	Numeric Forms
Billion Word	1,541,564	0.04%	90.21%	0.29%
Sleep Abstracts	59,578	0.80%	91.57%	7.63%
Brown	45,987	1.10%	97.99%	0.91%
WSJTreebank	39,910	1.07%	97.01%	1.92%
Technical Notes	12,218	2.38%	84.60%	13.02%
Airline Reviews	12,018	2.88%	93.03%	4.09%

	Total Forms	Stop Forms	Content Forms	Numeric Forms
Amazon Reviews	11,992	3.53%	93.89%	2.49%
VAERS	10,925	3.24%	84.16%	12.59%
Casino Reviews	7,338	5.37%	93.72%	0.90%
Park Reviews	6,753	5.51%	93.60%	0.89%
Skittles Tweets	3,579	7.57%	91.14%	1.29%

Table 12.3 contains the percentage in each group of all the words in the data set; each form is counted for how many times it appears.

Table 12.3. Types of Words per Corpus

	Total Words	Stop Words	Content Words	Numeric Words
Billion Word	663,930,711	47.19%	52.52%	0.29%
Sleep Abstracts	3,404,367	41.11%	58.27%	0.62%
WSJTreebank	1,082,713	44.62%	55.19%	0.18%
Brown	1,009,371	53.30%	46.64%	0.06%
Amazon Reviews	310,859	57.45%	41.50%	1.06%
VAERS	293,837	42.16%	56.49%	1.35%
Technical Notes	246,879	24.26%	73.50%	2.23%
Casino Reviews	187,554	54.88%	45.07%	0.04%
Park Reviews	162,829	50.44%	49.51%	0.04%
Airline Reviews	138,659	50.37%	48.78%	0.85%
Skittles Tweets	18,393	44.91%	54.77%	0.32%

In both tables, a reference data set is listed first; it is a large news-based data set (downloadable at https://arxiv.org/abs/1312.3005). The Billion Word Corpus is not the best possible reference data set, because it was not collected in accordance with scientific corpus analysis methodologies meant to create representative corpora. However, it is accessible and varied enough to represent some heterogenity in language. Keep in mind that it is primarily based on one type of document and therefore cannot be representative of the English language in either topic coverage or form.

If you decide to use use the Billion Word Corpus as a reference data set, then you can say that data sets that are showing denser information content have a lower stop word/form percentage than the reference data set. Figure 12.6 lists the corpora in order from highest to lowest percentage of stop words.

Figure 12.6. Percentage of Stop Words Compared to Total Words in Corpora

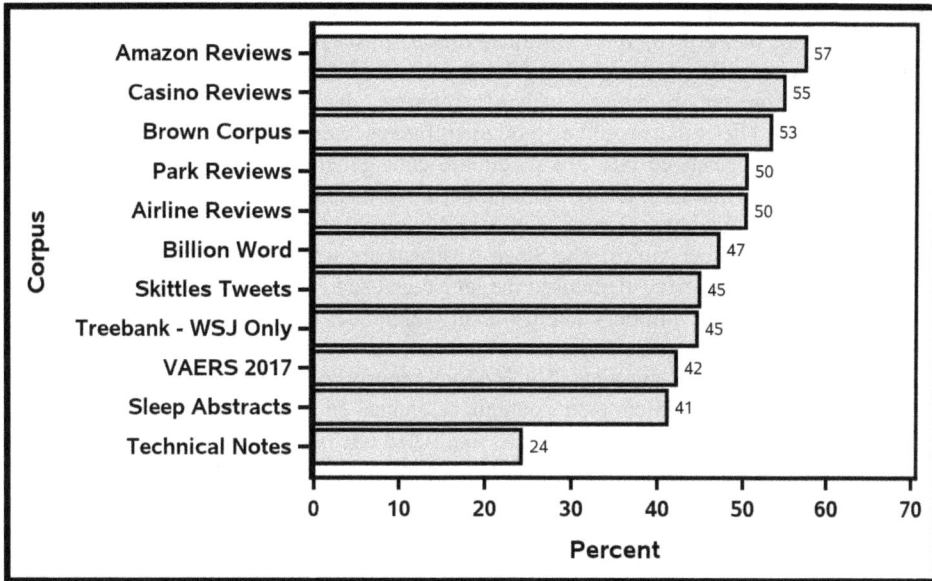

If you are looking at total words, then the reference data set has 47.19% stop words. Corpora with a smaller percentage of stop words are listed below the Billion Word Corpus and include the following:

1. Skittles Tweets (44.91%): a data set of tweets about Skittles
2. Wall Street Journal articles from Treebank data set (44.62%): newspaper articles
3. VAERS 2017 (42.16%): Medical reports of adverse reactions
4. Abstracts (41.11%): scientific research related to sleep
5. Technical Notes (24.26%): Automotive mechanic notes on car repair in progress

This set of corpora with higher information density either is technical in some way, or tends toward brevity, or both. The remaining corpora all have a higher level of stop word usage than the reference corpus. From most to least stop words are the following:

1. Amazon Reviews (57.45%): gamer console reviews
2. Casino Reviews (54.88%): guest reviews of hotel and casino experience
3. Brown Corpus (53.30%): 500 document reference corpus for American English compiled in the 1960s
4. Parks Reviews (50.44%): visitor reviews of camping facilities in Canadian parks
5. Airline Reviews (50.37%): customer reviews of airline service

Four of these lower-information-density corpora are sets of reviews written by the general public, representing a diverse set of authors. The Brown Corpus is a scientifically compiled reference corpus of 500 documents that was created in the 1960s to represent then-current American English. It is not used here as a primary reference corpus, because of its size and limitation to only American English, but it can serve as another comparison point.

Another comment to make about this analysis is that the numeric words also vary significantly between these data sets (Figure 12.7). Four corpora have fewer numeric words as a percentage of words than the Billion Word Corpus reference data set: Casino Reviews and Park Reviews, Brown Corpus, and Treebank—*Wall Street Journal* articles. In this case, the Brown Corpus may be a better view of a reference data set, because the Billion Word corpus contains URLs that would also be identified as "numeric." This reason is also likely why the Skittles Tweets corpus falls within the same general space. What is most interesting is the five corpora that have many more numeric words than expected: Sleep Study Abstracts, Airline Customer Reviews, Gaming Console Reviews, VAERS Medical Reports, and Technical Notes by mechanics. The Sleep Abstracts are scientific and bound to have measurements as a primary element in the language used. The Airline Reviews contain special terms for flight numbers and also many references to dates and times. The Amazon Reviews on gaming consoles contain both product names with numbers, as in "PS2," and also measurements and dollar amounts. The VAERS reports contain many biological measurements. The Technical Notes contain references to specific part numbers and measurements. Knowing your data means that when one of these numbers is different than you expected, or different from your reference corpus, you should research the reason for the difference to understand your data better.

Figure 12.7. Percentage of Numeric Words Compared to Total Words in Corpora

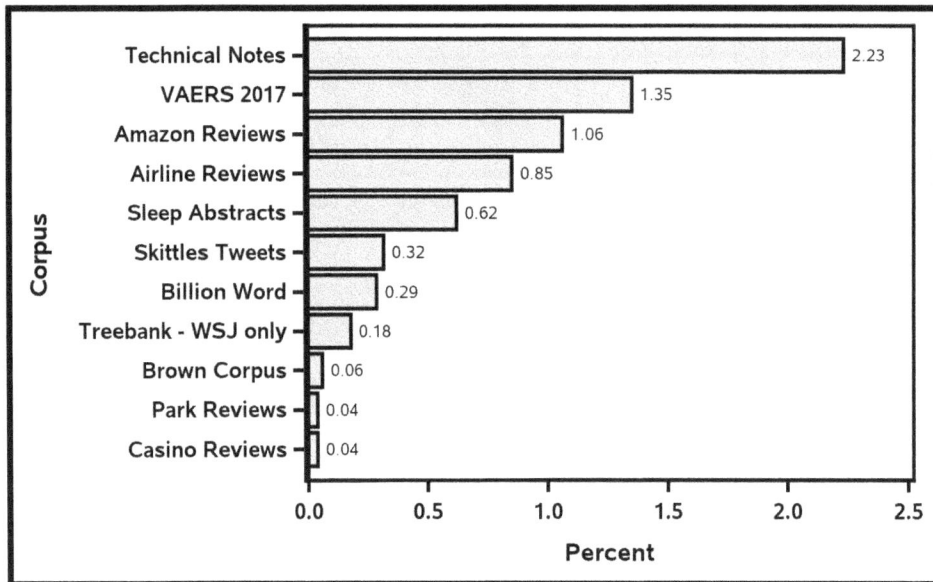

A third way to consider the density of information is to identify a way to recognize whether the information that you will be targeting with your model is likely or unlikely to be present in a particular document or part of a document. In other words, you represent not just a generic types-of-information density, but the density of the type of information you will target in your model. One way linguists do so is to identify a marker that frequently collocates with the targeted form. For example, adjectives are a good marker of sentiment. Finding the density of adjectives in your data is relatively easy compared with finding all of the statements relating to sentiment. See section 14.4 to review another example related to approximating the detection of dates in a corpus using LITI rules.

12.5.3. Language Formality

The style of language used in documents can be more informal or more formal. The more formal the language is, the more likely there will be proper usage of markers of structure like punctuation, capitalization, and grammar. Also, spelling and word usage will be more accurate and more consistent. These cues make models based on the language more accurate. The less formal data may have fewer of these cues or a less consistent use of them, making modeling more difficult. Some ways to approximate measures of formality include the following:

- Counting the number of contractions per document or as a total proportion of stop words
- Counting the number of first-person pronouns per document or as a total proportion of the stop words
- Calculating the proportional use of uppercase versus lowercase letters

For several corpora listed, the first-person pronouns as a proportion of the stop words can show you how these corpora compare in language formality for this dimension. The pronouns that were investigated include "I," "me," "my," "myself," "mine," "we," "us," "our," "ourselves," "ourself," and "ours." Some of the corpora contained all of these words at least once. The technical notes data contained only five of the forms, whereas all others contained at least nine of the forms.

As shown in Figure 12.8, the corpora that are review-oriented have the most first-person stop words as a proportion of the total number of stop words. News and generic corpora like Treebank, *Wall Street Journal*, and Brown have many fewer. Something unexpected is that the Technical Notes written by mechanics contain as many first-person stop words as news, perhaps as a reflection of the similar goal of reporting what is happening as they investigate the vehicle. The least number of first-person pronouns was found in the Sleep Abstract data, which is unsurprising, given the formality of this text genre.

Figure 12.8. Percentage of First-Person Stop Words in Each Corpus

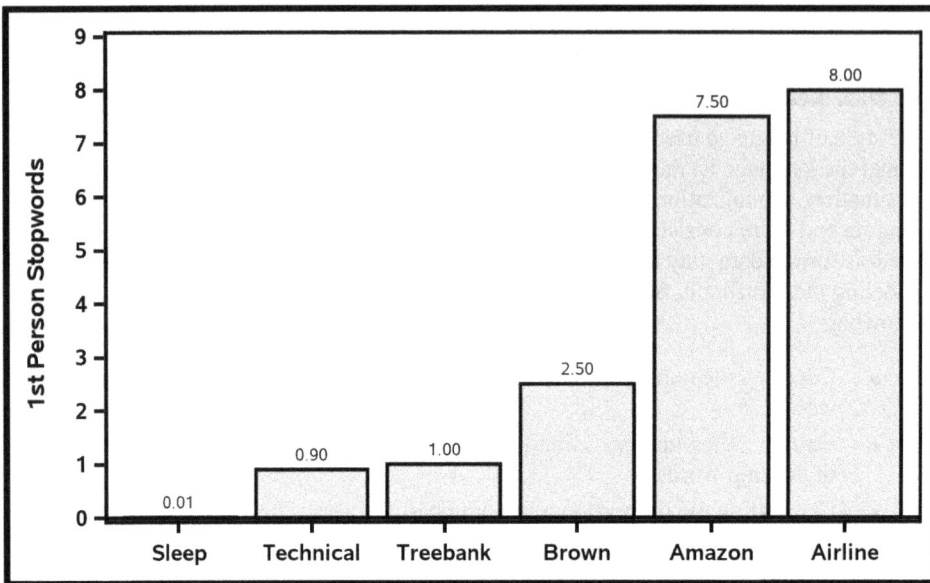

12.5.4. Information Complexity

One measure of information complexity is the length of sentences in your documents. First, you must have somewhat formal documents or shorter documents to be able to use this metric, because informal documents may not have clear sentence boundary indicators, resulting in the appearance of longer sentences that may continue to the end of the document. If your documents have detectable sentence boundaries, then you can detect how long each sentence is by token and chart the histogram of sentence length across the corpus. Longer sentences mean that more information is packed into each sentence, and shorter sentences mean that each sentence is more likely to contain fewer distinct propositions. Models that are based upon longer sentences must take into account more variation. Table 12.4 lists the sentence lengths for the corpora evaluated in this chapter.

Table 12.4. Sentence Length per Corpus

Data Set	Total Sentences	Average Number of Sentences per Document	Min/Max Sentence Length per Document	Average Number of Tokens per Sentence	Min/Max Tokens per Sentence
Airline Reviews	9,969	7.29	1/22	16	2/119
Park Reviews	16,704	2.52	1/37	12	1/86
VAERS	24,777	3.64	1/19	15	1/121
Skittles Tweets	2,350	1.69	1/6	11	1/39

Data Set	Total Sentences	Average Number of Sentences per Document	Min/Max Sentence Length per Document	Average Number of Tokens per Sentence	Min/Max Tokens per Sentence
Sleep Abstracts	160,916	9.38	1/95	26	1/325
Technical Notes	18,324	2.63	1/29	16	1/138
Amazon Reviews	17,889	9.77	1/109	20	1/456
Treebank WSJ	54,160	21.67	1/188	23	1/204

One way to use this data is to see how many longer documents (outliers) there are in your data. By looking at the Amazon reviews in Figure 12.9, you can see that most of the reviews are shorter than 20 sentences. Having 20–40 sentences in a document is rare, and more than that is highly unusual. It might even be worth looking at a few of the exceptionally long reviews to ensure that they are valid reviews. You can use this information to choose operators (SENT_n) and to decide whether to break up your documents into smaller chunks for analysis.

Figure 12.9. Longest to Shortest Amazon Review, by Number of Sentences in Each Review

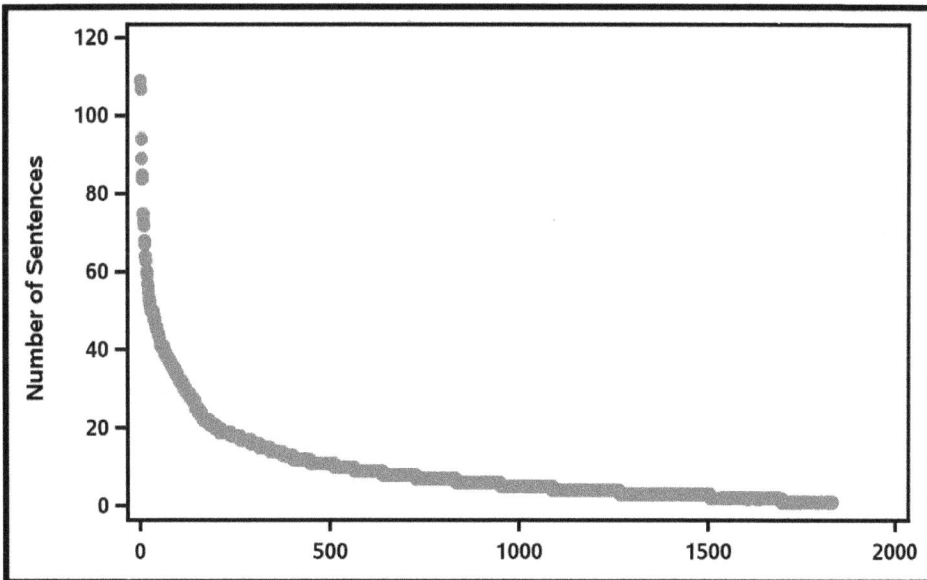

12.5.5. Domain Specificity

Domain specificity is another metric to investigate by looking at the vocabulary found in the documents. For this metric, a baseline reference corpus is used to specify the vocabulary in a language that is considered to be non-domain-specific. In this section, the baseline reference corpus is the BNC, a 100 million–word corpus, designed to represent written and spoken British English from the latter part of the 20th century (http://www.natcorp.ox.ac.uk/corpus/). The frequency word list for the corpus is available for download (http://www.kilgarriff.co.uk/bnc-readme.html).

To compare your corpus with the reference corpus (or with a third corpus), identify the terms from your corpus, and compare them with the reference corpus list. Identify any terms in your corpus that appear at least n times (start with $n = 3$ or 4) and are not found in the reference corpus. This is the proportion of your data that is likely to be domain-specific. More domain-specific corpora can be more difficult to build models for, but this challenge can be offset by domain-specific dictionaries.

When you compare the Sleep Abstract data set, described earlier, to the BNC data set, eliminating all tokens with no alphabetic characters, you find that about 43.4% of the vocabulary in the Sleep Abstracts is specific to the domain. The most frequent unique vocabulary items for the Sleep data are listed in Table 12.5.

Table 12.5. Most Common Domain Terminology in Sleep Abstracts Corpus

Word	Frequency
osas (obstructive sleep apnea syndrome)	2,564
Polysomnography	1,917
sleep-wake	1,133
Polysomnographic	905
sleep-disordered	834
sleep-related	781
ncpap (nasal continuous positive airway pressure)	675
Apneas	612
apnea-hypopnea	575
Hypopnea	572
osahs (obstructive sleep apnea-hypoapnea syndrome)	489
orexin (a hypothalamic neuropeptide)	488
Microg	463
Zolpidem	380
Adhd	379

Contrast the vocabulary in the Sleep Abstract data set with the Amazon reviews on game consoles, where the percentage of domain-specific terminology is only 6.2%. The most frequent unique vocabulary items for the Amazon reviews data are listed in Table 12.6. It is clear from these examples that when you work with data in a domain you are not personnaly familiar with, it is a good idea to use techniques like these to fully understand your data and to work with domain experts whenever possible.

Table 12.6. Most Common Domain Terminology in Amazon Game Console Reviews Corpus

Word	Frequency
wii	2,804
xbox	1,826
ps3	1,800
kinect	635
playstation	328
netflix	272
gamecube	229
blu-ray	226
dvd	173
250gb	143
hdmi	136
wifi	122
wiimote	107
xbox360	95
bluray	57

12.6. Business Goals and Targeted Information

When you have a good idea of what data you will work with and you have explored that data to see what topics occur and what possible insights might be found in the content, then you are ready to identify some business goals to build models for. Perhaps you have a predictive model that you would like to add lift to, or you have specific structured data that you would like to identify errors or plug gaps in, using unstructured data. Another type of business goal is to extract specific pieces of data from the unstructured text data in order to populate new structured data or databases to use in reports. An even more ambitious goal is to identify relationships between concepts to use in reports that drive business decisions. All of these goals are achievable with the tools SAS provides.

Once you have identified a particular business goal, you should identify the types of data that you need to extract to support that goal. This analysis may take you back into your data to explore with a new focus on particular types of questions. For example, if you want to support a categorization model that identifies potential fraud in unstructured documents by extracting the clues that may point to fraud in each document, then you will need to identify the types of clues you want to extract.

In another scenario, perhaps you want to extract each issue that a customer indicates about an aspect of your product. You first need to find mentions of your product, service, or aspects and then model how people discuss problems. In this case, you need to model both the product/service/aspect and the problems your customers describe.

Perhaps instead you are monitoring your company's reputation on social media. In that case, you will want to identify when your company or its products or services are being mentioned to focus on the data you want to analyze. The next step is to extract information about the details of risks that need to be addressed or positive feedback that can be used for marketing and other business decisions.

Each of these examples (and your own projects, as well) require that you also decide how to proceed to get the information that you need. As you think through your goals and explore how to achieve them with the data you have or can collect, you will decide exactly which tools you will need at each point of your analysis: categorization, IE, decision trees, SAS actions, DS2, and so on. It is a good idea to work through each part as an experiment to uncover issues and understand the challenges, and then use that information to plan your project from end to end.

12.7. Suggested Reading

To gain more background on the topics in this chapter, consult the following sources in the References list at the end of the book:

- De Roeck et al. (2004)
- Fothergill et al. (2016)
- Gablasova et al. (2017)
- Gries (2006)
- Lijffijt et al. (2011)
- Lu et al. (2017)
- Miller and Biber (2015)
- Németh and Zainkó (2002)
- Paquot and Bestgen (2009)
- Rayson (2008)
- Sanders and DeVault (2004)
- Sahlgren and Karlgren (2005)
- Sharoff (2010)

Chapter 13: Fundamentals of Project Design

13.1. Introduction to Project Design

In chapter 12, you learned about various ways to characterize the type of data you have and how to identify and align that data with your business goals. You also identified some of the information that you need to target in your data in order to reach your goals. Once you understand your data, your goals, and the information that you will target, you can turn to designing your project. In your design, you will make decisions based on answers to the questions that are addressed in this chapter:

- How to best target information for your models
- How to organize your taxonomy
- How to best leverage project-level settings

13.2. Definition of Targeted Information

After you identify a business goal or several related business goals that will target the same or similar information, you should define each of the pieces of information that you will need at a very specific and concrete level. In fact, the way the predefined concepts are described in chapters 3 and 4 is an example of the proper way to define each of the major parts of your model. You are encouraged to identify each item that you will extract, write a similar description of what each one entails and any related information that may be out of scope, and include examples as they would appear in the text.

The purpose of writing this standard definition (also known as an *annotation guide*) of each of your extracted items is threefold. This documentation on your model will guide the people building your model, annotating data, and testing your model accuracy. Even if these tasks are performed by the same person or the same group of people, the model will take time to build, and this document serves to keep the model and the envisioned target data aligned. This documentation can be updated as you proceed through the implementation and testing process so long as all of the participants of the project are aware of changes and the description remains both logical and feasible. To keep your target feasible, stay focused on the characteristics of the data, what actually appears in the text, rather than situations or meanings that are apparent only in the real world.

As you define the pieces of your model that you will need, you should consider the alignment between the data that you have and the data that would support your business goals. How well do they align? Are there any known risks? What is the complexity of the model or models that you will need to build? What is the required accuracy of the model to create useful results?

If you are not familiar with text analytics or information extraction (IE) and the model design is becoming very complex, you should either select a simpler project to start with or identify a piece of the larger project that you can start with. By starting with a simpler or partial project, you will more quickly learn about how you will need to set up your workflows and processes to support the model-building efforts and how you will deploy the model into a production environment. You will then be able to directly apply this knowledge to your next project, which could be larger or more complex.

13.3. Taxonomy Design

Now that you have identified the high-level concepts and relationships that you want to extract from your data, you are ready to design the rest of your model. A useful part of the SAS IE toolkit is the ability to put the pieces of your model into a tree-style format called a *taxonomy*. This structure will enable you to represent relationships between pieces of your model in an intuitive and flexible way.

The way you organize your model is your choice. In the research literature, you may see that the word "taxonomy" is used either generically as any tree structure containing information or depicting a type of hierarchy of inheritance, where the child nodes in the hierarchy always inherit the attributes of their parent nodes automatically. The SAS IE toolkit taxonomy does not restrict your usage, and it does not mandate inheritance as a feature of the taxonomy. You can easily add inheritance into the tree structure if you need it to function as a prototypical taxonomy through the addition of rules. However, you are also able to simply ignore the tree structure and represent the pieces of your model in a flat hierarchy or in any hierarchical configuration that makes understanding, building, and testing your models easy.

In Figure 13.1, a flat hierarchy is being used to extract information from legal contracts. No one piece of the model is dependent on any other pieces, and all seem to be of equal importance.

Figure 13.1. A Flat Taxonomy in SAS Enterprise Content Categorization

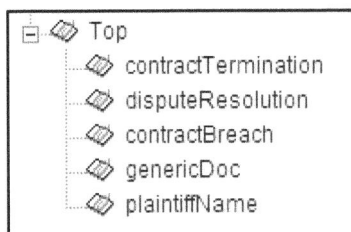

In Figure 13.2, the model is bigger and layered into three levels. The top level includes concepts such as contractTermination and disputeResolution, and the second level includes concepts such as terminationDate, startDate, and terminationReason, whereas the third level includes concepts such as dateMonth, dateDay, and dateYear. This tree structure shows that finding information about termination dates, start dates, termination reasons, terminated employee names, and company names all feed into the part of the model for contract termination. The pieces of the model that feed into an understanding of dispute resolution include the topic, start date, and resolution date.

Figure 13.2. A Hierarchical Taxonomy in SAS Enterprise Content Categorization

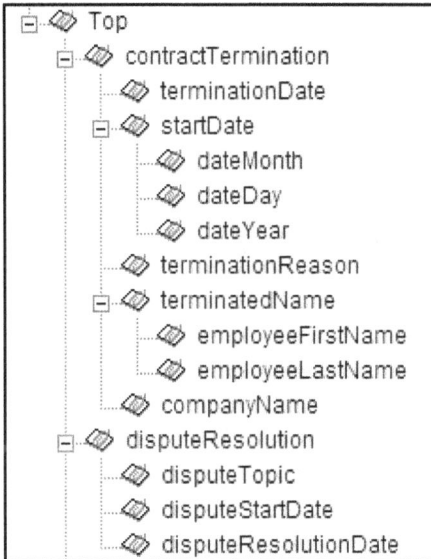

Part of the design diagram for Figure 13.2 is pictured in Figure 13.3.

Figure 13.3. Part of a Design Diagram for a Hierarchical Taxonomy

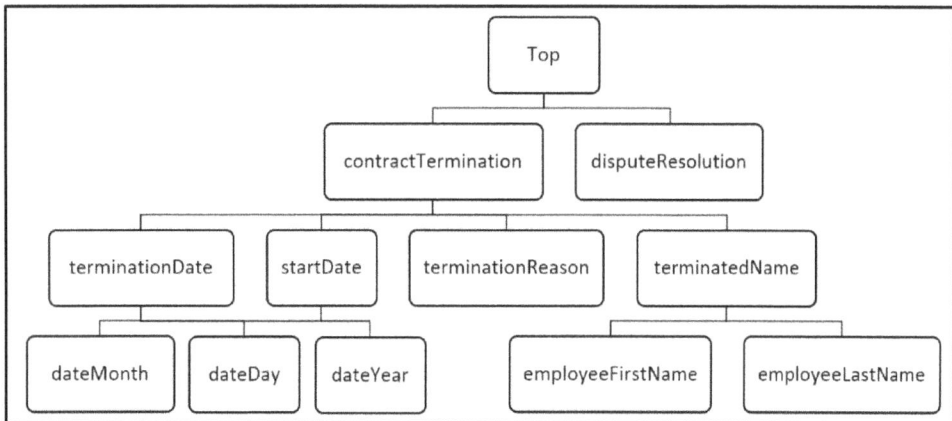

No specialized knowledge is required to use the SAS IE toolkit taxonomy structure, because it works in a similar fashion to folders on a computer in a directory structure. Just as each folder acts as a container for files and other folders on the computer, each concept node in the taxonomy acts as a container for one or more sets of rules. Although working with the SAS IE toolkit taxonomy is intuitive and open-ended, there are several best practice recommendations and options that will be described in this chapter to help you gain the greatest benefits from the taxonomy.

13.3.1. Decomposition

It is fundamental that each concept node in the taxonomy acts as a container for a set of LITI rules. Other rules can then reference this set of LITI rules by using the name of the concept node that holds them. This approach is the most important benefit of the taxonomy, because it enables you to build up a compositional design for your model of interconnected pieces in a manner similar to object-oriented programming methods. Each piece can be designed with one purpose and be limited in complexity, because you can combine the pieces together to describe more complex relationships between pieces of information in the text data.

This compositionality means that you do not need to try to put all of your rules for each of the high-level components that you have identified into one concept node. Instead, you should try to break each one down into the simplest pieces in order to be able to cover each part with a small set of more complex rules (like C_CONCEPT or CONCEPT_RULE types of rules) or a longer list of simple rules (like CLASSIFIER rules). Decomposition of the model into smaller pieces enables you to more easily test your model and discover problems and gaps as you build, because you can see the test results of each concept node in the taxonomy. You will also be able to more easily understand the purpose of each concept when you come back to maintain or update it later.

Tip: Break up complex concepts into simpler subconcepts for easier testing and maintenance.

A simple example of this principle is the predefined helper concept locAddrUSA, which is referenced by the predefined concept nlpPlace to find an address in the United States. The locAddrUSA concept is not designed with a list of rules that identify the patterns and elements of an address all in one place. Instead, the pieces of an address are decomposed into several sets of rules including lists for basic components like cities, states, state abbreviations, street words, and compass directions. There are also patterns defined in separate concepts like ZIP codes and house numbers. For example, Table 13.1 lists some of the basic components that define locAddrUSA.

Table 13.1. Helper Concepts that Define locAddrUSA

Concept Name	Description	Example
locHouseNum	REGEX rules to identify patterns that may be house numbers in context with other components	REGEX:[0-9]+[-]?[A-Z]

Concept Name	Description	Example
locStreetWord	List of words and abbreviations that are used to identify street names	CLASSIFIER:Boulevard
locCityNameUSA	List of city names in the USA	CLASSIFIER:Boston
locStateCodeUSA	List of two-letter codes	CLASSIFIER:MA
locZipUSA	REGEX rules to identify pattern of ZIP codes in the USA	REGEX:[0-9]{5}\-[0-9]{4}
compassPoint	List of directions and abbreviations	CLASSIFIER:South
digitSet	REGEX patterns that identify a subset of numeric patterns	REGEX:[0-9][0-9\,\.]+[0-9]
ordinalNum	List of word-based ordinals and REGEX to handle numeric ordinals	CLASSIFIER:eighty-first
wordNum	List of number words that may be ambiguous in the dictionary plus use of :Num tag	CONCEPT::Num CLASSIFIER:one
perFirstName	List of first names	CLASSIFIER:Abigail
perLastName	List of last names	CLASSIFIER:Alcott
perFirstNameAmbig	List of potential first names	CLASSIFIER:Ace
perLastNameAmbig	List of potential last names	CLASSIFIER:Almonds
perTitle	Rules point to different types of person titles	CONCEPT:sTitleReligious

The first five concepts are the basic components of a street address in the United States. The next four define generic concepts that can be used in many different types of rules, not just addresses. The final five concepts are some of the concepts borrowed from the person names rule set to help identify when streets are named after people. You can see that each of these concepts is designed to do a single thing in the model, which makes the models easier to build, test, and maintain.

Table 13.2 includes the three higher-level concepts that the concepts in Table 13.1 are used to define. You can see in the examples that the concepts listed above are used in combination to make the rules easy to understand and read. For example, you can see by reading the two rules illustrating locNameStreet that they would match street names like "Jane Alcott Avenue," "Michael Jones Blvd," or "Eighty-first St."

Table 13.2. Functional Concepts Defined with Helper Concepts

Concept Name	Description	Example
locNameStreet	Uses concepts like locStreetWord, perFirstName, locCityNameUSA, ordinalNum, and so on to define street names	CONCEPT:perFirstName perLastName locStreetWord CONCEPT:ordinalNum locStreetWord

Concept Name	Description	Example
ordComboNum	Uses ordinalNum and wordNum to derive larger ordinal numbers	CONCEPT:wordNum and ordinalNum
locAddrUSA	Uses all of the components listed above to model street addresses, full postal addresses, P.O. Box addresses, and so on.	CONCEPT:locHouseNum compassPoint locNameStreet CONCEPT:p.o. box digitSet locCityNameUSA locStateCodeUSA locZipUSA

This U.S. address model could be designed differently and still be correct. You can be confident that you have a successful design when you can document it clearly, test it easily, and maintain it without difficulty. If you are struggling with these items later in your development process, you may need to go back and modify your design. Look for places where you are trying to do too much in a single concept or where you have multiple or unclear goals for a single concept. In those areas, try to decompose the model further. Update your design as you learn more about your data and about how to build effective models. Figure 13.4 shows how some of the components combine in this example model for addresses.

Figure 13.4. Part of a Design Diagram for the locAddrUSA Concept

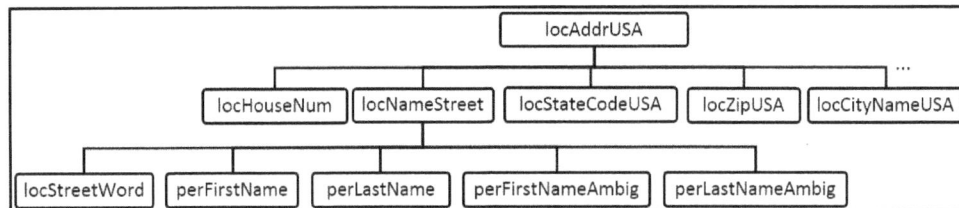

One way to encode this design in your taxonomy structure is presented in Figure 13.5.

Figure 13.5. Part of the locAddrUSA model in SAS Contextual Analysis

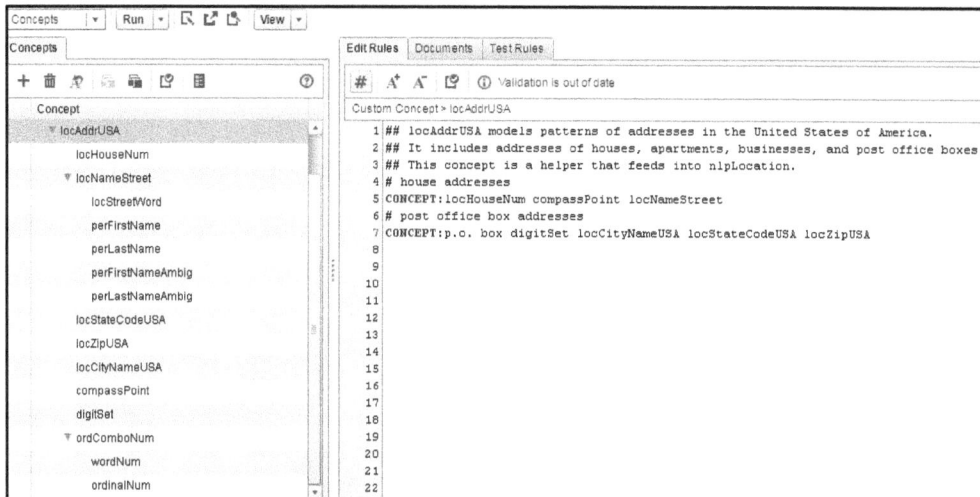

When you are working on your design, it is a good idea to test it out initially by putting in some exploratory rules and seeing whether you get the results that you were expecting when testing against your data. As you test, you may see that you are mixing many different types of rules, creating a messy concept model. Alternatively, you may see that the concept contains many more rules than you can easily test and maintain. In these cases, it is recommended to take a step back and decompose your design further.

Designing components in your model has many considerations beyond just being able to test and maintain your model. You also need to keep in mind the final purpose of your model and ensure that the design supports those goals. Also, you may need to take into account the content that you are finding in your data and structure some of your model around characteristics of that data.

An example of driving the model from the data is the distinction in person name rules between perFirstName and perFirstNameAmbig lists. The two separate lists indicate that through the building process some names were causing problems in the test results, because they were sometimes names and sometimes not names. These ambiguous names needed to be treated with more constrained rules, because simple rules that worked for less ambiguous names were problematic. Dividing the lists means that there will be more names rules, but they remain simpler and have better accuracy. Once you have the divided lists, you can make rules like the ones below in a concept called perSingleName in order to match a single person's full name:

```
CONCEPT:perFirstName perLastName
CONCEPT:perFirstNameAmbig perLastName
CONCEPT:perFirstNameAmbig perInitial perLastName
CONCEPT:perFirstName perLastNameAmbig
CONCEPT:perFirstName perInitial perLastNameAmbig
```

The first rule is a simple rule that combines relatively unambiguous first and last names. The other rules rely on at least one of the concepts being unambiguously a name and the pattern that reflects parts of a name being combined together. Consider the following first and last names:

- Jan
- Black
- Art
- Church
- Viola
- Hill
- Janelle
- Parson

- Tom
- Waits
- Josh
- Bell
- Tiger
- Woods
- April May
- Baby Ruth

Pause and think: Can you classify which of the tokens above are ambiguous names?

All the examples above except for "Janelle" are actually ambiguous names. Even the final two entries, containing two tokens each, could be person names or could be a list of months of the year and a candy bar name, respectively. For best matching results, these ambiguous names should be in a separate concept from unambiguous person names, and they should match only when there is evidence in the context that they refer to names.

13.3.2. Concept Types

Several aspects of good model design have already been discussed. Another important aspect is the ability to treat some of the concepts as foundational, just as a house or building has a foundation. No one usually sees the foundation of a building, because people usually interact with the more functional components like ground and upper floors, windows, doors, and the like. It works the same way in a well-designed concept model, where some concepts are hidden because they do not need to produce explicit output. These concepts are referred to as *helper* or *supporting concepts*, because their output is used only to feed other concepts and not produce directly observable results. *Functional* or *primary concepts*, on the other hand, are meant to provide output to be used for reports, databases, predictive models, and so on and produce matches that are visible to users.

Once you have divided your model into sections by concept and determined which concepts are helper versus functional ones, you can indicate this distinction in the model. Consult product documentation for specifics. But do not forget that, if you have marked certain concepts as helpers, then they no longer produce directly observable results. This is especially important when you are troubleshooting unexpected outputs.

Tip: When no results appear from your concept during testing, make sure that the concept that you are testing is not marked as a helper concept.

For example, in the design mentioned earlier for locAddrUSA, all of the concepts described are helper concepts and will not produce any output specific to each concept. Even locAddrUSA itself is eventually meant to be a helper concept that provides matches for the top-level predefined concept nlpPlace. The top-level concepts do not have to be the only ones to provide output, and lower-level concepts do not always have to be helper concepts. For example, perhaps you also want to generate output for whenever a city matches in an address—that match can be provided by not marking your locCityNameUSA concept as a helper, but letting it both contribute to other concept matches *and* also generate its own matches.

A third type of concept is a purely *organizational* one. It is used for structuring the taxonomy and for documentation purposes. An organizational concept contains no rules, but may contain some comments to document the purpose or restrictions of the concepts below it in the taxonomy. In fact, you can use this type of organizational concept node to break up your taxonomy into different sections. You can decide to place your foundational concepts all together and your functional concepts all together—each under such an organizational node, for example—if you like.

This approach is exemplified in Figure 13.6. Two organizational concepts, originConcept and destinationConcept, are shown. You can see that the definition for the originConcept is blank; it contains no rules. No matches will be returned for this concept, but it is used as a header to organize other match-producing concepts related to the country, date, and agency of origin of classified documents.

Figure 13.6. Organizational Concepts in a Taxonomy in SAS Contextual Analysis

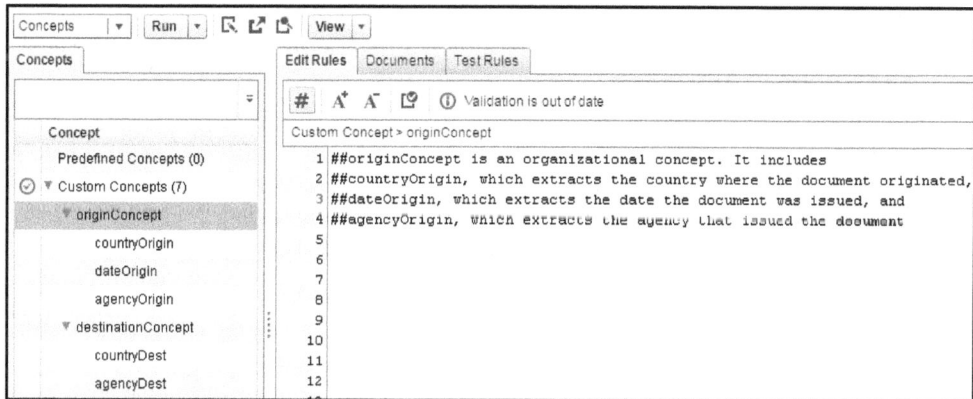

In this way, you can continue to divide your model into pieces and place each piece in a logical part of the hierarchy in order to help you and others find the pieces easily and understand the design of the model. Just as a blueprint has no direct effect on the building constructed from it, the taxonomy has no direct effect on how your model works through any mechanism like automatic inheritance. You are free to lay out the pieces of your model in the way that works best for you and your organization. If you want one concept to reference another, then you control that behavior directly through the rules in each concept.

13.4. Project Settings

There are additional decisions to make when you are setting up your project that are related to your design. They may not need to be made in order to work in the GUI and building models, but will definitely matter when it comes time to put your models into production. These decisions are grouped together because there are specific settings in the software that correspond to each one.

13.4.1. Match Algorithm and Priority

The first setting that you need to be aware of is the match algorithm. There are three possible match algorithms that may be used when you are running your model against data. They are called "all matches," "longest match," and "best match." These algorithms determine which matches to return and which matches, if any, to filter out.

Note, however, that the match algorithms do not modify the span of the match returned, but only determine whether the match will be returned or not. In other words, you should still use various rule types to control the span of matches. The rule types of CLASSIFIER, CONCEPT, and REGEX all return the full span of text defined by the rule, if matched in the text data. To return only a part of the defined span, you can use the C_CONCEPT or CONCEPT_RULE types. If you need to add a user-defined label to the returned span or return multiple spans, then you can use the SEQUENCE or PREDICATE_RULE types. SEQUENCE and PREDICATE_RULE types also return the full matched text from the first matched element to the last one.

"All Matches" Algorithm

The "all matches" algorithm is the default for the examples in this book. This algorithm does not filter out the matches of any two or more functional nodes—that is, nodes that have not been marked as helper nodes (these nodes may also be called "supporting" in your product documentation). Instead, all of the same (redundant) and overlapping strings of text that matched for more than one concept in the text are extracted. However, exact duplicates from within the same concept are always filtered out by the "all matches" algorithm. If multiple rules in the same concept match the exact same span of text, then only one match for that span will be returned. This match algorithm is useful in the following situations:

- If you have defined your model with many helper and few functional concepts
- If you are testing specific concepts
- If you are troubleshooting a full model
- If you are planning to post-process your results in a manner that makes this duplication irrelevant

Consider the following input document.

My steering wheel pulls to the left, especially when traveling at slower speeds.

When you built your rules, you wanted to match either "steering" or "steering wheel," so you have a rule for each in your vehicleFunctions concept like so:

```
CLASSIFIER:steering
CLASSIFIER:steering wheel
```

Regardless of whether these rules are in the same concept or different concepts, when using the "all matches" algorithm, two matches are returned, as shown in Figure 13.7.

Figure 13.7. Extracted Overlapping Matches for the Same Concept

Doc ID	Concept	Match Text
1	vehicleFunctions	steering
1	vehicleFunctions	steering wheel

Now consider the situation in which one functional concept references one or more other concepts. Then, two or more matches could be returned for the same matched span. For example, a hierarchical model contains two functional concepts, refrigeratorPart and appliancePart. The rules in refrigeratorPart include the following:

```
CLASSIFIER:unit top icemaker
CLASSIFIER:door shelf bin
```

The rules in appliancePart include the following:

```
CONCEPT:refrigeratorPart
CONCEPT:ovenPart
CONCEPT:dishwasherPart
```

With an input document such as the sentence "New unit top icemaker is not working properly," the same span of text would be extracted for both the refrigeratorPart and appliancePart concepts: "unit top icemaker." Both matches are returned with the "all matches" algorithm.

Consider another example, in which rules in different concepts match overlapping spans of text. If you are trying to find both mentions of person names and place names, then you may have two concepts with rules to match each type of name. One rule is in a concept named personName:

```
CLASSIFIER:Martin Luther King
```

The second one, streetName, might even be leveraging the first concept. An example rule in this concept is shown here:

```
CONCEPT:personName Expressway
```

Note that both concepts are functional in this example. Consider the following input document:

My accident occurred on Martin Luther King Expressway on November 3, 2003.

Pause and think: Assuming the model above, which contains two functional concepts, can you predict the matches for the input document above with the "all matches" algorithm?

The rules above find two overlapping spans matching for person name and street name as in Figure 13.8.

Figure 13.8. Extracted Overlapping Matches for Different Concepts

Doc ID	Concept	Match Text
1	personName	Martin Luther King
2	streetName	Martin Luther King Expressway

It is inevitable that with a set of rules with good coverage of concepts there could be more than one possible match to a single segment of text. The situation becomes even more complex when you consider that there may be multiple possible overlapping matches. For example, consider the text: "North Carolina Museum of Art African Art Gallery." Some of the extracted matches could be as follows:

- North Carolina as a place
- North Carolina Museum of Art as an organization
- North Carolina Museum of Art as a place
- African Art Gallery as a place
- North Carolina Museum of Art African Art Gallery as a place

There could be several ways of removing such overlapping matches. This filtering could be achieved through one of the following:

- Post-processing to remove duplicates or to select the right set of results
- Marking some of the concepts as helper concepts
- Using an alternative match algorithm (the "longest match" and "best match" algorithms are explained in subsequent subsections)

"Longest Match" Algorithm and Priority

One alternative algorithm to "all matches" is the "longest match" algorithm, which enables you to specify to extract only the longest of multiple overlapping matches. This filtering applies to matches within and across concepts. Consider again the three example models and input documents from the previous subsection. With the "longest match" algorithm, in the first example you would see only the matches for "steering wheel" because that is a longer match than "steering." In the third example, you would see only the match "Martin Luther King Expressway" because it is longer than "Martin Luther King."

The second example contains two matches for the same span of text: "unit top icemaker." This situation can also happen if the exact same span of text matches two or more concepts, as was mentioned previously for the string "North Carolina Museum of Art," which could be extracted as an organization or place. In this case, the "longest match" algorithm checks whether the matches that were produced for both concepts come from concepts with the same priority values.

Priority is a feature that allows users to specify which of two or more matches should take priority if the span is the same length. With the exception of early versions of SAS Visual Text Analytics, in all other SAS Text Analytics products that enable you to write custom concepts, priority can be set for any functional concept in your model. Priority is not taken into consideration for returning matches from helper concepts.

If you do not specify a priority for a functional concept, then the default value of 10 is used. Be cautious if you are using predefined concepts in your model: Be sure to consult product documentation for the default priority values for those predefined concepts. It is important to be aware of the priority settings in case there are potentially overlapping matches from your custom concepts and the predefined ones.

If one of the same-length matches is associated with a higher priority, then that match is returned. If not, then the extracted match is the one found in the text by the first concept that is compiled in the model. Keep in mind that the order of concept compilation into a model is not predictable.

If you want to avoid this outcome, make sure that you mark any concepts that, as helper concepts, are only feeding matches to another concept. In cases of referring concepts, as in the refrigerator parts example, even if the priority of a helper concept is higher than the priority of a functional concept, only the match for the functional concept will be surfaced. Alternatively, you can set the priority of one concept higher than the other to ensure that only the matches from the higher priority concept are shown in conflict cases such as this one.

The behavior of matches with the "longest match" algorithm is summarized in Table 13.3.

Table 13.3. "Longest Match" Algorithm Matches as a Function of Priority and Match Length

	Equal or No Priority Specified	**Not Equal Priority of Functional Rules**
Equal match length (in characters)	Matches to first rule that is compiled	Higher priority
Not equal match length (in characters)	Longest match	Longest match

"Best Match" Algorithm

Another alternative matching algorithm for removing multiple matches from the same or overlapping span of text is the "best match" algorithm. This algorithm relies on the priority of functional concepts to choose between matched spans that overlap partially or entirely: The match associated with the highest priority is returned.

Returning once more to the model and examples about person and address names above, understand that, if the priority of the personName concept is higher than that of the streetName concept, then the only match that will be returned will be "Martin Luther King" to the personName concept, in spite of its shorter length than that of the streetName concept match. With the example of "North Carolina Museum of Art" potentially matching place or organization, with the "best match" algorithm, if the priority of the place concept is higher than that of the organization concept, then only "North Carolina Museum of Art" would be returned as a match to the place concept.

Keep in mind that, if priority is the same or not specified, then the "best match" algorithm treats matches exactly the same as the "longest match" algorithm. In other words, with equal or no priority specified, if one of the matches is longer than the other, that one is the returned as the "best match." If the matches are of equal length, then the extracted match is the one found in the text by the first concept that is compiled in the model.

The behavior of matches with the "best match" algorithm is summarized in Table 13.4.

Table 13.4. "Best Match" Algorithm Matches as a Function of Priority and Match Length

	Equal or No Priority Specified	Not Equal Priority of Functional Rules
Equal match length (in characters)	Matches to first rule that is compiled	Higher priority
Not equal match length (in characters)	Longest match	Higher priority

Default Match Algorithm

In the SAS Text Analytics products, the default match algorithm is different in various contexts, so consult product documentation for details about the default match type for your product and version. For example, in SAS Contextual Analysis, the algorithm is "best match" when you are testing against documents, and "all matches" when you are testing snippets of test text. In addition, when combining multiple concept models together in products that support this option using the "litilist" parameter, you should be aware that this parameter orders the concept models in a sequence. In the case of overlapping or redundant matches, matches from the last model in the list are given preference, regardless of the match algorithm selection.

In most of the SAS Text Analytics products, it is possible to export score code, which you can then apply to large data sets in production or to smaller data sets for testing purposes. In score code, you can specify any of the different match types in a parameter that you can use to customize your output. For example, in the applyConcept action, the parameter to specify is matchType="ALL" | "BEST" | "LONGEST." In the SAS Contextual Analysis score code, the parameter that controls the type of match algorithm is the shaded value in the following code snippet:

```
status = cat.set_match_type(_apply_settings, 0);
```

A value of 0 represents "all matches," 1 is "longest match," and 2 is "best match." See the product-specific documentation for more details.

Keep the match algorithms in mind as you continue to work with LITI and IE. The type of match setting can be a master key in troubleshooting taxonomies and rules. A best practice when troubleshooting is to use the "all matches" algorithm, if possible. Remember that the other two match algorithms only remove matches from the set returned by all matches.

Therefore, you have a baseline set of matches in the "all matches" result that you can compare directly with any other match algorithm to see what was removed.

13.4.2. Case Sensitivity

Another project setting that can be applied at the concept level is case sensitivity. This setting is either on or off, depending on whether you want the system to match the exact case of the letters that you type in your rules (case-sensitive), or whether you want the rules to match the letters but ignore the case (case-insensitive). For example, if you are matching person names, you may want to define a set of ambiguous names and require that they each start with a capital letter to help distinguish them from common words. This use case is most appropriate for case-sensitive matching. Here are some rules in a case-sensitive concept called perFirstNameAmbig:

```
CLASSIFIER:Lot
CLASSIFIER:Joe
CLASSIFIER:Amber
CLASSIFIER:Mark
```

Alternatively, perhaps you have regular words in your rules and you want them to match, whether they are the first word in a sentence or not, or even when they are found in all-capital letters. Then you would want to set your concept to *case-insensitive* to handle these rules:

```
CLASSIFIER:steering wheel
CLASSIFIER:side panel
CLASSIFIER:engine
CLASSIFIER:windshield
```

Alert! In some products the REGEX rule type matches will reflect the case sensitivity setting, and in others it will not. Do not assume that the REGEX rule is not affected by the case sensitivity setting, because the user can easily specify by rule the case of each character to match. Instead, check that the rule syntax is not reinterpreted to ignore some of the characters that are explicitly specified in the rule before you rely on REGEX rule accuracy in the GUI.

13.5. Suggested Reading

To gain more background on the topics in this chapter, consult the following sources in the References list at the end of the book:

- Osborne and Maness (2014)
- Pagolu et al. (2017)

Chapter 14: Fundamentals of Model Measurement

14.1. Introduction to Model Measurement

Measuring the quality of your models for information extraction (IE) usually means leveraging the metrics of recall, precision, and potentially *F-measure* as introduced in chapter 1. You may remember that *precision* is the ratio of the number of correctly labeled spans to the total that were labeled in the mode; *recall* is the ratio of the number of correctly labeled responses to the total that should have been labeled by the model as represented in the answer key; and *F-measure* is the harmonic mean of precision and recall. Understanding these metrics and using them properly will help you understand the types of errors in your model and help you make improvements that will reduce errors. It is possible to use alternative metrics to gauge the quality of IE models, but these metrics are the standard across the field, so they will be the focus in this chapter.

In order to use these metrics to gauge model quality, you will need a sample that serves as your gold standard corpus. The steps and decisions to put this sample in place and use it effectively are covered in the sections below.

14.2. Use of a Gold Standard Corpus

In order to calculate metrics, you will need a *gold-standard corpus*, which is a sample that includes the answer key for your data and the target information that you intend to measure. In this sample, the answers are indicated by annotations on the spans of text that you want to extract. For each span your model extracts that is correct according to your gold standard annotation, you get credit toward your recall and your precision scores. If you are able to perfectly line up your annotations and your model's results, then you will have 100% recall and 100% precision. However, this perfection is never seen in IE models unless they are very simplistic, keyword-driven models. It is important to design your project with this understanding in mind and work toward accomplishing on each component the level of recall and precision that you need for your business purposes.

Figure 14.1 illustrates that two types of errors are *false negatives* and *false positives*. False negatives are items in the gold standard (lighter circle) that the model (black circle) did not find. The other type of error, *false positives*, are matches the model has found, but they are not in the gold standard. The *true positives* (found in both the gold standard and by the model) and *true negatives* (not found in both) illustrate agreement between the gold standard and the model.

Figure 14.1. Types of Matches When Comparing Gold Standard and Model Output

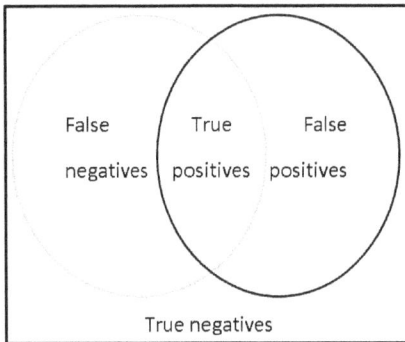

Note that the assumption is that the gold standard is accurate 100% of the time. This may not be true, and you may find that sometimes you need to update your gold standard to increase its accuracy. Be sure you are updating it because it does not align with your standards guide, not just because your model finds or does not find the span. Otherwise, you decrease the value of your gold standard to measure accuracy.

The following simple example illustrates the use of a gold standard that is accurate. Suppose you have 10 documents in your data sample, 8 of which contain a date, the concept that you want to extract.[1] Even if your model finds no date concepts at all, your model will correctly evaluate 2 of the documents, in which there is no date concept present. Across the 8 documents with one or more dates, there are multiple dates in some documents, for a total of 12 dates as shown in the Date Gold column in Table 14.1. In the Date Found column, your model found 11 dates. Because the two columns are side-by-side, it is easy to see where the misalignments occurred.

Table 14.1. Misalignments between Gold Corpus and Model Matches

DocID	Date Gold	Date Found
Doc1	None	None
Doc2	None	Today
Doc3	May 13, 1992	May 13, 1992
Doc3	today	today
Doc4	the day after tomorrow	tomorrow
Doc5	16JUN1995	16JUN1995
Doc5	JUNE1995	None

DocID	Date Gold	Date Found
Doc6	in 1996	None
Doc7	June 04th 1995	June 04th 1995
Doc7	after Oct 16th	Oct 16th
Doc8	from 5-16 October	from 5-16 October
Doc9	JUN 2002	JUN 2002
Doc10	Apr 2016	Apr 2016
Doc10	None	May
Doc10	week17	None

In Doc2 the model found "Today," but it was in the context of the organization name "USA Today," which is not a date. In Doc7, your model also identified "May" as a date, but it was actually a person's name. So far, you have two errors in precision: false positives. Now for a check on recall: the model has completely missed three dates—two in Doc5 and one in Doc7. In addition, the model does not match the exact same span for Doc4 and Doc7. In the typical calculation for text extraction metrics, these four errors, including the two total misses and the two partial misses, are all treated as misses for the recall calculation. The two partial misses are also treated as errors for the precision calculation. So a partial miss is treated as a miss twice. Some more forgiving approaches to measurement treat a partial match as a recall match and as a precision miss, because a match was found at the right location, but the span is incorrect. The stricter approach to measurement is used in the examples in this book.

The calculation of precision, recall, and *F*-measure for the example is in Table 14.2.

Table 14.2. Precision, Recall, and *F*-Measure Calculations

Description	Value
Correctly found by model	7
Total found by model	11
Total in gold corpus	12
Precision	7/11 = 63.6%
Recall	7/12 = 58.3%
F-measure	$2 * \frac{58.3*63.6}{58.3+63.6} = 60.8$

14.3. Setup of a Gold Standard Corpus

You may have realized by this point that the annotations for the gold standard have to come from somewhere. The best source of these annotations is human subject matter expert assessments. A human can use both his or her human expertise, and the information in the standard definition or annotation guide, to place annotations on a data sample. Ideally, a rigorous process would be used that incorporates redundancy and *interannotator agreement* metrics. A good process includes multiple human experts with training on the annotation guide and some duplication of assigned document or sentences to annotate. In this way, areas of disagreement between annotators can be identified and assessed.

Ideally, the annotators are different from the people building the model. Also, ideally, the computer model is leveraged to uncover areas of inconsistency in the annotations. When approached in this manner, the sample is truly a golden corpus and reliable for informative metrics calculations. In other words, you can use the sample to project metrics across the full corpus of documents, in accordance with your sampling procedure. Another benefit of this rigorous approach to building your gold standard is that the process can be an early warning system: If human annotators are struggling to use your annotation guide or to get high interannotator agreement, then you may need to go back to your design phase and revisit your goals. Building a model that can carry out tasks that humans cannot do consistently is very difficult, partially because it is difficult to assess and refine the model.

If you cannot follow this ideal process to build a gold standard corpus, then there are several modifications that you can use with a rule-based model, because the rule-based approach creates some flexibility for you from the start. If you were trying to train a statistical model, then you would need a fairly large gold standard corpus to use for training, developing, and testing your model. This data would need to be as accurate and complete as possible from the beginning of your project to be effective. For a rule-based model, you have options to modify this approach, because a human does not have to start with perfect knowledge from the beginning, but can learn and assess the model that he or she is building and the data iteratively.

When building a rule-based model, remember that the uses of an annotated corpus include both developing and testing. Developing includes research into patterns in the data, representing key patterns in LITI, and checking that you have extracted the right results with your model. This is an iterative process, and can actually be applied separately to different components of your model, as well as to the model as a whole. When working in this manner, it is useful to already have the annotations in place on a development sample, because that speeds up the process of evaluating your work. However, it is also possible to add annotations to your development sample as you work, or to update a starting set of approximate annotations. If you have a clear definition of what is targeted by the model, then you should be able to assess, on the basis of that description, whether a given document has the text spans you intend to extract.

When you are developing rules, it is fine to simply place or update annotations for your data as you read and interact with documents. You can still calculate recall and precision from the result of this effort. This recall and precision score will be the metric on your development sample. However, you still need to use an unseen sample of data if you want to assess how your model will perform against new data. For text models, this metric is essential for seeing how the model generalizes. Many model builders have trouble with constructing models that are specific enough to find the key information, without being too specific, or they generalize by relying only on keywords. Using a testing sample iteratively as you build will provide feedback on these tendencies.

In the best-case scenario, this test sample is built using the human annotation process already described, with multiple people and a rigorous process. However, it is also possible, though not ideal, to do this annotation with your model builders. They should enter this task with only the standard definition in hand and do this task completely separately from interactions with the model (in whatever state it might be). This artificial wall between tasks will help make the assessments more valid, though the model builders' results will be somewhat skewed toward the lessons learned from building the model. Using some combination of model builders and non-model-builders is also an option. A best practice to be followed if at all possible is to ensure that your annotators cover some of the same documents; this overlap in assessment will enable you to calculate interannotator agreement. Knowing how often your annotators agree helps you diagnose training issues or possible errors in your design or standards guide documentation.

You can build your test sample all at once and use it from then on, but if your model builders are involved, then doing so is not the best approach. If your model builders have seen and interacted with the testing data directly, then that data no longer represents unseen data. To avoid this pitfall, you can iteratively stop periodically to take a smaller sample to use for testing. After assessments have been given, you can generate the metrics and then continue model development. At that point, you can add the testing sample to the development sample and use it to continue to improve the model. The next time you want to generate metrics, pull a new testing sample and repeat this process. This type of iteration can continue until the model reaches the level of quality that is desired.

The human assessment of a testing sample can begin with temporary assessment that the humans evaluate and update, or can be done completely by hand. It can also happen in iterations. In fact, this practice of having a smaller testing sample that is used for metrics calculation and then added to the development sample is a common way to iterate rules development. The process is shown in Figure 14.2.

Figure 14.2. Workflow for Iterative Annotation and Testing of IE Model

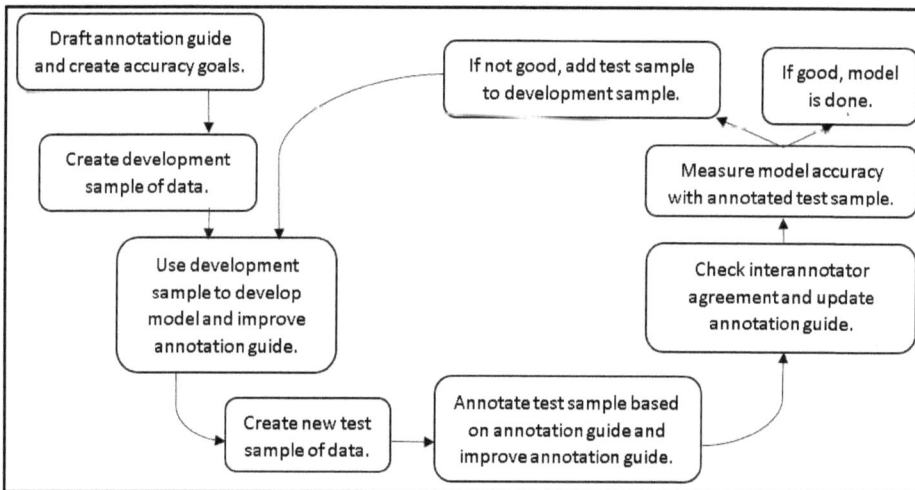

First, the development sample is created and used to build a candidate model. Then a new, often smaller sample is created for testing. The test sample should not have been used for development and ideally is drawn from a different data set with similar characteristics as the development sample. The test sample is used for calculating quality metrics. If quality thresholds are met, then the development is complete. If the quality is not yet good enough, the test sample is added to the development sample and used to further improve the model.

Then a new test sample is drawn, and the metrics are calculated again. This process continues until the quality threshold is met or the project's design, goals, data, or targets are adjusted.

14.4. Setup of Approximate Annotations

When you are first setting up your project, one way to start with a set of annotations that are approximate guesses of the right answer is to use another variable in your data as a placeholder or temporary annotation. This kind of placeholder annotation can be derived from several sources, including the following:

- Structured data that you already have
- Categories that you have already sorted documents into
- Loose, keyword-driven, or pattern-driven models built using the categorization or concepts functionality in the IE toolkit to identify documents or text spans that you want to assume are positive examples of your concept until you are able to assess them more closely

Here is an example of using a rough pattern-driven model to generate approximate annotations. If you want to find dates in your data, but do not have an annotated corpus to use for testing, you can explore your data to identify patterns that can be represented by a few rules. You can use them to try to find matches that might be dates and later update those assessments. A few rules that you could start with include the following:

```
##Find tokens that are alphanumeric; Jan06
REGEX:[A-Za-z0-9]*(?:[A-Za-z][0-9]|[0-9][A-Za-z])[A-Za-z0-9]*

##Find number sets separated by hyphens or slashes; 12/23/84
REGEX:[0-9]+[-\/] [0-9]+[-\/] [0-9]+

##Find 4 digits in a single token; 1922
REGEX:[0-9]{4}

#List of keywords for days: January, Tuesday, today, etc.
CONCEPT:dateKeyword
```

The first rule finds tokens that are alphanumeric. The second rule finds number sets separated by hyphens and slashes. The third rule finds 4-digit tokens. The fourth rule refers to a list that includes keywords such as month names, day names, words like "today," and the like.

This rule set will identify matches that may be dates in your data. You can apply the rules by using the applyConcept CAS action from a SAS Viya release from 2019 or later, and generate as output the ruleMatchOut table, a new output table related to rule generation. The output is represented in Table 14.3.

Table 14.3. RuleMatchOut Table as a Result of the applyConcept CAS Action

docid	_sentence_	_start_	_end_	_match_text_
38	San Jose and several other California cities mounted major campaigns during the summer to woo the group, which was founded in June by seven electronics concerns.	128	131	June
38	The venture plans to announce a final site by late November.	51	58	November
39	The record price for a full membership on the exchange is $550,000, set Aug. 31, 1987.	81	84	1987
45	The company reported that net profit climbed 30% in the first half of 1989 and said that it expects a gain of about 25% for the full year.	76	79	1989
45	The French group said consolidated net profit after payments to minority interests rose to 749 million francs (US$119.2 million) from 575 million francs in the first half of 1988.	190	193	1988
46	As a presidential candidate in 1980, George Bush fortnightly expressed his position on abortion in an interview with Rolling Stone magazine published that March.	38	41	1980

Table 14.3 includes the document ID, the sentence in which a match was found, the start and end offsets for the match, and the match text. When you use approximate annotations in your gold standard, you do not have high-quality assessments when you begin; both your model and your gold standard annotations on the development sample are incorrect to some degree. So part of your process will be aligning both to the documented standard definition or annotation guide for each concept that you are targeting. This means that your early metrics are not very reliable, but they should be useful enough to start development alongside the manual evaluation process during development to help you drive your model in the right direction. In your testing sample, human assessments should replace the temporary ones before you generate final metrics.

Exporting the table to Microsoft Excel makes it easier to create an annotated key based on the matches. First move the match_text column next to the sentence column, and then apply a Microsoft Visual Basic macro to highlight the text in the _sentence_ column. Now you can add a column called Annotation to place assessments; in Table 14.4 you see the use of 1 if the annotation is a date, and 0 if it is not. In the _sentence_ column in Table 14.4, the matches being evaluated are shaded.

Table 14.4. Approximate Annotations

docid	_sentence_	_match_text_	Annotation
1	When he died in 1959, Charles left behind four chapters of . . .	1959	1
1	The stock closed yesterday at $33.625, giving Mrs. Kelvin 33.6 million shares at a value of . . .	yesterday	1
1	These individuals may not necessarily be under . . .	may	0
1	The exchange also may step up the disclosure of firms engaged in program trading.	may	0
1	In September, the company was the 11th biggest program trader on the Big Board . . .	September	1
1	The corporation, on Wednesday, as expected, reported a net loss for the third quarter of $1.11B . . .	Wednesday	1
1	But they have obtained 8300 forms without court permission . . .	8300	0

At the time of the publishing of this book, you cannot do annotations in the graphical user interface for SAS Visual Text Analytics, but a similar feature is on the roadmap. As always, customer requests can help prioritize developing the feature sooner.

14.5. Creation of Samples for Development and Testing

When you are developing an IE model, one goal is to get access to data examples that represent the patterns and variety of your data as it relates to items of interest. Seeing as many of these examples as early as possible results in better coverage of your model and better overall recall scores. If the examples represent your targeted content in terms of its variability, then you can build models that generalize to new data more quickly. To do so, you can use the same methods already described to create strata in your data and then use the strata to create stratified samples. This method will enable you to sample more or less from each stratum, depending on your development and testing needs.

For example, you could use a filter like the date filter rules in the previous section to identify documents with many date candidates, documents with moderate numbers of date candidates, documents with few date candidates, and documents with no date candidates. These four sections of your data could then be used for stratified sampling, so that you could use the documents with many date candidates first to see the types and variety of date candidates found in those documents. This will help you build more generalized rules faster, because you will see more true examples of dates from your data and see more false positive examples, as well. You will also be able to see how much your rules are generalizing over each of the different strata.

In general, if your targeted concepts are very common in your data, you may be able to use simple random sampling to create your gold standard corpus or working data. However, if your concepts are fairly infrequent in your data, or if you are targeting more complex facts or relationships, then you will probably benefit from stratified sampling. In this way, you can ensure that you are seeing the most useful data for building models sooner. You can use this approach for developing and also when you want to put candidate documents in front of subject matter experts for annotation. To keep human annotators engaged, it is helpful to present them with frequent examples for them to assess rather than burdening them with a large quantity of data that is irrelevant. This avoids the needle-in-a-haystack problem, because most humans do not focus well enough for long enough periods to be effective in such tasks.

Taking time to plan your gold standard corpus and your methodology for development will save you a great deal of time in building and testing your model later. A purposeful approach will also enable you to take advantage of knowledge you gain from exploration of your data, helping you identify whether any automatic or machine learning tools can aid in your development work. You may also find that some lists already exist in your organization or online, which can save you time in developing rules for things like product names, body parts, disease names, machine parts, and the like.

14.6. Model Quality and Decisions

Once you have a good test sample and you have run your model against it, you will be able to calculate recall and precision metrics. Understanding what to do with this information is critical, and earlier decisions about how to decompose your model into components and what concepts to measure affect how useful this information will be. For example, perhaps one of your target concepts is blood pressure measurements. Your initial design looks something like Figure 14.3, where three subcomponents feed into the primary component.

Figure 14.3. Blood Pressure Measurement Model Design

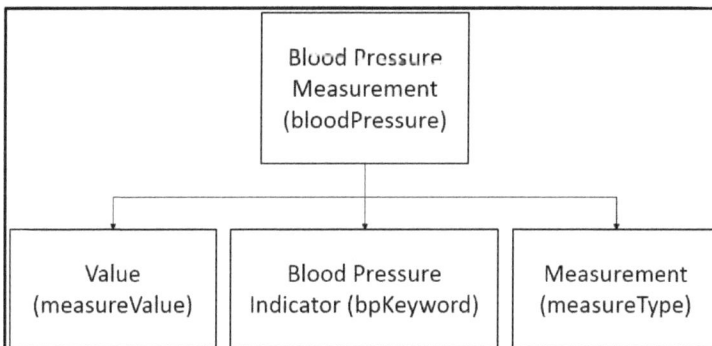

You apply your model to your test sample and get following metrics: recall = 70%, and precision = 82%. For IE models, recall will frequently vary between 15% and 35% for poor models, 35% and 55% for models with limited value, 55% and 75% for a good model, and 75% and 95% for an excellent model. This guideline will vary if you have not carefully defined your target, or if your target is very complex and hard to distinguish in textual content. Precision is usually easier to test and easier to achieve with rule-based models, so the standards for a good model are higher: 60–80% for a good model and 80–95% for an excellent model. You generally do not see models reaching much more than 95% unless the target is very simplistic or the data is very homogeneous, very simple, or small.

14.6.1. Strategies for Overcoming Low Recall

If you have an acceptably good model with high precision, but recall is below what you wanted to achieve, then the model is probably missing rules, or the rules are not general enough. If you have three subcomponents in your model, how can you tell which ones needs adjustment?

One way to start is by running your model components separately over your development sample to see how each one compares with your target. You can then evaluate the errors in recall for the weaker components by looking at the annotations that your rules failed to identify. It is also possible to run each component against your test sample; however, it is important to avoid using the results to identify areas for improvement, or else you risk polluting your metrics. However, if you are taking multiple test samples and rolling them into your development sample as you work, then evaluating the errors after getting the metrics is not a problem.

What if you still have some problems in your model and you are not sure how to proceed with improvements? Another strategy is to compare sets of alternative rules with each other. This can be done at either the component level or the model level. Some SAS Text Analytics products will assist you in doing so, but you can do so even in products without extra support by putting the two sets of rules in two different concepts and then using a REMOVE_ITEM rule to extract the differences, as shown in section 9.2.1. Alternatively, you can use operators like NOT and UNLESS. Here is an example using NOT with rules for blood pressure extraction.

The starting rules reflect your model design in Figure 14.3; the names of concepts used in the software are in parentheses after the design names. The measureType concept corresponds to your Measurement component and consists of rules intended to detect the type of measurement (millimeters of mercury):

```
CLASSIFIER:mm hg
CLASSIFIER:mmhg
```

The measureValue concept corresponds to your Value component and consists of rules that find numerical values in the patterns commonly used to discuss blood pressure in your data:

```
CONCEPT::digit +/- :digit (SD)
CONCEPT::digit +/- :digit
CONCEPT::digit/:digit/:digit
```

Finally, you have a keyword-based component called bpKeyword that corresponds to the Blood Pressure Indicator component. It contains rules that find words and phrases that commonly indicate that blood pressure is the topic under discussion:

```
CLASSIFIER:blood pressure
CLASSIFIER:systolic
CLASSIFIER:diastolic
CLASSIFIER:pulmonary pressure
```

As you started building your rules, you initially put the following into your bloodPressure concept, using only two of your three supporting concepts:

```
CONCEPT:measureValue measureType
CONCEPT:measureValue (_w) measureType
C_CONCEPT:_c{measureValue} _w measureValue measureType
```

You run this model over your data and see many good matches, and you start to wonder whether perhaps you do not need your bpKeyword concept after all. To use your bpKeyword concept, you will want to interact with the rules currently in your top-level node (bloodPressure); therefore, you would need to modify your design as shown in Figure 14.4.

Figure 14.4. Blood Pressure Measurement Alternative Model Design

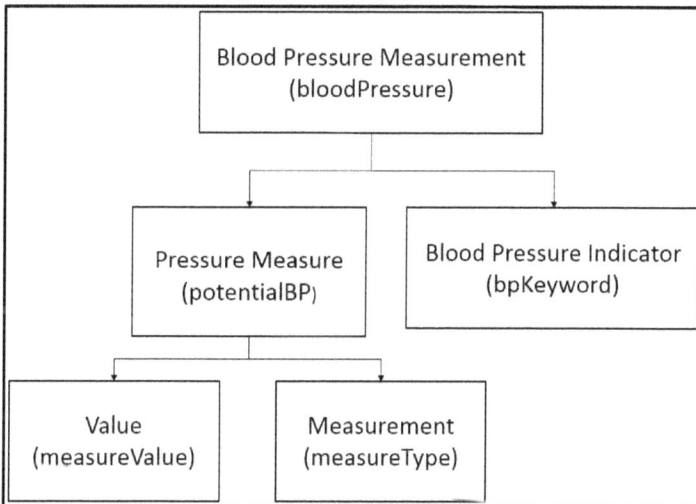

In order to investigate further whether this change is desirable, you move these initial rules from your bloodPressure concept into a new concept called potentialBP and run that concept, finding 280 matches, including the ones in Figure 14.5.

Figure 14.5. Matches in SAS Contextual Analysis.

Terms and Synonyms	Concept ▼
☐ 100 +/- 3 mm hg	potentialBP
☐ 0.78 +/- 0.32 mm hg	potentialBP
☐ 8 +/- 10.1 mmhg	potentialBP
☐ 14 +/- 1 mm hg	potentialBP
☐ 18 +/- 4 mm hg	potentialBP
☐ 12.9 +/- 2.7 mm hg	potentialBP
☐ 19 +/- 3 mm hg	potentialBP
☐ 36 +/- 12 mm hg	potentialBP

You like many of these matches and just want to know how many of the good ones you might lose if you add the keywords as a restriction. Here is the rule that you are planning to add to the bloodPressure concept; it says to find your blood pressure match within a distance of 8 sentences of one of your blood pressure keywords:

```
##Blood pressure rule focused/limited by keywords in the context
CONCEPT_RULE:(SENT_8, "_c{potentialBP}", "bpKeyword")
```

In order to see how many of the good matches from potentialBP you will lose with this restriction, you use a test rule like this one in a tempTest concept, which finds all the potentialBP matches that cannot be found by the previous rule:

```
##Blood pressure rule excluding those documents that contain the
keywords in any distance
CONCEPT_RULE:(AND, (NOT, "pbKeyword"), "_c{potentialBP}")
```

Running this rule, you see 137 matches, so you know that of your original 280 matches, you would lose a significant number with the more constrained approach that you were planning. The matches of this test rule included the shaded text as follows:

1. The mean preoperative intraocular pressure was 40.0 +/− 14.1 mm Hg (mean +/− standard deviation).

2. In a stable portal hypertensive rat group (no hemorrhage or transfusion) a standard vasopressin dose, 2.5 mU X kg−1 X min−1, resulted in a significantly lower portal pressure (11.5 +/− 0.7 vs. 14.4 +/− 0.6 mmHg) with a concomitantly lower portal venous inflow (8.5 +/− 0.3 vs. 11.1 +/− 0.6 ml X min−1 X 100 g body wt−1) when compared with rats receiving placebo.

3. Compared to placebo, nifedipine significantly decreased distal esophageal contraction amplitude (mean +/− SEM, 198 +/− 11 mmHg to 123 +/− 9 mmHg; p less than 0.005), as well as duration and lower esophageal sphincter pressure.

4. No change was noticed in mean pulmonary artery wedge pressure, which was 20 +/– 3 mm Hg at the beginning of the study and 19 +/– 3 mm Hg at the completion (P greater than .05, NS), nor in other hemodynamic and blood gases parameters.

5. The endolymphatic pressure of the ear operated on was significantly higher (0.78 +/– 0.32 mm Hg) than that of the perilymph.

6. Although the BP was maintained when furosemide was given alone, when given with prazosin and captopril, the mean BP fell by 13 +/– 5 mm Hg (P less than 0.05).

7. At a left atrial pressure of 30 +/– 5 mmHg, ventilation of the LLL with the hypoxic gas mixture caused QLLL/QT to decrease from 17 +/– 4 to 11 +/– 3% (P less than 0.05), pulmonary arterial pressure to increase from 35 +/– 5to 37 +/– 6 mmHg (P less than 0.05), and no significant change in rate of LLL weight gain.

8. However, at last follow-up arm-to-leg pressure gradients were lower in 9 infants after subclavian flap (8 +/– 14.1 mmHg) than in 5 infants of similar age who had resection (34 +/– 23.9 mmHg) (P less than 0.05).

9. Coronary wedge pressure was significantly higher in arteries with spontaneously visible and recruitable collaterals (41 +/– 12 and 36 +/– 12 mm Hg, respectively) than in arteries without collaterals (18 +/– 4 mm Hg).

10. Aortic pressure fell from 108 +/– 3 to 100 +/– 3 mm Hg (p = 0.02) and mean distal left anterior descending coronary artery pressure fell from 81 +/– 4 to 69 +/– 5 mm Hg (p = 0.02) after circumflex occlusion.

11. A steep decrease in arterial blood oxygen tension was obvious immediately after the institution of one-lung ventilation, reaching the lowest mean value of 63 +/– 2 mm Hg (+/– SEM) at 12 minutes.

12. Immediately following balloon inflation in the caudate nucleus of rats, there was a significant increase in intracranial pressure to 14 +/– 1 mm Hg (mean +/– standard error of the mean), accompanied by a reduction in cerebral blood flow (CBF) in the ipsilateral frontal cortex, as measured by the hydrogen-clearance technique.

13. The intraocular pressure in untreated eyes (controls) increased by an average of 12.9 +/– 2.7 mm Hg.

14. The PaO2 increased in all patients from 60.5 +/– 12.6 to 66.5 +/– 13.6 mm Hg (p less than 0.05), whereas the venous admixture was unchanged. This was attributed to an increased PVO2 (27 +/– 7 to 30 +/– 5 mmHg, p less than 0.01) secondary to a reduction of calculated peripheral oxygen consumption during ketanserin infusion.

Your conclusions, after reviewing the results and consulting with a medical subject matter expert, are that various types of pressure are measured in a similar way in the body and that you will need to narrow your matches. For example, the first match is pressure in the eye; the second you consulted an expert about and decided to include; the third is pressure in the digestive system; and the fourth is clearly blood pressure. However, you also learn that your current keyword list is too limited and will cause recall problems, so you add various additional rules to pbKeyword as a result of your investigation and leverage it to focus your matches on blood pressure measurements only.

Errors in recall can frequently be tied to the practice of using larger chunks of information from your documents as elements in your rules rather than looking at each token and neighboring tokens for clues about what pieces are really contributing to the meaning that you want to extract and which ones are not contributing. To determine whether this is an issue for you, examine whether your rule set includes many strings that include function words. You can eliminate the error by evaluating which pieces of the rule really contribute to the meaning that you need to extract, and which ones can be eliminated. You can set up comparative sets of rules to see whether your revised rules produce improved matches.

14.6.2. Strategies for Overcoming Low Precision

If your model has errors in precision, then you may be overusing keywords, missing some necessary function words, or missing an entire component in your model. To address this issue, you can use some of the strategies mentioned already to diagnose the rules against your development or test sample. You can also compare sets of rules with each other to see whether you can find the rules that are too broadly defined. To "drill down" even further on precision errors, you can look for missing components.

One way to find missing rule elements or missing model components is to leverage the features of topic identification or categorization rule generation in SAS Text Analytics products. First, use the methods already explained to identify the component or components of your model that are contributing the most to your problem. Then, construct a data set of sentences (or other small chunks of the documents) from your gold standard, using only the chunks that have your key component or components present. If you are working on a single component, find a pattern of characters that can generate candidates as you saw in the date example. You need the data set that you are creating to have both positive and negative examples of your targeted content—in other words, data that is a true match, and data that might be close in some way but is not a true match.

Next, run topic identification on your sentences or chunks and analyze whether you see any topics that are associated only with documents that are positive examples or only with documents that are negative examples. If so, then you should review and consider adding terms that define those key topics to constrain your rules. If you are not sure about this, then you can make your gold standard annotations into a target variable and generate categorization rules. These rules are somewhat similar to a basic version of the CONCEPT_RULE format, but do not use all the operators that are available in a CONCEPT_RULE. However, they may help you uncover a word, set of words, or concept that you can try adding to your rule set. If you are missing patterns between words in your analysis or think that this is a possibility, then use the same strategy without removing stop words from your terms list before generation of topics or categories. Alternatively, try it with bi-grams or tri-grams as your terms. The *n*-grams represent a series of *n* tokens; bi-grams are a series of any two neighboring tokens.

Here are some rules that you can use to generate *n*-grams; the specific rules here will generate bi-grams. You can put a Concepts model (node) in your pipeline before your Text Parsing node to see these terms in your terms list. Note that this approach will greatly expand the size of your terms list.

Keep in mind that overlapping pairs of tokens may be removed in some SAS Text Analytics products because of the selection of "best match" or "longest match" algorithms. Consult the documentation to learn what match algorithm is default for the Text Parsing node in your product.

In the bigramTerm concept, you can place this rule:

```
CONCEPT:inputToken inputToken
```

The inputToken concept can be as simple as a single rule (or more complex, if you want to limit this concept in some manner):

```
CONCEPT:_w
```

A REMOVE_ITEM rule will help you exclude any token types that you do not want to see in your *n*-grams, like punctuation. You can put this rule into your globalRules concept:

```
REMOVE_ITEM:(ALIGNED, "_c{inputToken}", "excludeThese")
```

You can eliminate punctuation, digital locations, and numbers from your *n*-grams, with these three rules in the excludeThese concept:

```
CONCEPT::sep
CONCEPT::digit
CONCEPT::url
```

You can also experiment with variations to get trigrams or even *skip-grams*, which skip over intervening tokens. An idea for skip-grams might look like this:

```
CONCEPT_RULE:(ORDDIST_2, "_c{inputToken}", "inputToken")
```

Remember the exploratory model for dates in section 14.4? You can also use rules like the *n*-gram ones to further explore how to refine your model. For example, after creating the ruleMatchOut table with the applyConcept CAS action, exporting it to Microsoft Excel, and adding annotations, you can import the table as new data into a product like SAS Visual Text Analytics. When you set up the Data node, make your annotations and the matched text into display variables, and use the sentence column as your text variable. After doing so, you add a rule to your model, along with the rules above, to more clearly see the context before each matched item:

```
C_CONCEPT:_c{bigramTerm} dateKeyword
```

When you run this rule, you can see what is working and not working by sorting your annotations as illustrated in Figure 14.6.

Figure 14.6. Matches in SAS Visual Text Analytics

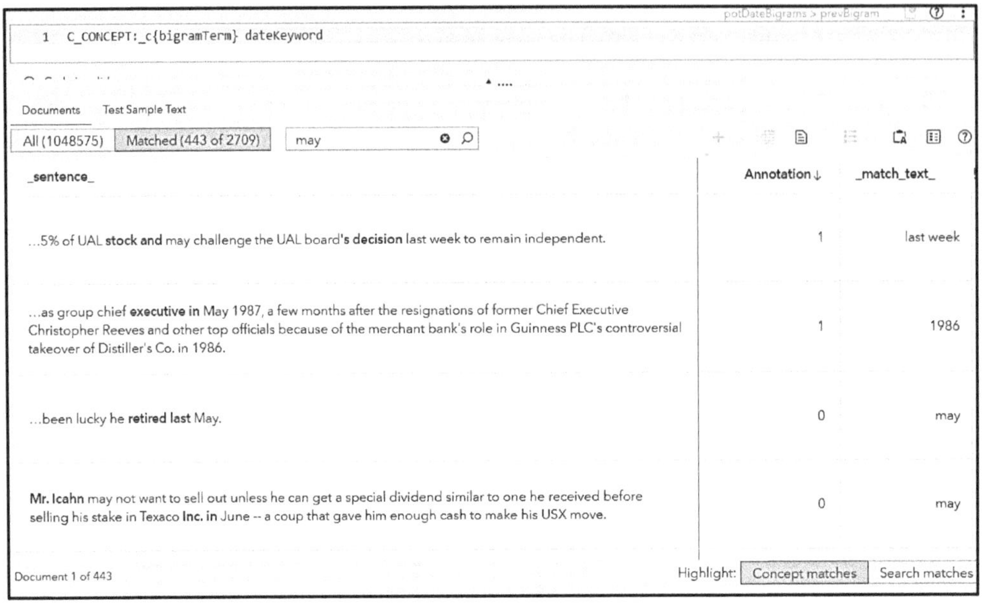

For example, you notice that the word "may" is finding many matches that are not month-related. You then look for the list of documents containing the match "may" with a positive annotation of 1 and see whether there is any prior context that will help disambiguate dates from other contexts. You realize from exploring the patterns that "may" is often a verb when it does not start with an uppercase letter, and sometimes a verb or name, when it does start with an uppercase letter. The most useful preceding keywords in your data mark "May" as a date after "in" and "next." When you explore what comes after keywords, you also notice that, if a digit follows a keyword, then it is also usually a date. You refine your rule set to reflect these patterns.

14.7. Model Monitoring

Once you have a good model in place, that model can be used indefinitely. However, you will probably want to monitor the performance of the model over time to identify when something has changed that might affect the usefulness of the model. Changes that will be discussed here include differences in the data that your model is processing, changes in the real world that affect the topics or keywords in your data, or changes in language or trends in how people talk about their experiences. Another type of change could be the business goals that the model is supporting.

Periodically you should identify whether the performance of the model has changed significantly. To do so, take a random or stratified sample from new data that your model is consuming, manually annotate the data, and then run the model on the data and calculate the metrics. If the metrics are significantly lower than they were when you put your model into production, then further analysis of the errors will help you assess what has changed in your data. You can identify when to do so by analyzing the relative proportion of items that you are extracting from your data and track whether the proportions change significantly.

Analysis of relative proportions through time is also a useful way to apply your model, so it will not be an additional step to monitor the model separately from using the model.

As you assess the changes, you can periodically profile your data, as you did before setting up your gold standard, to see how different the data is from when you first analyzed its properties. Comparing the properties that you noted initially to the properties that you can assess later will help you know whether the whole nature of the corpus has changed, whether topics have shifted, or whether some other element has been introduced. If your data sources have changed significantly, then you may need to redesign your model or add a filtering step to narrow down the data to a targeted subset for future use.

You should also assess ways that business processes, product lists, customer services, and other related situational elements could have changed during this time. Are the business goals of the model still valid? Did any of the assumptions that held previously change since the model was set up? It may be that updating your model is as simple as adding new products or services into the relevant components of your model. You can set up such updates to occur regularly and then monitor for larger changes separately. If your model is less effective and these analyses do not uncover why, then the best path forward is iterating in the same fashion that you did when building your model. In this way, you can detect which components are weak or strong. Once you discern what needs to be updated, you can set up a plan to make the updates and create a new baseline to monitor.

14.8. Suggested Reading

To gain more background on the topics in this chapter, consult the following sources in the References list at the end of the book:

- Pagolu (2017)
- Piskorski and Yangarber (2013)

---

[1] This unrealistically small example is used to enhance understanding of how metrics are calculated; actual samples will be much larger.

References

Abdelmagid, Muawia, Mubarak Himmat, and Ali Ahmed. 2014. "Survey on Information Extraction from Chemical Compound Literatures: Techniques and Challenges." *Journal of Theoretical and Applied Information Technology* 67(2): 284–289.

Aggarwal, Charu C., and ChengXiang Zhai. 2012. "An Introduction to Text Mining." In *Mining Text Data*, edited by Charu C. Aggarwal and ChengXiang Zhai, 1–10. Boston: Springer. https://doi.org/10.1007/978-1-4614-3223-4.

Albright, Russell, Janardhana Punuru, and Lane Surratt. 2013. "Relate, Retain, and Remodel: Creating and Using Context-Sensitive Linguistic Features in Text Mining Models." Paper 100-2013. *Proceedings of the SAS Global Forum 2013 Conference. Cary, NC: SAS Institute, Inc.* https://support.sas.com/resources/papers/proceedings13/100-2013.pdf

Belamaric Wilsey, Biljana, and Teresa Jade. 2015. "Text Analytics through Linguists' Eyes: When Is a Period Not a Full Stop?" SAS Voices Blog. https://blogs.sas.com/content/sascom/2015/07/13/text-analytics-linguists-eyes-period-not-full-stop/.

Burdick, Doug, Mauricio Hernandez, Howard Ho, Georgia Koutrika, Rajasekar Krishnamurthy, Lucian Popa, Ioana R. Stanoi, Shivakumar Vaithyanathan, and Sanjiv Das. 2011. "Extracting, Linking and Integrating Data from Public Sources: A Financial Case Study." *Bulletin of the Technical Committee on Data Engineering* 34(3): 60–66. .

Chiticariu, Laura, Yunyao Li, and Frederick R. Reiss. 2013. "Rule-based Information Extraction is Dead! Long Live Rule-based Information Extraction Systems!" *Proceedings of the 2013 Conference on Empirical Methods in Natural Language Processing*, 827–832. http://aclweb.org/anthology/D13-1079.

De Roeck, Anne N., Avik Sarkar, and Paul H. Garthwaite. 2004. "Defeating the Homogeneity Assumption: Some Findings on the Distribution of Very Frequent Terms." *Technical Report* No. 2004/07.

De Ville, Barry. 2006. "Text Mining with 'Holographic' Decision Tree Ensembles." Paper 072-31. *Proceedings of the Thirty-first Annual SAS Users Group International Conference. Cary, NC: SAS Institute, Inc.*

Fedschun, Travis. 2019. "Vaccinations at Workplaces in Kentucky, Ohio and Indiana Linked to 'Multiple Infections,' Officials Say." Fox News Online, February 3. https://www.foxnews.com/health/vaccinations-at-workplaces-in-kentucky-ohio-and-indiana-linked-to-multiple-infections-officials-say.

Feinburg, Jonathan. 2014. Wordle. http://www.wordle.net/create.

Fothergill, Richard, Paul Cook, and Timothy Baldwin. 2016. "Evaluating a Topic Modelling Approach to Measuring Corpus Similarity." In *Proceedings of the Tenth International Conference on Language Resources and Evaluation.*

Friedman, Carol, Lyudmila Shagina, Yves Lussier, and George Hripcsak. 2004. "Automated Encoding of Clinical Documents Based on Natural Language Processing." *Journal of the American Medical Informatics Association* 11(5): 392–402.

Gablasova, Dana, Vaclav Brezina, and Tony McEnery. 2017. "Exploring Learner Language Through Corpora: Comparing and Interpreting Corpus Frequency Information." *Language Learning* 67(S1): 130–154.

Gao, Emily. 2018. "How to Tokenize Documents into Sentences?" *SAS Users Blog* (July 26).

Giordanino, Marina, Claudio Giuliano, Damjan Kužnar, Alberto Lavelli, Martin Možina, and Lorenza Romano. 2008. "Cross-Media Knowledge Acquisition: A Case Study," 59–66. In *Proceedings of the Workshop on Cross-Media Information Analysis, Extraction and Management, CEUR Workshop Proceedings Series* Vol. 437.

Golshan, Parisa Naderi, Hossein Ali Rahmani Dashti, Shahrzad Azizi, Leila Safari. N.d. "A Study of Recent Contributions on Information Extraction."

Gries, Stefan Th. 2006. "Exploring Variability Within and Between Corpora: Some Methodological Considerations." *Corpora: Corpus-based Language Learning, Language Processing and Linguistics* 1(2): 109–151.

Grishman, Ralph and Beth Sundheim. 1996. "Message Understanding Conference—6: A Brief History." *Proceedings of the 16th International Conference on Computational Linguistics* 1: 466–471. https://doi.org/10.3115/992628.992709.

Hogenboom, Alexander, Frederick Hogenboom, Flavius Frasincar, Kim Schouten, and Otto van der Meer. 2013. "Semantics-based Information Extraction for Detecting Economic Events." *Multimedia Tools and Applications* 64(1): 27–52.

Iria, Jose, Spiros Nikolopoulos, and Martin Možina. 2009. "Cross-Media Knowledge Extraction in the Car Manufacturing Industry," 219–223. In *21st IEEE International Conference on Tools with Artificial Intelligence*.

Jiang, Jing. 2012."Information Extraction from Text." In *Mining Text Data*, edited by Charu C. Aggarwal and ChengXiang Zhai, 11–41. Boston: Springer. https://doi.org/10.1007/978-1-4614-3223-4.

Jurafsky, Daniel, and James H. Martin. 2018. "Information Extraction." In *Speech and Language Processing*. Unpublished draft of September 23, 2018. https://web.stanford.edu/~jurafsky/slp3/17.pdf.

Kadra, Giouliana, Robert Stewart, Hitesh Shetty, Richard G. Jackson, Mark A. Greenwood, Angus Roberts, Chin-Kuo Chang, James H. MacCabe, and Richard D. Hayes. 2015. "Extracting Antipsychotic Polypharmacy Data from Electronic Health Records: Developing and Evaluating a Novel Process." *BMC Psychiatry* 15: 166.

Kelly, A.P. 2007. "Qualitative Data Analysis." In *Social Research Methods: SC2145 Subject Guide*. London: University of London International Programmes Publications Office. https://reengineering2011.webs.com/documents/Social_research%20CH_4-1.PDF.

Li, Qi, Louise Deleger, Todd Lingren, Haijun Zhai, Megan Kaiser, Laura Stoutenborough, Anil G. Jegga, Kevin Bretonnel Cohen, and Imre Solti. 2013. "Mining FDA Drug Labels for Medical Conditions." *BMC Medical Informatics and Decision Making* 13: 53.

Lijffijt, Jefrey, Panagiotis Papapetrou, Kai Puolamäki, and Heikki Mannila. 2011. "Analyzing Word Frequencies in Large Text Corpora Using Inter-arrival Times and Bootstrapping." In *Machine Learning and Knowledge Discovery in Databases: European Conference, ECML PKDD 2011*, edited by D. Gunopulos, T. Hofmann, D. Malerba, and M. Vazirgiannis. *Lecture Notes in Computer Science* 6912. Heidelberg: Springer.

Liu, Jiawen, Mantosh Kumar Sarkar, and Goutam Chakraborty. 2013. "Feature-based Sentiment Analysis on Android App Reviews Using SAS Text Miner and SAS Sentiment Analysis Studio." Paper 250–2013. *Proceedings of the SAS Global Forum 2013 Conference*. Cary, NC: SAS Institute, Inc. https://pdfs.semanticscholar.org/063a/b0519e4b498489397e3108f1ad47e07af06d.pdf.

Lu, Jinghui, Maeve Henchion, and Brian Mac Namee. 2017. "Extending Jensen Shannon Divergence to Compare Multiple Corpora." In *Proceedings of the 25th Irish Conference on Artificial Intelligence and Cognitive Science*.

Massey, J. Gregory, Radhikha Myneni, M. Adrian Mattocks, and Eric C. Brinsfield. 2014. "Extracting Key Concepts from Unstructured Medical Reports Using SAS Text Analytics and SAS Visual Analytics." Paper SAS165-2014. *Proceedings of the SAS Global Forum 2014 Conference*. Cary, NC: SAS Insitute, Inc.

Meystre, Stephane M., Guergana K. Savova, K. C. Kipper-Schuler, and John F. Hurdle. 2008. "Extracting Information from Textual Documents in the Electronic Health Record: A Review of Recent Research." *IMIA Yearbook of Medical Informatics* 17(1): 128–144. .

Miller, Don, and Douglas Biber. 2015. "Evaluating Reliability in Quantitative Vocabulary Studies: The Influence of Corpus Design and Composition." *International Journal of Corpus Linguistics* 20(1): 30–53.

Moens, Marie-Francine. 2006. "Information Extraction from an Historical Perspective." In *Information Extraction: Algorithms and Prospects in a Retrieval Context*, 23–45. Dordrecht: Springer. https://doi.org/10.1007/978-1-4020-4993-4.

Németh, Géza, and Csaba Zainkó. 2002. "Multilingual Statistical Text Analysis, Zipf's Law and Hungarian Speech Generation." *Acta Linguistica Hungarica* 49(3–4): 385–405. https://doi.org/10.1556/ALing.49.2002.3-4.8.

Nikolopoulos, Spiros, Christina Lakka, Ioannis Kompatsiaris, Christos Varytimidis, Konstantinos Rapantzikos, and Yannis Avrithis. 2009. "Compound Document Analysis by Fusing Evidence Across Media," 175–180. *Seventh International Workshop on Content-based Multimedia Indexing*.

Osborne, Mary, and Adam Maness. 2014. "Star Wars and the Art of Data Science: An Analytical Approach to Understanding Large Amounts of Unstructured Data." Paper 286-2014. *Proceedings of the 2014 SAS Global Forum Conference.* Cary, NC: SAS Institute, Inc.

Owda, Majdi, Pei Shyuan Lee, and Keeley Crockett. 2017. "Financial Discussion Boards Irregularities Detection System (FDBs-IDS) Using Information Extraction," 1078–1082. In *Intelligent Systems Conference (IntelliSys).*

Pagolu, Murali, Christina Engelhardt, and Cheyanne Baird. 2017. "Exploring the Art and Science of SAS Text Analytics: Best Practices in Developing Rule-based Models." Paper SAS587-2017. In *Proceedings of the SAS Global Forum 2017 Conference.* Cary, NC: SAS Institute, Inc.

Pagolu, Murali. 2017. "Breaking through the Barriers: Innovative Sampling Techniques for Unstructured Data Analysis." Paper SAS761-2017. *Proceedings of the SAS Global Forum 2017 Conference.* Cary, NC: SAS Institute, Inc.

Paquot, Magali, and Yves Bestgen. 2009. "Distinctive Words in Academic Writing: A Comparison of Three Statistical Tests for Keyword Extraction." In *Corpora: Pragmatics and Discourse: Papers from the 29th International Conference on English Language Research on Computerized Corpora (ICAME 29)*, edited by Andreas H. Jucker, Daniel Schreier, and Marianne Hundt, 247–269. Amsterdam: Rodopi.

Piskorski, Jakub and Roman Yangarber. 2013. "Information Extraction: Past, Present and Future." In *Multi-source, Multilingual Information Extraction and Summarization. Theory and Applications of Natural Language Processing Series,* Vol. 11, edited by Thierry Poibeau et al., 23–49. Berlin: Springer. https://doi.org/10.1007/978-3-642-28569-1.

Rayson, Paul. 2008. "From Key Words to Key Semantic Domains." *International Journal of Corpus Linguistics* 13(4): 519–549.

Renkema, Jan (editor). 2009. *Discourse, of Course: An Overview of Research in Discourse Studies.* Amsterdam: John Benjamins.

Sabo, Tom. 2014. "Uncovering Trends in Research Using Text Analytics with Examples from Nanotechnology and Aerospace Engineering." Paper SAS061-2014. *Proceedings of the 2014 SAS Global Forum Conference.* Cary, NC: SAS Institute, Inc.

Sabo, Tom. 2015. "Show Me the Money! Text Analytics for Decision-Making in Government Spending." Paper SAS1661-2015. *Proceedings of the SAS Global Forum 2014 Conference.* Cary, NC: SAS Institute, Inc. http://support.sas.com/resources/papers/proceedings15/SAS1661-2015.pdf.

Sabo, Tom. 2016. "Extending the Armed Conflict Location and Event Data Project with SAS Text Analytics." Paper SAS6380 2016. *Proceedings of the SAS Global Forum 2016 Conference.* Cary, NC: SAS Institute, Inc.

Sabo, Tom. 2017. "Applying Text Analytics and Machine Learning to Assess Consumer Financial Complaints." Paper SAS282-2017. Proceedings of the *SAS Global Forum 2017 Conference.* Cary, NC: SAS Institute, Inc. http://support.sas.com/resources/papers/proceedings17/SAS0282-2017.pdf.

Sahlgren, Magnus, and Jussi Karlgren. 2005. "Counting Lumps in Word Space: Density as a Measure of Corpus Homogeneity." In *String Processing and Information Retrieval: 12th international conference, SPIRE 2005*, edited by Mariano. Consens and Gonzalo. Navarro. *SPIRE 2005. Lecture Notes in Computer Science* 3772. Berlin: Springer.

Salager-Meyer, Françoise. 1992. "A Text-Type and Move Analysis Study of Verb Tense and Modality Distribution in Medical English Abstracts." *English for Specific Purposes* 11(2): 93–113. https://doi.org/10.1016/S0889-4906(05)80002-X.

Sanders, Annette and Craig DeVault. 2004. "Using SAS at SAS: The Mining of SAS Technical Support." Paper 010-29. *Proceedings of the Twenty-Ninth Annual SAS Users Group International Conference.*

Sarawagi, Sunita. 2008. "Information Extraction." *Foundations and Trends in Databases* 1(3): 261–377. https://doi.org/10.1561/1900000003.

Sharoff, Serge. 2010. "Analysing Similarities and Differences between Corpora." In *Proceedings of the Seventh Language Technologies Conference (Jezikovne Tehnologije), Ljubljana, Slovenia: Institut Jozef Stefan.*

Small, Sharon G., and Larry Medsker. 2014. "Review of information extraction technologies and applications." *Neural computing and Applications* 25(3–4): 533–548. https://doi.org/10.1007/s00521-013-1516-6.

Stubbs, Michael. 1997. "Whorf's Children: Critical Comments on Critical Discourse Analysis (CDA)." In *Evolving Models of Language: Papers from the Annual Meeting of the British Association for Applied Linguistics*, edited by Ann Ryan and Alison Wray, 100–116. Clevedon, UK: Multilingual Matters. https://www.uni-trier.de/fileadmin/fb2/ANG/Linguistik/Stubbs/stubbs-1997-whorfs-children.pdf

Sun, Weiyi, Anna Rumshisky, and Ozlem Uzuner. 2013. "Annotating Temporal Information in Clinical Narratives." *Journal of Biomedical Informatics* 46 (December): S5–S12.

Tao, Jie, Amit V. Deokar, and Omar F. El-Gayar. 2014. "An Ontology-based Information Extraction (OBIE) Framework for Analyzing Initial Public Offering (IPO) Prospectus," 769–778. In *47th Hawaii International Conference on System Sciences*.

Titscher, Stefan, Michael Meyer, Ruth Wodak, and Eva Vetter. 2000. "Methods of Text and Discourse Analysis." London: Sage.

van Dijk, Teun A. 1985. *Discourse and Communication: New Approaches to the Analysis of Mass Media Discourse and Communication.* Berlin: Walter De Gruyter.

Waltl, Bernhard, Georg Bonczek, and Florian Matthes. 2018. "Rule-based Information Extraction: Advantages, Limitations, and Perspectives." *Jusletter IT*, February 22. https://wwwmatthes.in.tum.de/pages/1w12fy78ghug5/Rule-based-Information-Extraction-Advantages-Limitations-and-Perspectives.

Wang, Yanshan, Liwei Wang, Majid Rastegar-Mojarad, Sungrim Moon, Feichen Shen, Naveed Afzal, Sijia Liu, Yuqun Zeng, Saeed Mehrabi, Sunghwan Sohn, Hongfang Liu. 2018. "Clinical information Extraction Applications: A Literature Review." *Journal of Biomedical Informatics* 77 (January): 34–49.

Windham, K. Matthew. 2014. *Introduction to Regular Expressions in SAS*. Cary, NC: SAS Institute Inc.

Wood, Linda A., and Rolf O. Kroger. 2000. *Doing Discourse Analysis: Methods for Studying Action in Talk and Text.* Thousand Oaks: Sage.

Woodie, Alex. 2018. "Mining New Opportunities in Text Analytics," October 9. Datanami. https://www.datanami.com/2018/10/09/mining-new-opportunities-in-text-analytics/.

www.ingramcontent.com/pod-product-compliance
Lightning Source LLC
Chambersburg PA
CBHW081054220326
41598CB00038B/7089